W9-BAH-683

RENDEZVOUS WITH DEATH

RENDEZVOUS WITH DEATH

The Americans Who Joined the Foreign Legion
in 1914 to Fight for France and for Civilization

DAVID HANNA

REGNERY
HISTORY

Regnery History™ is a trademark of Salem Communications Holding Corporation; Regnery® is a registered trademark of Salem Communications Holding Corporation

Library of Congress Cataloging-in-Publication Data

Names: Hanna, David, 1967- author.
Title: Rendezvous with death : The Americans who joined the Foreign Legion in 1914 to fight for France and for civilization / David Hanna.
Description: Washington, DC : Regnery Publishing, 2016. | Includes
   bibliographical references.
Identifiers: LCCN 2016004232 | ISBN 9781621573968
Subjects: LCSH: World War, 1914-1918--United States. | World War,
   1914-1918--Biography. | Americans--France--History--20th century. |
   France. Armâee de terre. Lâegion âetrangáere--History--World War,
   1914-1918.
Classification: LCC D570.1 .H27 2016 | DDC 940.4/1244092313--dc23
LC record available at https://lccn.loc.gov/2016004232

ISBN 978-1-62157-396-8

Published in the United States by
Regnery History
An imprint of Regnery Publishing
A Division of Salem Media Group
300 New Jersey Ave NW
Washington, DC 20001
www.RegneryHistory.com

Manufactured in the United States of America

10 9 8 7 6 5 4 3 2 1

Books are available in quantity for promotional or premium use. For information on discounts and terms, please visit our website: www.Regnery.com.

Distributed to the trade by
Perseus Distribution
250 West 57th Street
New York, NY 10107

For John A. Ware

(1942–2013)

New Yorker, agent, mentor, friend, man about town...

... fighting, dying, not only for Christianity, but for civiliza-
tion. On the result of this clash...depends the preservation of
the world.
—Jack Bowe, 1918

I do not consider that I am fighting for France alone, but for
the cause of humanity, the most noble of all causes.
—Kiffin Rockwell, 1914

And on the tangled wires
The last wild rally staggers, crumbles, stops.
Withered beneath the shrapnel's iron showers:
Now heaven be thanked, we gave a few brave drops;
Now heaven be thanked, a few brave drops were ours.
—Alan Seeger, 1916

CONTENTS

Map courtesy of Midori Tuzu

PARIS
(with numbered arrondissements)

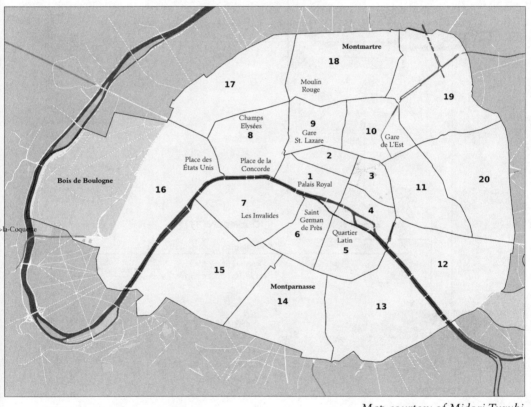

Map courtesy of Midori Tuzuki

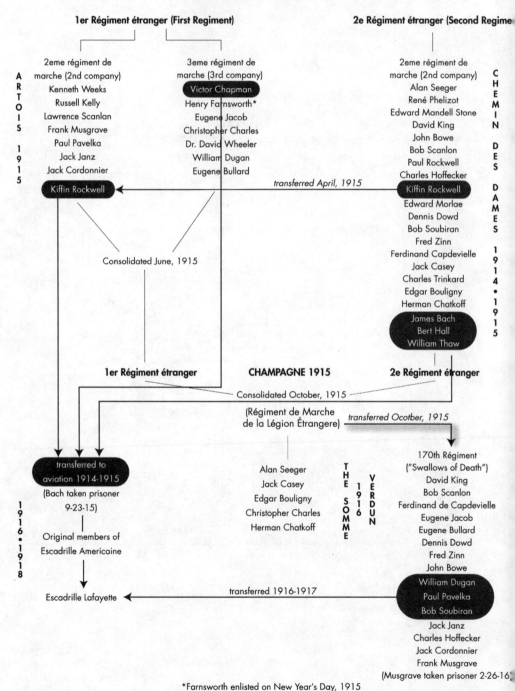

THE VOLUNTEERS OF 1914 (listing those mentioned in book, not all inclusive)
LA LÉGION ÉTRANGERE (Foreign Legion)

1er Régiment étranger (First Regiment)

2e Régiment étranger (Second Regime

A R T O I S 1915

2eme régiment de marche (2nd company)
Kenneth Weeks
Russell Kelly
Lawrence Scanlan
Frank Musgrave
Paul Pavelka
Jack Janz
Jack Cordonnier

Kiffin Rockwell

3eme régiment de marche (3rd company)
Victor Chapman
Henry Farnsworth*
Eugene Jacob
Christopher Charles
Dr. David Wheeler
William Dugan
Eugene Bullard

2eme régiment de marche (2nd company)
Alan Seeger
René Phelizot
Edward Mandell Stone
David King
John Bowe
Bob Scanlon
Paul Rockwell
Charles Hoffecker

transferred April, 1915   Kiffin Rockwell
Edward Morlae
Dennis Dowd
Bob Soubiran
Fred Zinn
Ferdinand Capdevielle
Jack Casey
Charles Trinkard
Edgar Bouligny
Herman Chatkoff

C H E M I N D E S D A M E S 1914 • 1915

James Bach
Bert Hall
William Thaw

Consolidated June, 1915

1er Régiment étranger

CHAMPAGNE 1915

2e Régiment étranger

Consolidated October, 1915

(Régiment de Marche de la Légion Étrangere)

transferred Ocotber, 1915

transferred to aviation 1914-1915

(Bach taken prisoner 9-23-15)

Original members of Escadrille Americaine

1916 • 1918

Alan Seeger
Jack Casey
Edgar Bouligny
Christopher Charles
Herman Chatkoff

T H E S O M M E   1916   V E R D U N

170th Régiment
("Swallows of Death")
David King
Bob Scanlon
Ferdinand de Capdevielle
Eugene Jacob
Eugene Bullard
Dennis Dowd
Fred Zinn
John Bowe

William Dugan
Paul Pavelka
Bob Soubiran

Escadrille Lafayette

transferred 1916-1917

Jack Janz
Charles Hoffecker
Jack Cordonnier
Frank Musgrave
(Musgrave taken prisoner 2-26-16)

*Farnsworth enlisted on New Year's Day, 1915

Chart courtesy of Midori Tuzuk

PROLOGUE

What would you risk your life for? For most of us, fortunately, this is a purely hypothetical question. One's family and friends come immediately to mind. For some of us, our hometown or neighborhood might, as well. The patriotism that motivates a relative few to serve in our country's armed forces fell out of fashion with the great majority of citizens long ago. What about an idea? Would you risk your life to defend something not linked to you by ties of blood or friendship, community or country? As the last days of July 1914 were swept into the past and the first frantic days of August hurried Europe and the world into an uncertain future, a group of Americans volunteered their services to the French government. The *Légion étrangère*—the Foreign Legion—would be their vehicle. These men were inspired by what they saw as a clear case of democratic values, culture, and civilization itself under attack from the forces of autocracy and a modern barbarism embodied by Kaiser Wilhelm's Germany. With rare exception absolute amateurs, they chose to risk their lives for an idea. To see it protected, many of them would make the ultimate sacrifice.

These American citizens left behind promising careers and their families to join in combat with a foreign army and defend a country some of them had never even been to. For many of them, though, their previous experiences in France were a deep part of what motivated them to enter the fight. This was a country and a culture they identified with and believed was worth dying to defend. Their service would take them to the battlefields of Artois, Champagne, and Verdun. Their sacrifices preceded by nearly three years the eventual commitment by President Wilson to take America into the fight and finish what these men started.

This is not just the tale of the conventionally glamorous Lafayette Escadrille. Some of the men whose stories appear in this book would indeed go on to found that all-American air squadron. But the experience of fighting the Germans on the ground, both before and after the squadron's creation, has been largely ignored in other accounts. While the Lafayette Escadrille has an undeniable appeal, the overwhelming majority of the Americans who volunteered in those first few giddy and terrifying months of the war would serve on the ground, in the army, and in the trenches. They asked for no special considerations, only the honor of helping defend France in her hour of greatest need.

Among those Americans were a number of individuals whose motivations and experiences set them apart. Their stories are the richest and the most revealing: men such as poet Alan Seeger; Southern gentleman and knight errant Kiffin Rockwell; blue bloods David

King, William Thaw, and Victor Chapman; African-American boxer Bob Scanlon; and Spanish-American War veteran Jack Bowe. They represented a cross-section of American society at that time. What set them apart was either a heightened sense of idealism, a thirst for action, or both. Added to this was smoldering rage against imperial Germany—and everything they perceived it stood for. For the most part they carried it all off with remarkable *sangfroid* and *bonhomie*. They knew how to enjoy themselves. And with rare exception, they didn't regret the decision they had made, even once the realities of war were thrust upon them. They were exceptional men.

It was not simply the bravery and idealism of the original American volunteers that was exceptional, it was the degree to which they stood out from their fellow citizens back home. Most Americans were willing to sit on the sidelines, even after credible reports of German atrocities in Belgium and France reached the public. It was "not our fight." And yet there were those boys over there fighting in the Foreign Legion—a number of them writing columns for newspapers back home. What they had seen with their own eyes couldn't be so easily dismissed. The risks they were taking could not be trivialized. Barely perceptible at first, the slow and steady shift in American public opinion towards intervention owed much to the efforts of a handful of Americans holding the line in a trench in Champagne. America entered the war in 1917; *Americans* entered it in 1914. This was a case of the people leading the government to act by the force of their example and their words.

★ ★ ★

Both on account of the available source material and for the sake of the narrative, I have chosen to focus on some of the American volunteers of 1914 more than others. Some are mentioned only briefly. A number who volunteered in 1914 are not mentioned at all. However, all of them chose to risk all for a country, and an ideal. This demands respect. I would recommend Paul Rockwell's book, *American Fighters in the Foreign Legion*, published in 1930, for those who wish to pursue their stories in more detail. To those with a special interest in the aviators, I would recommend Herbert Molloy Mason Jr.'s excellent book, *The Lafayette Escadrille*, published in 1964. Mason was a pilot himself, as well as a fine writer.

I also recognize that a number of the American volunteers are perhaps deserving of a full-length biographical treatment of their own (Alan Seeger certainly comes to mind). This book, however, is about the group, not any one individual. They were comrades-in-arms in the truest sense. This is also an American story. Those like-minded men from other lands that volunteered in 1914 as well are largely absent. But their story, too, is one worth telling. And finally, the year is important. All the Americans featured here volunteered in 1914—when the world, or at least the world as it existed before August 1914, was turned upside down.

CHAPTER 1

BELLE ÉPOQUE

One winter day when he was about eight years old, Alan Seeger and his older brother Charles were sledding with some neighborhood children. As they sped down the hill, a delivery wagon pulled by two horses appeared in front of them. All of the other boys veered off and piled into nearby snow drifts, but Alan raced on through the horses' legs, earning a scolding from the frightened driver. Charles hurried down the hill with the others to see if he was all right. Later, Charles recounted Alan explaining his actions as a sort of test: "It's hard to explain, Charlie. But I couldn't turn away. Don't you get it? I had to prove to myself that I had the nerve. You know what I mean?"[1] Charlie felt there was something prophetic about the incident: "That was Alan. Tilting against windmills. As a boy, he was a leader, always dreaming up games. His favorite one was where he played a knight on a

1

predoomed quest against impossible odds. Alan's knight always died nobly...."[2]

Alan Seeger was born on Friday, June 22, 1888, at his family's home on East 73rd Street in New York.[3] He was fortunate—not only were his parents and older brother loving people, their station in life was comfortable. And to have a lifestyle that was comfortable, if not opulent, in that era provided the young boy with a sense of security and possibility that is now largely lost to us. The year 1888 marked not quite the halfway point of an historical period known as the *Belle Époque*, or "beautiful time," which stretched from the close of the Franco-Prussian War in 1871 through midsummer 1914. It was a confident age full of technological wonders and increasing trade and communication across the globe. For the overwhelming majority of people in Europe and America, the standard of living exceeded anything experienced in previous centuries. The characteristic sentiment of the age was optimism—confidence that science equaled progress, that progress was irresistible, and that mankind itself was constantly improving.

In the two decades just before Alan Seeger's birth, America had seen the completion of the first transcontinental railroad, the advent of the telephone and the incandescent light bulb, and the electrification of much of the country, beginning with New York. The internal combustion engine, automobiles, recorded sound, motion pictures, X-ray machines, airplanes, and radio would all be introduced in Seeger's brief lifetime. The Panama Canal would be completed in 1914. Already in his childhood, with refrigerated boxcars and refrigerated compartments in the holds of steamships, Alan Seeger and his family could eat a much wider variety of foods throughout the year than previous generations. The United States was experiencing an unprecedented industrial, technological, and financial revolution. Wealth was unevenly distributed, with "robber barons" such as steel magnate Andrew Carnegie, oil tycoon John D. Rockefeller, and above all banker J. P. Morgan dominating the nation's affairs. Still, the middle class was expanding and living a lifestyle that even European nobility could not have hoped to enjoy just a few generations earlier. In America the *Belle Époque* was actually two separate but linked historical periods. The first was known as the "Gilded Age," lasting from approximately the assassination of President Abraham Lincoln in 1865 until the assassination of William McKinley, the last Civil War veteran to serve as president, in 1901. The age acquired its sobriquet from a book by Mark Twain that insinuated that the era's glossy exterior hid cheaper substances beneath (corruption, poverty, culture without taste, knowledge without wisdom). The advent of McKinley's vice president, Theodore Roosevelt, to the White House in 1901 heralded a new age, the "Progressive era," of which this accidental president was a vocal champion. For Alan Seeger, Theodore Roosevelt would come to embody the ideals of American democracy and America's special role in the world.

The Seeger family lived an interesting as well as a comfortable life. Alan's father was a partner in an export-import firm with significant business interests in Mexico. Described as "tall and handsome" with "a ready laugh, a quick wit" and "some talent as an artist,"[4] Charles Seeger Sr. had a passion for music. His wife Elsie was noted for her beauty and her vitality. In 1890 they moved their young family to a stately home atop Tompkins Hill on Staten Island overlooking New York's Upper and Lower Bays and the Narrows between. Alan's younger sister Elsie was born there. It was in this idyllic setting that Alan Seeger first manifested the character traits that would bring him to his destiny across the Atlantic.

As much as he was a reckless daredevil, there was also a side to Alan Seeger that was very sensitive to romance and beauty. An early biographer described how from the window of the children's nursery one could see vessels of various descriptions entering New York's Upper Bay and "the outgoing stream which carried the imagination seaward.... The children did not look without curious eyes upon this stirring scene."[5] Where were the ships going? What exotic destinations might lie ahead? What perils, hardships, and beautiful sights might they encounter? The children were moved sufficiently to cover the walls of their nursery with drawings of the ships they observed. In addition, from his own room Alan had a fine view of lower Manhattan. He treasured the visits the children made to the great metropolis with their mother. "Everything about them excited him: the shops, theaters, restaurants, the bustle and the noise."[6]

In 1898, the Seegers had to give up their home on Staten Island when the family business began to founder. They moved back to New York. The magic city seen from afar was now home. As Alan Seeger grew he appreciated that New York was not only all he had imagined it to be but also something more: a city with hundreds of thousands of immigrants living in poverty and squalid conditions. He missed the hill back at home on Staten Island. This element of perspective would become one of the defining elements of the poetry he would write as a young man. The family fortunes did not improve, and Alan's father decided to make a bold move to Mexico City, taking the entire family along with him. This new setting provided Alan Seeger with raw material for his first works of verse. He found himself tremendously moved by the twin smoking volcanoes of Popocatépetl and Ixtaccihuatl looking down at the Valley of Mexico, the whiteness of sunbaked adobe, the vivid greens of the tropics interspersed with occasional reds, blues, and yellows. The antiquity of the valley and the people who lived there also moved him to write:

> Here, among trees whose overhanging shade
> Strews petals on the little dives below,
> Pattering townward in the morning weighed
> With greens from many an upland garden-row,
> Runs an old wall; long centuries have frayed
> Its scalloped edge, and passers to and fro
> Heard never from beyond its crumbling height
> Sweet laughter ring at noon or plaintive song at night.[7]

In a time of technological wonders, Alan Seeger was trying to capture the essence of a deserted garden in Mexico. It is important to remember that as much as this age was one of science and progress, it also embraced color, emotion, and expression. By the time he was sent off to boarding school in 1902, Alan Seeger was a being transformed. Many awkward moments still lay ahead, but his sensitive nature had borne fruit, and his path was to be that of the poet.

★ ★ ★

Feelings like those stirring in the youthful Alan Seeger were already being expressed in truly breathtaking scope in France. The composer Claude Debussy had made his reputation in the Paris *avant-garde* in the 1890s with compositions such as *Deux*

Claude Monet, *La Gare Saint-Lazare*, oil on canvas, 1877.

Arabesques and *Claire de Lune*. These pieces departed from the understood order of things in the musical world of the time in a fashion that mirrored the style of the Impressionist and Post-Impressionist painters, such as Claude Monet, Pierre-Auguste Renoir, Vincent van Gogh, and Paul Cezanne. Monet found a smoky and noisy symbol of the modern age such as the Gare Saint-Lazare railway station worthy of study; rather than painting a realistic picture of a train arriving at a station, he depicted it in a gauzy amorphous manner that captured the essence of the age of steam. By 1900, Monet and his peers in the Impressionist Movement had found a degree of acceptance in French society and officialdom. They had come a long way from being described—in *Le Figaro* in 1875—as monkeys who had gotten hold of a box of paints. Paris, and France as a whole, had come a long way since the early 1870s, the decade that saw the birth of both the Impressionist Movement and the Third Republic.

Eighteen years before Alan Seeger was born, France had undergone one of the most difficult episodes in its history. In 1870, provoked by the clever diplomacy of Otto von Bismarck, France declared war on Prussia. Bismarck hoped to use this war to rally the other German states around Prussia's leadership and form a unified German Reich. France's leader, the Emperor Napoleon III (Louis Napoleon, the nephew of Napoleon Bonaparte) hoped to use the war to revive the lagging support for his regime inside France. The result, chronicled in Émile Zola's novel *La Débâcle*, was a series of devastating French military defeats at Sedan and Metz, followed by a lengthy siege of Paris and finally a humiliating peace. The worst occurred, however, after the Germans stopped firing. Angered by what they perceived to be the capitulation of a conservative government to German demands and resentful of socio-economic inequality, ordinary Parisians rose up in class revolt and established the "Paris Commune." Before it was all over, nothing less than pitched battles had occurred in the streets of Paris between opposing armies of Frenchmen. The Communards' reign in the city was bloody, but the government's crackdown was worse still. The hilltop village of Montmartre had been the site of the initial rising, and it was there that the rising's final defenders were executed. The schisms in French society ran deep, and few believed that the Third Republic, established in the wake of the crisis, would live very long. Yet it did live. Neither France's conservative elements nor its leftists could agree on a future that was inclusive of the other, and therefore both permitted the Third Republic to survive as a temporary solution; in fact it would last for nearly seven decades—from 1871 to 1940.

View of the Eiffel Tower and the grounds of the *Exposition Universelle* on the Champs de Mars with the Seine and the Pont d'Iena in the foreground, 1889.

Bismarck's Reich was proclaimed in the Hall of Mirrors in Louis XIV's palace at Versailles. The Prussian army marched in triumph down the Champs-Élysées, while France was forced to pay an indemnity of 5 billion francs (an enormous sum in 1871). Most of Alsace and a large portion of Lorraine were annexed by the new Germany, with little consideration for the sentiments of their inhabitants. This defeat was a shock to the psyche of France, which had been accustomed to treating the German states as political pawns for centuries. But out of this collective national trauma emerged a society perhaps more central to the cultural and intellectual life of Western Civilization than any that had preceded it. Germany had won on the battlefield, but as would become evident in the decades ahead, France would win in its contributions to the arts, theater, science, literature, fashion, and culture. This rejuvenation of France, and of

Paris specifically, was on display for all to see at the 1889 Paris *Exposition Universelle*—especially in the giant wrought iron tower erected by Gustave Eiffel to commemorate the beginning of the French Revolution one hundred years before. It was the tallest man-made structure in the world, surpassing the Washington Monument in America, a distinction it maintained until the completion of the Chrysler Building in New York in 1930. To be sure, the "temporary" structure was derided by many of the Exposition's critics as a monstrosity, but it quickly gained popular favor and permanence in the city's vision of itself. Plans to dismantle it after the Exposition ended were quietly dropped.

Beaming a set of powerful searchlights into the night from its spire, the Tower came to represent France's rebirth from the ashes of 1871. Moreover, there was nothing in Berlin that could match it in daring of conception, audacity of design, or the effect it had on the international consciousness. Soon after its completion, American inventor Thomas Edison met with Eiffel in his personal apartment at the top of the Tower. The Wizard of Menlo Park presented the Magician of Iron with a fresh copy of one of his new phonograph records. It was a moment that encapsulated the dizzying and intoxicating heights of the modern age and all its possibilities.

Something quite different, however, was intoxicating the German people and their leaders. The new Kaiser, Wilhelm II, had come to power the year before the *Exposition Universelle*, following the untimely death of his father. Germany's new leader was vain, thrusting, and colossally arrogant. One of his first important decisions was to dismiss the very man who had created the empire he had inherited. Otto von Bismarck understood how crucial

France's diplomatic isolation was to German security. In a few short years, Wilhelm had reversed this situation—isolating Germany diplomatically and driving Russia's Czar into an alliance with the French republic. But with Germany's industry and military the envy of Europe, its population the best educated and paid in the world, and its universities the most widely admired, the Kaiser felt he had little to worry about. By the end of the 1890s he had decided to construct a navy as well: one that would rival and alarm his British cousins. And for the most part his people—the most industrious and obedient in Europe—were with him. Even before Wilhelm's ascension to power, the mood in Germany had changed. Historian Barbara Tuchman remarked how "the banker Edgar Speyer, returning to his birthplace . . . after twenty-seven years in England, found that three victorious wars and the establishment of the Empire had created a changed atmosphere in Germany that was 'intolerable' to him. German nationalism had replaced German liberalism. Great prosperity and self-satisfaction had acted, it seemed to him, like a narcotic on the people, leaving them content to forgo their liberty under a rampant militarism and a servility to Army and Kaiser that were 'unbelievable.'"[8]

Germany was now exercising its right, as it saw it, to become the preeminent world power. The nineteenth-century writings of naturalist Charles Darwin, historian Heinrich von Treitschke, and philosopher Friedrich Neitzsche all seemingly pointed to a struggle in which Germany had no choice but to assert itself. In fact it was the "right and duty of the nobler, stronger, superior race to extend its rule over inferior peoples, which, in the German view, meant over the world."[9] The half-mad Neitzsche became the unwitting seer of this new Darwinian understanding of international relations: "The sap was rising in Germany and Germans responded eagerly" to Nietzsche's "theory of the rights of the strong over the weak."[10]

And it was not just in Germany that nationalism and a new readiness to strive for mastery were on the rise. From his eyrie atop Tompkins Hill, ten-year-old Alan Seeger had been able to observe the mighty new vessels of the U.S. Navy in the hurried weeks of the summer of 1898 as the United States itself looked to impose its vision of a new order on the Western Hemisphere and in Asia. The Spanish-American War signaled a turn towards a more robust international role for the United States, with significant implications for the new century that was about to dawn.

★ ★ ★

John "Jack" Bowe was to play a part in this imperial drama. In many respects he was an unusual volunteer; even by the time he saw action in the Spanish-American War he was already an unlikely candidate for service on account of his age and responsibilities. Born in England in 1869, Bowe had settled on the edge of the Great Prairie in Canby, Minnesota, married a local widow, and put down roots. Yet he was there with the 13th Minnesota Regiment when it embarked from San Francisco on June 26, 1898, and when it arrived at its destination halfway across the globe in the Philippines on July 31.

The Filipinos (like the Cubans, whose aspirations were the original cause of the war) wanted to gain their independence from Spain. President McKinley, however, wanted the island nation as a base to project American economic power onto the Asian mainland. Jack Bowe and his comrades first fought the Spanish in the Battle of Manila on August 13, 1898, seizing the city;[11] they then fought the Filipinos in the insurgency that followed. Once the Filipinos realized America's true intentions, they became grimly determined to expel their erstwhile liberators. The Filipino Insurrection of 1899 to 1902 was one of the ugliest conflicts in U.S. military history. Fighting an asymmetrical war thousands of miles from home was not a simple matter. The ruthlessness of the struggle on both sides shocked observer and participant alike. Torture, mutilation, and—most distressingly of all—reprisals involving atrocities perpetrated against unarmed civilians characterized the fight. When word of what was occurring reached home, a debate ensued in the press and Congress over whether America was discarding its most cherished ideals for the allure of riches and power abroad. For his part, Theodore Roosevelt, campaigning as William McKinley's vice presidential running mate in the 1900 election, emphasized the absurdity of these claims by pointing out the treatment of Native Americans and the seizure of their lands. Would anyone seriously consider giving Arizona back to the Apaches, he queried?[12] No. In the end, the U.S. asserted its control over the Philippines; Jack Bowe returned to Minnesota, wrote a book about his experiences in the war, and was elected mayor of Canby. He fathered four children and appeared to be a man whose greatest adventures were behind him.

One unintended consequence of the Spanish-American War was the first genuine reconciliation between the states of the old Confederacy and the rest of the Union. For the first time since the War with Mexico in 1846–1848, officers and enlisted men from both sides of the Mason-Dixon Line served together against a common foe. In fact, the overall commander of the force that liberated or invaded Cuba (depending on one's point of view) was an ex-Confederate officer, General Joseph Wheeler. The South had suffered terribly during the Civil War and was just now beginning to reemerge and participate in the dynamic changes occurring in the rest of the country, something the Cotton States and International Exposition of 1895 in Atlanta was meant to celebrate.

Two of the young men who would grow up in the "New South" heralded at the Exposition were Paul Rockwell and his brother Kiffin. Born four years apart, in 1888 and 1892, the two boys had lost their father to typhoid in 1893, and subsequently had been raised mostly by their maternal grandfather, Enoch Shaw Ayres. Ayres owned a large tobacco plantation in the lowlands of South Carolina, with wooded areas and rivers nearby full of wild game. The boys' characters took shape in a rich natural and historical environment. Ayres regaled his two admiring grandsons with tales of his service in the Confederate Army under Robert E. Lee. Their grandfather was proud of the fact that when news reached him of the substance of the meeting between Lee and Ulysses S. Grant at Appomattox Courthouse he had simply, "ridden away to his South Carolina home without waiting to be paroled, and therefore "had never surrendered to the 'Yankees.'"[13] The stories of the "Lost Cause" made an especially strong impression on the youthful Kiffin Rockwell. His brother Paul was steady and studious. Kiffin was a more restless soul. In his memoir of his brother, Paul captured the essence of Kiffin Rockwell in these formative years: "He was accounted a good shot, and was an excellent fisherman.... For his books he did not especially care, although he learned his lessons well and quickly, having a keen and clever mind. His favorite reading books were books of travel and adventure.... But his best hours were those spent out in the open; he was a good swimmer and an excellent horseman...."[14]

These pursuits would provide an ideal foundation for the life that Kiffin Rockwell would one day lead. In 1909 he entered the Virginia Military Institute, the school where Thomas "Stonewall" Jackson had once taught. But he didn't stick. He next wangled an appointment to the Naval Academy at Annapolis, in the hope that the sea would be a more direct route to actual action, but he soon grew disillusioned with this line of thinking and instead wound up at his brother's college, Washington & Lee, located near VMI in Lexington, Virginia. Kiffin Rockwell's years there proved to be largely pleasant ones. He was described as tall, graceful, blue-eyed, and handsome, and "much sought after by the girls."[15] In his studies, only history seemed to make any impression. Years later Paul remarked on this time in his brother's life: "As I look back, it is clear to me that Kiffin was all this while only unconsciously marking time. He was in school more from family habit and tradition than from a real desire to follow classical studies. He usually had a far-away, dreamy look in his eyes, and often seemed to be living in another world from that surrounding him."[16]

Kiffin Rockwell had all the makings of the knight errant, but without a quest worthy of his abilities and temperament. For him the *Belle Époque* was seemingly too serene and self-satisfied. The next few years would find him restlessly moving from one place to another, trying on occupations, until at last he found himself back in the South, in Atlanta, working in an advertising agency and sharing an apartment on West Peachtree Street with his brother Paul, waiting for...what? He couldn't explain.

★ ★ ★

For Bob Scanlon, the "New South" looked a lot like the "Old South." Growing up African-American—or, in the parlance of the time "Negro" or "colored"—in the South in the 1890s and early 1900s made one an object of both derision and suspicion. If one was male, the threat of mob violence was never far from the surface. It was during this period that lynching reached epidemic proportions in the South, with nearly two thousand African-Americans losing their lives in this manner.[17] Bob Scanlon of Mobile, Alabama, had limited options. The one thing he did have going for him was an athletic physique. The first decade of the twentieth century witnessed the rise of the first black sports hero in American history: the heavyweight boxing champion of the world, Jack Johnson. Johnson's rise to the top of the ranks generated fear and anger in many whites. For blacks such as young Bob Scanlon, Johnson represented hope and racial pride. It was no surprise, then, that Scanlon himself used boxing to change his stars. He followed in Johnson's historical wake and eventually found himself in what was, for him, a new world: Europe.

Between 1907 and 1910, Bob Scanlon fought thirteen bouts in the United Kingdom and France, primarily as a light heavyweight but also as a welterweight. London and Paris were a revelation to the young American. The venues for his fights were in some of the most notorious enclaves of these two cities: primarily London's Whitechapel district and the village of Montmartre in Paris. The Moulin Rouge, the Hippodrome, and the "Élysée Montmartre" drew the paying crowds to see the cards Scanlon boxed on in Paris. But there was much more, oh so much more, going on in Montmartre than merely boxing. The site of Scanlon's first bout, the Moulin Rouge, with its eponymous windmill decorated with bright red lights, had become an icon of the Paris *demi-monde* (literally the "half-world," a term coined in the nineteenth century to describe the less reputable side of society inhabited by actors, gamblers, courtesans, artists, and addicts). Artist Henri Toulouse-Lautrec had immortalized a number of the cabaret's top performers in mass-produced promotional posters in the years before his death in 1901. High-kicking red-headed can-can dancer Jane Avril and black-gloved night club singer Yvette Guilbert drew both starving artists and wealthy aristocrats to the Moulin Rouge, the Chat Noir (Black Cat), and the Lapin Agile (Agile Rabbit). The latter was favored by Pablo Picasso, who had arrived in Paris from Barcelona in 1900 and like so many other artists had been drawn to Montmartre for its cheap rents and unapologetically Bohemian lifestyle.

Sex drove most of the cabarets' business, or rather sex mixed with art, alcohol, and drugs. Of these the most fashionable, and the most dangerous, was absinthe. First developed in the eighteenth century, the green-colored liquor was incredibly potent, with a distinctive taste as a result of the anise and wormwood used in its production. Pernod was the preferred brand of connoisseurs, though many labels competed for the French market. The addictive, deleterious, and hallucinogenic effects of absinthe made it an object of criticism from social conservatives who feared it would corrode the health and morals of French society. But the socio-political divide between the right and left in France extended beyond the bottle. It had its roots, arguably, as far back as the French Revolution. One party believed they represented tradition against radicalism; the other was sure they represented progress in the face of reaction.

In the years prior to Bob Scanlon's debut as a professional fighter at the Moulin Rouge, France had nearly torn itself apart over the conviction of a captain of artillery on charges of espionage. The tremendous strides that had been made since the debacle of 1870–1871, put on such glorious display at the *Expedition Universelle* in 1889, were jeopardized by *l'affaire Dreyfus* (the Dreyfus affair), which had begun in 1894 with the discovery that *someone* in the French Army was passing secrets to the Germans. Dreyfus, a Jew from Alsace, was wrongly accused and convicted. When he was sent to the French penal colony in South America, it seemed a closed matter. But over time the truth of what had happened came to light. Dreyfus's Jewish background became a source of some of the most poisonous invective France had ever witnessed. The army and its anti-Dreyfusard supporters saw this as a struggle ultimately more significant than one man's guilt or innocence—as nothing less than a battle for the soul of France. They believed the Dreyfusards were undermining France when it was in a vulnerable and dangerous situation—by attacking the army as it stared down the Kaiser and his generals. But the Left had one significant advantage going for it in this instance: the truth. In the end, as a result of tireless efforts on his behalf by his brother, the novelist Émile Zola, and others, Dreyfus secured his release and eventual reinstatement in the army. But *l'affaire Dreyfus* had forced France to decide what it stood for—and, in the end, what it stood for was the rights of the individual and the rule of law. One other thing that *l'affaire Dreyfus* brought attention to was just how paranoid the French High Command was regarding Germany. It was all the Kaiser and his top officials could do not to snicker as France turned itself upside down and inside out. But as the second decade of the new century began, Frenchmen, of whatever political persuasion, had begun to rally around a common national identity. As subsequent events would demonstrate, it would prove to be none too soon.

The Moulin Rouge, Montmartre, Paris, 1900.

* * *

For David King and Victor Chapman, Paris meant the pursuit of artistic improvement and accomplishment, as well as personal freedom. Both had been raised in wealthy cocoons, never experiencing physical deprivation, accustomed to all doors being open to them because of who they were. Both men attended Harvard soon after that hallowed institution had undergone significant change brought about by university president Charles William Eliot. It was still largely a preserve of the wealthy. But the modern university with its emphasis on research and professional schools—of which Harvard is now the premier example in the popular mind—had its genesis during Eliot's time as president. There's nothing to suggest that either King or Chapman was an especially gifted or promising student at Harvard. In certain respects, like their future brother-in-arms Kiffin Rockwell at Washington & Lee, they seemed to be in college because it was the usual thing for someone of their station to do at that period in their lives. In fact, both men possessed artistic souls and looked across the Atlantic to Paris, as so many Americans had done before them—author James Fenimore Cooper, painters Samuel F. B. Morse and Mary Cassatt, sculptor Augustus Saint-Gaudens, and arbiter of the *avant garde* Gertrude Stein, to name but a notable handful—to find an outlet for artistic expression: one with a notebook and pen and typewriter; the other with a sketchpad, a piece of charcoal, and a box of paints.

Considering their social backgrounds, these young men were refreshingly lacking in snobbery. They enjoyed sharing a table, a bottle, and a laugh with anyone who shared their passion for life, and for life in Paris in particular. Diminutive and easy-going, David King did not write the great American novel, or much else, during this period, but he did develop a fondness for Pernod and the *demimonde*.[18] Victor Chapman was a handsome, gregarious giant with the build of a lumberjack and the generous nature of a child. His youth had been marked by loss—first when his beloved mother died when he was six years old; then when his brother drowned in front of him. There is no doubt that his inability to save his brother affected him deeply. For the rest of his life he would never shirk from putting himself at risk to aid others. Children liked him; so did dogs. On the other hand, his father remarked that there was "something about him of silence, mystery" and "part of the Middle Ages in his piety."[19] Yet, he "could eat anything, sleep on anything, lift anything, endure anything."[20] Chapman graduated from Harvard in 1913 and soon thereafter embarked for Paris to study at the *atelier* of a noted French architect. But true to form, the young man always had his box of watercolors with him: ready to paint any scene that captured his attention.

The year before Chapman arrived in Paris, Alan Seeger had found his way to the city as well. He had graduated from Harvard in 1910, in the same class with David King, having followed his brother Charles, who was studying music there, to the Ivy League school. Seeger had distinguished himself to a certain degree with the publication of some poems in the *Harvard Monthly*. But he was a social misanthrope. His reputation was that of an intelligent yet immature young man. To some degree his social awkwardness and literary posturing continued on his return from Harvard to New York. Taking to the Bohemian lifestyle of Greenwich Village, Seeger worried both family and friends with his brooding nature, lack of hygiene, and obvious penury. Finally, in the spring of 1912, with the assistance of a generous and loving father, Alan Seeger booked passage to the city of his desires, to start over.

Settling in Paris's Latin Quarter, he rented a small studio at 17 Rue Sommerard in the city's 5th arrondissement. Soon after taking the apartment he confided to a friend that he "chose it for the view." He was particularly fond of the towers of Notre Dame Cathedral just across the Seine. Seeger wrote that he could see them "even from pillow, gray and spectral against the lustre of the city lights as I go to bed at night."[21] It was here that he would find his voice as a poet, with the city itself as his muse. Few have ever absorbed Paris as Seeger did. The free-flowing wine of the cafés aside, he was drunk on it.

> Oh, go to Paris... In the midday gloom
> Of some old quarter take a little room
> That looks off over Paris and its towers
> From Saint Gervais round to the Emperor's Tomb
> ...And looking out over the domes and towers

That chime the fleeting quarters and hours,
While the bright clouds banked eastward back of them
Blush in the sunset, pink as hawthorn flowers
You cannot fail to think, as I have done,
Some of life's ends attained, so you be one
Who measures life's attainment by the hours
That Joy has rescued from oblivion.

To Seeger, Paris was a universe in itself. When his brooding nature threatened to take possession of him he enjoyed "walking for hours along the Seine or through the winding streets of Montmartre; then carousing with friends, making the rounds of Left Bank cafés." At dawn they would head to Les Halles, the city's great open-air market, to "a stall where steaming onion soup and hunks of still-warm bread could be bought for a few centimes."[22] The conversation, running the gamut from the passionate to the ridiculous, never lagged until the morning sun rising into the sky forced them "home to a garret room or studio, to sleep a few hours and awaken ready for work, play, or love."[23] And Seeger was tasting his first modest literary success since his Harvard days. His posturing, haughty, and defensive demeanor gave way to a more mature, lighter, confident, and humble personality. With this new more agreeable disposition, Seeger made friends easily and widely. His social circle reached out beyond the Parisian literary scene to include old classmates like David King and painters and composers as well. He crossed social, ethnic, and racial lines to form new bonds.

Among his friends was a working class Brooklyn native named Herman Chatkoff. Chatkoff had had a falling out with his parents and subsequently signed on as a deck hand aboard a cattle boat to work his way across the Atlantic to France. He was currently employed at a garage washing cars. On the side he "painted bad Parisian street scenes" occasionally selling one "to an American tourist with more money than taste."[24] Bob Scanlon, the African-American boxer from Mobile, Alabama, also became one of Seeger's good friends. Scanlon had returned to the United States in 1910 and again in 1912 to fight in New York and Milwaukee, but he always found his way back to Europe. He won more than he lost,[25] and he was game. People wanted to see him. As a sort of poor man's Jack Johnson, Scanlon enjoyed personal freedom abroad that would have been all but unthinkable for a "colored" man back home. France in particular had been very good to him. It was an exciting place. It was a hopeful time. And ultimately it was worth fighting for.

Paris was at its very best in the years just before the outbreak of war in 1914. Some, it is true, saw in the *Belle Époque* an over-ripe decadence. As early as the 1890s, Max Nordau had written with near hysteria of "Anarchism, Socialism, women's dress, madness, suicide, nervous diseases, drug addiction, dancing, sexual license, all of which were combining to produce a society without self-control, discipline or shame which was 'marching to its certain ruin.'"[26] What, then, would he have thought of Pablo Picasso's *Les Demoiselles d'Avignon*? This painting shocked the Parisian art community when it was first given a private showing in 1907. It heralded Cubism, the new method adopted by Picasso and his collaborator the French painter Georges Braque. It also heralded new notions about art, beauty, and meaning. Picasso's great rival Henri Matisse had initially made light of the painting, but then moved even more boldly in the radical direction it pointed to. Instead of representing the inevitable devolution of

Western Civilization, the work of Picasso and Matisse demonstrated in no uncertain terms the vitality and continued evolution of *Belle Époque* society.

And it was not just in art that this vitality was evident in the Paris of the time.

The changes in fashion, particularly in women's clothing, were also quite bold and imaginative. The days of wasp-waisted ladies being tied into constricting corsets was at an end. Coco Chanel, a girl from the provinces who had gotten her start design-

Alan Seeger in Paris, 1912.

ing hats, had begun a revolution in French haute couture. Her women's styles were "inspired by menswear, and all modeled on the simplicity of design that suited her and (in her own estimation) enhanced the youthfulness of the wearer."[27] François Coty was in turn revolutionizing the perfume industry while funding the creation of works of art by René Lalique in the design of bottles for his ever more subtle and complex scents. In the automobile industry, Louis Renault and André Citroën were on the cutting edge of innovation in both design and production.[28] Marcel Proust was nearing completion of the first volume of his great work *In Search of Lost Time*. In the laboratory Pierre and Marie Curie were discovering polonium and eventually, at great personal risk, radium. As Mary McAuliffe has pointed out, "Instead of patenting the technique that Marie had developed to isolate it, they decided to publish the results of their work in accord with the scientific spirit."[29] It was far from a decadent age.

Then what was it? It was all these things, and something more. Barbara Tuchman in her great work *The Proud Tower*, written at a time when the *Belle Époque* was still a living memory for tens of millions of people, described it as "an edifice of grandeur and passion, of riches and beauty and dark cellars. Its inhabitants lived, as compared to a later time, with more self-reliance, more confidence, more hope; greater magnificence, extravagance and elegance; more careless ease, more gaiety, more pleasure in each other's company and conversation, more injustice and hypocrisy, more misery and want, more sentiment including false sentiment, less sufferance of mediocrity, more dignity in work, more delight in nature, more zest."[30]

There were few passions pursued with "more zest" during this era than flight. Aviation had taken hold of the popular imagination as nothing else had or could, given its ancient, even dreamlike, connotations. But unlike Icarus, these new men in their flying machines would not be defeated by the elements. It had all started in 1901 at the less-successful sequel to the 1889 *Exposition Universelle*, when the fair's promoters had offered a prize to the first person to successfully pilot an airship around the Eiffel Tower. A Brazilian inventor named Alberto Santos Dumont was the first to successfully do so, in a motor-powered dirigible of his own design. He claimed the 125,000-franc prize and became the toast of Paris. But two years later, on the other side of the Atlantic, brothers Orville and Wilbur Wright outdid Santos Dumont by inventing the first functioning airplane. Their successful test at Kitty Hawk, North Carolina, on December 17, 1903, was nothing less than revolutionary in its implications for both travel and warfare. Interestingly enough, the Wright brothers' work was not appreciated in their home country to nearly the same degree that it was in Europe—and, above all, in France. Within six years of the Wright brothers' first flight, Louis Blériot had piloted a monoplane of his own design across the English Channel, capturing first laurels for France in international aviation prestige. His fellow Frenchmen Henri and Maurice Farman, Gabriel Voisin, and Roland Garros followed on the trail Blériot had blazed. Again, *Belle Époque* France was in the vanguard.

Back in the United States, a daring few also took the skies, most notably motorcycle innovator and racer Glenn Curtis. A fair number of the early pilots had previous experience as either motorcycle or automobile racers. Flying certainly called to the daredevil streak in certain people. Broken limbs, burns, and death were always one critical miscalculation, one crucial malfunction away. It wasn't for everyone. Though the masses were fascinated by flight, only an elite group of pilots actually experienced the exhilaration and the dangers. At Yale in the years before the war, one of those aspiring to this elite of the skies was a student from Pittsburgh named William Thaw. Thaw came from a different branch of the same family that produced the notorious Harry Thaw, who had married showgirl Evelyn Nesbit, the former teen mistress of architect Stanford White, in 1905 and in a fit of jealous rage shot and killed White while he was dining on the roof of Madison Square Garden. Harry Thaw was a drug addict and sadist who pleaded "temporary insanity" in his defense. He won at the trial, but had his personal life dragged through the muck of the sensationalist press. His kinsman William enjoyed the high life as well. His name was seen in the gossip pages of the press of the day with claims that, if even partly true, were impressive indeed. One article claimed that he had once drunk

"68 brandies at one sitting at a country club," lost "$200,000…in a poker game," and given "a dinner at the Waldorf for twenty stage beauties" with the "sky as the limit."[31] Bill Thaw knew how to have a good time. But there was more to him than this. He loved beautiful women and consuming large amounts of alcohol, but he loved flying more.

William Thaw had dropped his studies at Yale altogether in 1913 to pursue a full-time career in aviation, both in design and as a pilot. In one of the most daring achievements of the early age of flight, William Thaw and his partner Steve MacGordon flew their flying boat underneath the four main bridges (as they then existed: the Brooklyn, Manhattan, Williamsburg, and Queensboro Bridges, respectively) spanning the East River, connecting Manhattan to Long Island. It was audacious—and dangerous—and intended to make New Yorkers, and Americans in general, sit up and take notice.[32] Within a few months, Thaw found himself in France trying to convince the French to purchase his brother Alexander's idea for a stabilizing device. He and his brother eagerly anticipated word from the government: a $100,000 prize was at stake. Meanwhile, he entered the Schneider Trophy Race held in Monaco Bay in April 1914, but failed to place.[33] In France, spring turned to summer.

* * *

The previous spring, a new performance by the Ballets Russes dance company had premiered at the Théâtre des Champs-Élysées in Paris. The music for the ballet, *Le Sacre du printemps* (The Rite of Spring), was written by composer Igor Stravinsky to evoke pagan rites. As a virgin danced herself to death in a fertility ritual, the strains of Stravinsky's music filled the hall with a sense of unease, mixed with excitement and anger. The crowd in attendance that night was split between the exhilarated and the outraged; a riot broke out and spread into the nearby streets and cafés. It was as if something both deeply ancient and disturbingly new had been birthed that evening. Its roots were in Nietzsche's writings, in the plays of Gabriele D'Annunzio, and perhaps most significantly in Sigmund Freud's pioneering work in psychoanalysis. Freud's "id," fully unrestrained, seemed to be on display that night in Paris. The conjuration of pre-Christian pagan rites suggested something unnerving. For all of the dismissive vitriol leveled by the Left at the Catholic Church and its conservative supporters, the civility and respect for the rule of law that all enjoyed and took for granted had its foundation in Christianity. If Western Civilization became unmoored from the Christian religion, the future began to look potentially as ferocious as the unrecorded past. With the removal

Those magnificent men in their flying machines—William Thaw (at right) after successfully flying under the four bridges spanning the East River, New York, 1913.

of the moral constraints Judeo-Christian civilization had imposed on itself, the use of power—exponentially enhanced by the new technology—in pursuit of national, racial, or ideological goals was now unlimited. In Germany, this mindset found fertile ground.

Germans had been late to form a national identity in a defined political and geographic form. Once it was securely in place, however, it superseded all other loyalties. When Nietzsche had proclaimed that God was dead, he was hoping that religion would be replaced by his Superman. But, as Barbara Tuchman explained, "ordinary people substituted patriotism. As faith in God retreated before the advance of science, love of country began to fill the empty spaces in the heart. Nationalism absorbed the strength once belonging to religion."[34] And this new religion had its own high priests—the Kaiser and his coterie of Junker generals (Prussian noblemen, with large agrarian estates) and sycophantic advisors. In their effort to hold German society and Germany's political institutions firmly under their control, they looked to exploit the country's vast industrial capacity to create a war machine unlike any the world had yet seen. To be fair, they were not alone in inciting nationalistic hysteria or building ever more—and ever more powerful—armaments. Many nations used the government-funded public education systems (seen as a great advance by progressive reformers in the nineteenth century) to inculcate a belief in their people's special place in the world, to nurse old grudges, and to justify future aggression. The business community did its part, but was also looking to exploit other markets: "Krupp, the colossus of Essen, was the largest single business in Europe. Skoda, Schneider-Creusot, Vickers-maxim, the distended combines of many mergers with harsh names that grated on the ear, had interests in every camp."[35]

Yet Germany held special place in this circle of rivals. While its militarism and growing industry (particularly in the Ruhr basin) and the political tone-deafness of its Kaiser threatened its neighbors, Germany itself suffered from the dangerous delusion that it was being threatened. The "encirclement" by Russia to the East and France to the west, aided at sea by Britain's Royal Navy since the *Entente Cordiale*—a diplomatic "understanding" (with military implications) between longtime rivals France and Britain, aimed at restraining Germany—had been made public in 1904, made Germany's leaders not only powerful and potentially unrestrained, but paranoid. This was a toxic combination. Russia in particular made German generals nervous. As early as December 1912, Helmuth von Moltke, the chief of staff of the German Army, stated, "In my opinion war is inevitable, and the sooner the better."[36] He subsequently ordered a premeditated publicity campaign to prepare public opinion for war against Russia. Because of the Franco-Russian alliance, however, war with Russia meant war with France—and finishing the unfinished business of 1871. For Germany to break out of its self-perceived "encirclement" and achieve its goal of world supremacy, France must be broken. For France to be broken, Paris must be captured. The French, for their part, had erected a statue of a female figure representing "Strasbourg," the capital of the lost province of Alsace, in the Place de la Concorde and kept it draped in a black cloak in mourning.

And what of the calls for an international court to settle conflicts through arbitration, a view fervently espoused by American captain of industry Andrew Carnegie, and more disingenuously by Kaiser Wilhelm's own cousin, Czar Nicholas II of Russia? The Kaiser answered this question for himself, and for his countrymen: "I shit on all their decisions."[37]

CHAPTER 2

ERUPTION

Those living during the *Belle Époque* had a vague unease over the European political situation, akin to the disquiet felt by prosperous villagers tending their vineyards and livestock on the green slopes of a long-dormant yet smoking volcano. Ever since Germany had fought a series of wars to achieve unification in the previous generation, the existing Great Power balance in Europe had been disturbed by the newcomer's sense of entitlement. The European nations were lined up like dominoes waiting only for someone, or something, to start the chain reaction of a general European war—or so conventional wisdom has it.

★ ★ ★

The assassination of the Austrian Archduke Franz Ferdinand and his wife on June 28, 1914, triggered the eruption that would alter Europe forever. Before it was all over, four empires would be swept away, the world's first communist state would be created, and the United States would emerge as a great power. But why did it happen? What was it about the assassination of these two people that caused such catastrophic upheaval?

The archduke was the heir to the throne of Austria-Hungary, a dual monarchy with the ancient Hapsburg family at its head. As a Hapsburg, Franz Ferdinand was all too familiar with the vulnerability of his family's empire to the yearnings of the various ethnicities within it for greater autonomy. None of these ethnic groups was more problematic than the Serbs—a proud people with a long history of fiercely independent stands and tragic defeats. After centuries of being dominated by Muslim Turks, they were in no mood to be dominated by German-speaking Catholics. Austria-Hungary had taken advantage of the Turks' weakness after a war with Russia to seize control of the provinces of Bosnia-Herzegovina in 1878. Bosnia was home to the majority of Europe's nine million Serbs. Making the situation even more volatile, a land-locked rump Serb state existed nearby as a catalyst for discontent and ultra-nationalist conspiracies. One of these conspiracies involved Serbia's intelligence chief, Dragutin Dimitrijević, also known as Colonel Apis, and an organization known as "Young Bosnia." Apis himself also played a leading role in a shadowy Serb organization known as the "Black Hand." Even today some of the details remain murky, but what is clear is that the Black Hand armed a small band of Bosnian Serbs with bombs and revolvers and assisted them in crossing the imperial frontier undetected just days before the archduke's arrival in Sarajevo, the provincial capital of Bosnia.[1] Ultimately,

Princip is apprehended after firing his fatal shots in Sarajevo, June 28, 1914.

one of these Bosnian Serbs named Gavrilo Pincip—little more than a boy really—got up the nerve to shoot Franz Ferdinand after an earlier attempt with a bomb had failed. As the archduke's chauffeur backed into a side street off Appel Quay, Princip walked over and aimed into the open limousine.

Princip hoped that the assassination of the empire's leading figure—Franz Ferdinand's uncle, the Emperor Franz Joseph, was a doddering old man by this point—would lead to a war that would ultimately result in an enlarged Serbia. This new entity would then unite all Serbs and their fellow Southern Slavs in an independent state. It was an example of the rash, act-with-violence line of thinking that had been popularized in the preceding century by the anarchist movement. After emptying his revolver, Princip gamely tried to commit suicide by chomping down on a cyanide capsule that had been conveniently supplied by the Black Hand. It failed to have the desired effect, only making him

violently ill. He would die in prison during the war, a largely
forgotten figure.

Within hours of the assassination, the Austrian government
began formulating a response. Both the foreign minister Leopold
von Berchtold and chief of staff of the army Conrad von Hotzendorf viewed the tragedy as an opportunity that they had to be
especially careful not to squander. They viewed the rump Serb state
as the main problem facing Austria-Hungary. Its very existence
served as a beacon for fanatics like Princip. Now the time had come
to fight a preemptive war and stomp it into oblivion. The problem
for Berchtold and Hotzendorf was that Serbia had a powerful
protector in imperial Russia. The Russians shared ethnic, religious,
and cultural ties with the Serb people and would not permit their
archrival in the Balkans to bully their fellow Slavs. Czar Nicholas
II's army was the largest in Europe, and the shared border between
the two empires meant that by invading Serbia, Austria-Hungary
would open itself up to invasion. It was an apparently intractable
dilemma. Yet Foreign Minister Berchtold had a possible ace up his
sleeve.

Going back to the formation of the Dreikaiserbund (Three
Emperors' League) in 1873, Germany had maintained a formal
alliance with the Hapsburgs. Austria-Hungary's more powerful
northern neighbor was on the cusp of hegemony, not only in con-
tinental Europe, but in the world at large as well. Or so its most
ardent admirers *and* detractors claimed. The reality of the situation, however, was more complex than this. Though Germany had
the most powerful (if not necessarily the largest) army in Europe,
it was a nation riddled with anxiety. The leaders of the country
were primarily drawn from the old landed aristocracy of Prussia,
conservative by nature and suspicious of any move toward a more

inclusive, democratic society in Germany. The Junkers, the Kaiser, and his ministers pushed for a place of primacy for Germany in world affairs (*weltpolitik*); on the other hand they feared their own primacy slipping away within Germany itself (*innenpolitik*).[2] The country's military leaders' obsession with "encirclement" in turn, led to a disastrous conclusion: war was inevitable (for both foreign and domestic reasons), and the sooner the better, as Russia's project of modernizing its army was well underway and would place Germany at a disadvantage by the decade's end.

In later years, Germany's desire for war in 1914 was dismissed in the more fashionable interpretation of events in Europe in favor of an indictment of all the Great Powers for somehow letting events slip away from them. As Britain's wartime prime minister David Lloyd George remarked in hindsight: "The nations slithered over the brink into the boiling cauldron of war without any trace of apprehension or dismay.... The nations backed their machines over the precipice...not one of them wanted war, certainly not on this scale."[3]

But this view conveniently overlooks the decision-making by Germany's leaders in the months leading up to that fateful summer of 1914. To be fair, Lloyd George would have had no way of knowing much of what we now know about that crucial period. It wasn't until the 1960s, when German historian Fritz Fischer with access to the imperial archives in Potsdam—then on the other side of the Iron Curtain—brought new attention to these documents, that the "collective guilt" thesis was called into serious question. Fischer upset decades of smug, self-righteous scholarship on the causes of the war. His most damning piece of evidence was the diary entry of one Admiral Müller on a German War Council meeting held late in 1912 in which Chief of Staff Helmuth von Moltke and

Kaiser Wilhelm II (left) and Army Chief of Staff Helmuth von Moltke. Both felt war was necessary and "the sooner the better."

Kaiser Wilhelm agreed that war was necessary. In the supercharged environment of July and August 1914, those Americans who flocked to France's defense *instinctively* understood something that it would take generations of historians to finally, fully recognize: Germany wanted war in 1914. It was the aggressor. Its semi-feudal nobles wanted to impose their authority at home and abroad, in no uncertain terms. In approaching Germany, Austrian Foreign Minister Berchtold was going to be reaching out to a far more receptive audience than even he suspected. His ace would prove to be a relatively simple card to play.

The July 5, 1914, meeting between Berchtold and the Kaiser and his chancellor Theodobald von Bethmann-Hollweg would lead to the greatest war in human history up to that time. Today historians commonly refer to this meeting as the "blank check," implying that that's exactly what Germany gave Austria-Hungary, to proceed against Serbia however it saw fit—the understanding being that, regardless of the consequences, Germany would stand by Austria militarily. This apparently reckless behavior on Germany's part makes far more sense in the light of Fischer's thesis. To paraphrase historian David Fromkin's description, Germany essentially "piggy-backed" its preemptive war against Russia (and Russia's ally France) onto Austria-Hungary's preemptive war against Serbia.[4]

The latter served to mask Germany's true aims perfectly. Armed with Germany's guarantee, Berchtold returned to Vienna in a greatly strengthened position *vis-a-vis* Serbia. Of course if Serbia, or the other powers of Europe for that matter, had known what had transpired at this meeting, perhaps the war could have been avoided. However, the meeting's secret nature all but guaranteed war—exactly as Germany had intended.

By the time Austria-Hungary presented Serbia with an ultimatum containing ten separate demands, the wheels of war had already been set in motion. The form and timing of the ultimatum on July 25 was intended to catch both the Serbs and the Triple Entente powers off their guard. Serbia had to accept all the demands or none, leaving it virtually no room for diplomatic maneuver. As it was the weekend, most of the British cabinet had gone home to be with their families. The French president, Raymond Poincaré, who had been in Russia on a state visit, had just left his eastern ally and was on a steamship in the Baltic Sea en route to France. All of this was quite cleverly intended. Now that Germany had the perfect cover for its preemptive war against Russia and France, it was not about to allow cooler heads to prevail. Too much was at stake.

This was a time, mind you, when Social Darwinist thinking was very much in vogue. The idea that a Power was either expanding or in decline was accepted as gospel by most. The concept of peaceful, mutually beneficial cooperation was totally alien to Germany's statesmen and military leaders. War was inevitable. Why not strike while the odds were still in one's favor? Britain's foreign secretary, Sir Edward Grey, suspected what was afoot, but the speed with which events unfolded left him playing a hopeless game of diplomatic catch-up. Russia, self-conscious of its role as protector of Europe's Slavs, marched ponderously but resolutely towards the precipice. The lack of imagination on the part of Russia's leaders at this point gives one the impression of men hypnotized by their adversaries, unable or unwilling to recognize what Germany was doing. Czar Nicholas II reached out to his cousin the Kaiser, but their correspondence proved fruitless in heading off the crisis. The fact that both were essentially well-meaning simpletons likely had something to do with that failure. By the last day of July, Austria-Hungary had declared war on Serbia and shelled its capital, Russia had mobilized in support of Serbia, and Germany had issued an ultimatum to Russia to stand down or face the consequences. When this ultimatum went unanswered, Germany went to war with Russia and her ally France.

* * *

For her part, France had no vital interest at stake in the quarrel between Austria-Hungary and Serbia. Because of her treaty obligations with Russia, however, which originated in the alliance formed between the two countries in 1893, France *was* involved. It had forged this alliance more than twenty years earlier to counter Germany's growing might on the continent of Europe. The scars of her defeat in the earlier Franco-Prussian War of 1870–1871 had

motivated French leaders to align France with the most conservative and autocratic of the Great Powers of Europe. The lost provinces of Alsace and Lorraine needed to be redeemed. Germany
would be unable to resist the justness of France's cause and the
sheer numbers of her less sophisticated ally. Or so the more opti-
mistic members of the government believed. At the very least, it
was understood that the Russian alliance would always force
Germany to pause before acting rashly. The idea that Russia would
suck France into a general war was certainly not the conventional
view at the time—the alliance was supposed to prevent the war
with Germany, not precipitate one. Yet France was presented with
an ultimatum by its archrival on August 2: stand down or face war
with the Kaiser's army. The fact that they had been preparing for
this moment for over forty years did little to soften the impact of
what was about to transpire. France was going to war. All Paris
was electric and terrified—emboldened, resigned.

★ ★ ★

In the midst of these heady, panicked hours the American expatriate community was as swept along by events as their hosts. There
was a general sense that France's fight was their fight, too. Within
days of Germany's formal declaration of war, a group of American
men sought the counsel of U.S. ambassador Myron Herrick to determine the legality of joining the French Army. Herrick explained to
them that it would be impossible to do so and retain their U.S. citizenship. Fortunately, France had a curious institution known as the
Légion étrangère. The French Foreign Legion, formed in 1831 to
help subdue Algerian insurgents, actively recruited foreigners to fight
for France. It asked only that its members swear "to serve with

faithfulness and honor" and "to follow the corps...wherever the government may wish to send it."[5] No formal oath of allegiance to France was necessary.[6]

For its part, the giant French military machine appreciated the Americans' keen desire to help, but it had far larger concerns as plans formulated and tweaked for more than a generation were put into effect. The innocuous-sounding "Plan 17" called for an enormous French offensive east into the lands taken by Germany in 1871—Alsace and Lorraine—then on to the Rhine and beyond. The French High Command, despite ample evidence to the contrary from the Boer War and the Balkan Wars earlier in the youthful century, insisted that the ferocity of the bayonet would trump the Maxim machine gun and high explosive. Relying on the combination of *élan* and *cran* (guts), they expected to sweep the German Army before them in an *attaque à outrance* (attack to excess). Millions of young Frenchmen mustered on village greens and in town and city squares, their hobnailed shoes clattering on ancient cobblestoned streets, boarded railway cars long diverted for just this purpose, and traveled through a green and golden countryside towards the German frontier.

For Alan Seeger and his circle of friends in Paris, these days were filled with a high degree of pathos and an otherworldly detachment from the events screaming at them from the headlines of the city's dailies. Life went on. On the day after Serbia failed to agree to all of the terms of Austria-Hungary's ultimatum, so pregnant with dread, Belgian cyclist Philippe Thys completed the final stage of the Tour de France. He entered Paris after a 210-mile ride from the port of Dunkerque on the English Channel, claiming his second consecutive title.[7] The heated discussions in the cafés continued far into the evenings, but with an urgency now, as radical socialists and anarchists argued against those in support of heeding the nation's call to arms.[8] In the end, there were far more of the latter (including many socialists), and the tables began to empty as *patrie* trumped ideology—in what would come to be known as the *union sacrée* or "sacred union" between French citizens and the state, though some did refuse to take part in the war. (The French authorities had actually anticipated a 5–13 percent refusal rate from call-ups. In fact, the rate was only 1.5 percent). For his part, Pablo Picasso, a citizen of Paris for fourteen years, chose to stay in the city, but stay out of the fight. His fellow cubist Georges Braque volunteered.

In the meantime, the Americans in Paris were forced to wait until August 21 to formally enlist. In the intervening weeks they held daily drill under Charles Sweeney, West Point class of 1904, in the courtyard of the Palais Royal in the 1st arrondissement. Curious crowds of onlookers watched admiringly as they earnestly adopted a military posture in civilian dress. The initial nucleus of men that had sought out Ambassador Herrick had grown daily with new arrivals from elsewhere in France, and from the United States itself.

Among these were the brothers Paul and Kiffin Rockwell, most recently of West Peachtree Street, Atlanta, Georgia. As news of the war blared across the headlines of the city's newspapers, the Rockwells felt first outraged, and then compelled to join France in its coming fight. Their work at the Massingale Advertising Agency, which had seemed to hold some promise, now appeared banal at best. They contacted the French Consulate in New Orleans and offered their services for the war effort, caught a train to New York, and booked passage aboard the liner St. Paul for Europe. In short order they reached France.[9] It was the great adventure that had been calling Kiffin Rockwell all his life.

Adventure had little to do with what drew another American to Paris that summer. Jack Bowe—the Spanish-American War veteran who was now a forty-five-year-old father of four and ex-mayor of Canby, Minnesota—was a man with a deep sense of right and wrong. Bowe saw the coming struggle as one between France, "a people with an army," and Germany, "an army with a people."[10] As such this fight was a fight in defense of free peoples everywhere and their most cherished values. It was his fight.

For the varied assortment of Americans still frequenting their old haunts, there was a general sense of gratitude to the city that had served as both inspiration and playground. They owed it to the Parisians. Thus it was a mix of idealism, duty, and sentimentality that spurred their efforts to get into the fight against Germany. Swiss poet Blaise Cendrars and a number of like-minded expatriates published a proclamation in the Paris papers that captured this mood perfectly:

> The hour is grave. Every man worthy of the name should
> act to-day, should forbid himself to remain inactive in
> the midst of the most formidable conflagration history
> has ever enregistered. Any hesitation would be a crime.
> No words, actions....[11]

Aspiring architect and artist Victor Chapman made his way to England to first consult with his father, John Jay Chapman. He had left France when news of mobilization reached Paris. This was a difficult encounter, with the father trying to be both considerate of his son's wishes, while at the same time encouraging him to reconsider his decision to join a fight that was not his own. He later recounted his meeting with his determined son: "Victor had been prowling about in a lonely way for twenty-four hours, and he now, with a sort of hang-dog humility, suggested he was going to enlist. I reasoned with him. With that stupidity which is the natural gift of parents, I probed his conscience and suggested that perhaps it was merely a random desire to see life and get rid of his serious duties that led him to the idea of enlistment.... But my own idea was that I was only preventing the lad from doing something which was not fundamentally his duty.... Within a week, he was in France."[12]

Alan Seeger had also been in England visiting with his father just before the outbreak of the war. He had intended to find a publisher there for his first volume of poems, but it was not to be. Seeger bid his father farewell on July 25 and was back on the continent soon thereafter, in Bruges, Belgium, placing his manuscript with a printer in a country that was about to be overrun by the German army. The streets of Paris were charged with news of war, but the tables in his favorite local café were deserted "but for the proprietor, a querulous old man named Léon Barreaux. He told Alan that most of his French customers had been called to the colors, while the foreigners among them had joined *La Légion*."[13] Seeger sprinted down the street, eager to join his countrymen "playing soldier" at the *Palais Royal*.[14] He arrived in time to be chewed out by Charles Sweeney for failing to "fall in" when directed to do so—it made little difference to Sweeney that Seeger had no idea what "falling in" meant.

The group of men that eventually coalesced around daily drill in the courtyard of the *Palais Royal* was nothing if not diverse: a well-meaning but motley collection of Ivy Leaguers, tramps, and adventurers motivated by the same overriding passion to defend France—and by extension civilization—in her hour of greatest need. Along with Kiffin and Paul Rockwell, prizefighter Bob Scanlon, and Brooklyn tough kid Herman Chatkoff, Alan Seeger was joined by Harvard classmate David King, Yale dropout turned stunt pilot William Thaw, and professional racecar driver Bob Soubiron. Veteran Edward Morlae, who, like Jack Bowe, had fought in the Philippines, also joined them; he claimed to have seen fighting in the Mexican Revolution as well. New Yorker and Columbia University graduate Dennis Dowd was rumored to have been disappointed in love and was making good on his promise to a young lady to whom he had proposed that he would go to France to fight in the war if she refused him.[15] Edgar Bouligny of New Orleans, James Bach of St. Louis, Fred Zinn of Battle Creek, Michigan, and San Franciscans Charles Hoffecker and Jack Casey, another artist, were there too, as were Harvard graduate Edward Mandell Stone, taxicab driver Bert Hall, jeweller's engraver Charles Trinkard of Ozone Park, New York, and Ferdinand Capdevielle, the son of a New York fencing master.

Perhaps the most interesting of the lot was one René Phelizot of Chicago, by way of Africa. Phelizot had led the kind of life that was the stuff of boys' dime novels. After running away from home in the Midwest at age thirteen, he had worked as a cabin boy on a Mississippi riverboat, then later worked his way across the Atlantic. Eventually he found his calling as a big game hunter in Africa. He dealt in elephant tusks and gained wide renown in the Lake Chad region for his very specific set of skills.[16] Phelizot's father was a Frenchman. On holiday in France in July 1914, he too was swept up in the desire to aid France. But he would do so as an American—representing the country of his birth.

By the end of the third week in August, most of the original contingent of Americans was in place. There were fewer than fifty of them, a drop in the bucket of France's potential military strength, but collectively they possessed great symbolic significance. The foreign volunteers—not just Americans but Greeks, Russians, Jews, Armenians, Alsatians, Danes, Colombians, Peruvians, Italians, and Spaniards (many nationalities raised volunteer contingents to join the *Légion étrangère*)—demonstrated to the wider world that France's cause was just and universal. The American volunteers in particular carried an added significance in that their home country was an industrial giant and potentially potent military power as well. If their commitment could sway American public opinion, then perhaps the U.S. government could eventually be convinced to abandon its stated policy of strict neutrality. On August 21 the Americans officially signed their enlistment papers and were granted three days to get their affairs in order before embarking. For Alan Seeger this decision sparkled with a clarity rare in life:

> I have talked with so many of the young volunteers here. Their case is little known, even by the French, yet altogether interesting and appealing. They are foreigners on whom the outbreak of war laid no formal compulsion. But they had stood on the butte [Montmartre] in springtime perhaps, as Julian and Louise stood, and looked out over the myriad twinkling lights of the great city. Paris— mystic, maternal, personified, to whom they owed the happiest moments of their lives—Paris was in peril. Were they not under a moral obligation, no less binding than [that by which] their comrades were bound legally, to put their breasts between her and destruction? Without renouncing their nationality, they had chosen to make their homes here beyond any other city in the world. Did

The American volunteers cross the Place de l'Opera on their way to the Gare Saint-Lazare on August 25, 1914.

not the benefits and blessings they had received point
them a duty that heart and conscience could not deny?[17]

And on a deeper level, the war was calling Seeger and his comrades to defend one side in an ancient feud, in modern form.
According to this historical interpretation the Allied side that they
were joining was "a pan-Latin front, a classical civilization united
against the German barbarians."[18] As art historian Kenneth E.
Silver has explained, in the larger historical context for those living
in Paris in 1914, "The very people who invaded France are the
same ones who sacked Rome."[19] And they were now coming to
sack Paris. The day after the Americans officially enlisted, the
French Army met the enemy in the climax of what would come to
be known at the "Battle of the Frontiers." As the name suggests,
the fighting was concentrated along the border between the French

Republic and the German Empire. From the Ardennes Forest in the north to Mulhouse in the south, French soldiers attacked the Germans, trusting in their élan and their bayonets to sweep their long-time foe before them. In the age of modern warfare, however, rapid-firing machine guns and powerful and accurate artillery fire more than offset these perceived strengths. On this single day— August 22, 1914—the French Army lost approximately 27,000 soldiers killed. This figure does not reflect French soldiers who were wounded or taken prisoner, only those who lost their lives. To place this figure in some historical context: the single deadliest day in U.S. military history was September 17, 1862, when both the Union and Confederate forces *combined* lost a total of 3,654 killed in the Battle of Antietam. One can't help but contemplate what France lost on that terrible day. Certainly more than a battle.

As Paris reeled under the news of the disaster to the east, it looked anxiously to the north where the German general Alexander von Kluck had pushed through Belgium and now looked to descend on the city. Would the French cause be lost before the Americans volunteers could even fire a shot? This wasn't as preposterous a question as it might seem. But the ominous news did little to dim the ardor of the Americans. When the day scheduled for their departure arrived, they were buoyant, proud, unafraid. A number of years later Jack Bowe explained how his future comrades-in arms began their journey to war: "Starting from the Palace Royale in the Latin Quarter, that corner of old Paris where, in by-gone days, Camille Desmoulins jumped on a chair and made the speech that started the French Revolution."[20] Except now it was they who were playing their part in history.

Dressed in civilian clothes, the volunteers began their march in the morning sunshine to the Gare Saint-Lazare that Claude Monet had painted, about a half mile away in the 8th arrondissement. Crowds gathered along their route, pitching chocolates and flowers, while pretty girls proffered kisses. René Phelizot and Alan Seeger took turns holding aloft the oversized American flag at the front of the procession, and managed to monopolize the attentions of many of *les demoiselles* along the route.[21] Who could blame them? To be a hero, warranted or not, if only for a few moments in Paris in the late summer, was as close to being a god as any living man was likely to come. And then, at the station, their golden moment already fading into obscurity, the volunteers boarded a train for Rouen—and their new life in the *Légion*, in the war, in a new age.

CHAPTER 3

LA LÉGION

The train to Rouen was crammed with volunteers from all over the world, bound by a common commitment to serve France in what was becoming increasingly clear was her desperate hour. The *Légion* intended to use Rouen, a historic town in Normandy, for training raw recruits, and few could have been more raw than this lot. Many were put up in a former girls' school that had been converted into a barracks. Compressed bales of straw covered the floor and served as beds.[1] The town itself, only seventy miles from the nearest positions of the advancing Germans, was in a state of flux, as was evident to the Americans. David King later recounted, "The city was teeming with a marvelous, heterogeneous collection: wounded from the British Army, stragglers from the Belgian Army, refugees, French reservists, British Army Service Corps units, all wandering around the streets aimlessly, some terribly depressed, others hilarious and singing, and a good portion of them drunk."[2]

William Thaw was bemused by the incredible racial, ethnic, national, linguistic, and occupational diversity of his new companions, approximately twelve hundred of them in all. But he gleaned something else from the human flotsam and jetsam described by King that had washed up in Rouen ahead of the German tide. Thaw wrote at the time, "I am going to take a part, however small, in the greatest and probably last, war in history, which has apparently developed into a fight of civilization against barbarism. That last reason may sound a bit grand and dramatic, but you would quite agree if you could hear the tales of French, Belgian and English soldiers who have come back here from the front...."[3]

The stories Thaw and his comrades heard about the conduct of the German Army on its march through Belgium and into France could move even the most jaded. Certainly rumor and exaggeration played some part in magnifying the nature and scope of the atrocities, but the sheer volume of reports could not be denied. Perhaps the best known act of barbarism, both then and now, was the sack of the Belgian town of Louvain. The city was burned and hundreds of civilians were lined up and shot in revenge for the actions of *franc-tireurs* along the route that had taken the German army through the town on its way to Brussels. *Franc-tireurs* was the name given to Belgian guerilla fighters that used the civilian population as a shield from behind which to strike at the invaders. There is debate over the scale and intensity of *franc-tireur* activity in August 1914, but the German High Command had made up its mind how to deal with this anticipated threat in advance: collective responsibility for German deaths. This meant murdering innocent civilians to cow the population into cooperating. Louvain's famous library and university, founded in 1426, were left in ashes as well. But what occurred a few days before the burning of Louvain in the nearby town of Dinant was even worse. As historian Barbara Tuchman relates in her book, *The Guns of August*, "They [the town's residents] were kept in the main square until evening, then lined up, women on one side, men opposite in two rows, one kneeling in front of the other. Two firing squads marched to the center of the square, faced either way and fired till no more of the targets stood upright. Six hundred and twelve bodies were identified and buried, including Felix Fivet, aged three weeks."[4]

For those that claim all this was simply Allied propaganda, it was: the most effective kind. That doesn't mean these atrocities did not happen. In Tuchman's time, cemeteries in towns and villages throughout Belgium were full of row after row of headstones bearing the date 1914 and the inscription, *"Fusillé par les Allemands"* (shot by the Germans).[5] They still do.

★ ★ ★

Clearly, Rouen in its current state was no place to train recruits. It was too close to the fighting. The military recognized the inadvisability of continuing with the original plan for the foreigners and re-embarked them for a long journey to the south, far away from the front, to the Pérignon barracks at Toulouse. This was where the Americans and their multi-national comrades-in-arms would be initiated into the life of a *légionnaire*.

The French Foreign Legion, a unique institution composed of foreign volunteers serving under French officers, had initially been formed in 1831 to help subdue Algeria for France. The fact that the soldiers had no ties to France made it far easier for politicians to send

LÉGION ÉTRANGÈRE
(1862)

Nineteenth-century illustration of a
légionnaire in the field.

them abroad to do the dirty work of the empire. This famed unit already enjoyed a certain roguish mystique by the time the war in Europe broke out. By way of example, in one instance in 1863, sixty-five *légionnaires* held off two thousand Mexican soldiers for over ten hours at the Battle of Camaróne. The last five surviving defenders mounted a bayonet charge when their ammunition ran out.[6] This gritty reputation, however, should not be confused with the glamorous luster of later depictions of the *Légion*, in the 1939 film *Beau Geste*, for instance. In 1914 *légionnaires* were seen as a hard lot: men running from something—perverts, deserters, thugs, and worse. The discipline was severe; the conditions often harsh. No one with better options signed up for the *Légion*.

Serving primarily in the far-flung reaches of the French colonial empire, *la Légion Étrangère* took in any foreigner, no questions asked—or at least that was the popular understanding. It was largely true. The Spanish-American War veteran Jack Bowe sketched an outline of a professional *légionnaire*: "He is taken at face value.... He does not impair his citizenship.... He retains his own individuality. No one pries into his private affairs. His troubles are his. He carries them, also his fame, without advertising...."

Whatever his status in civilian life, in the *Légion*, he is simply a *Légionnaire*. This is not the place for weaklings. Invariably they are used up in the training. Here are only the strong...who neither give nor ask favors."[7]

The *Légion* contained men from nearly every country in Europe (including Germany), as well as a significant contingent of North African Arabs and others. These men asked little from life materially. Their sustenance was extreme unit pride (*esprit de corps*) and a bottle and a wench in the off hours. To help meet the crisis that began in 1914, the French military recalled significant numbers of *légionnaires* from abroad, ultimately forming four companies to feed into the line (the *2ᵉ*, *3ᵉ*, and *4ᵉ régiments de marche* of the *1ᵉʳ étranger*, and the *2ᵉ régiment de marche* of the *2ᵉ étranger*).[8] The Americans, and various other idealistic volunteers (*bleus*), were to be mixed with seasoned veterans (*anciens*). The wisdom of this policy would be questioned later on, but at the time it appeared sound.[9]

The trip from Rouen to Toulouse was a purgatory of sorts: the recruits jammed into cars with little space and even less water. A journey that should have taken no more than twenty-four hours stretched into an interminable ninety-hour trip, with the train moving at a crawl. Thirst was aggravated by the salted meat that was issued as rations. Added to this was the body odor of hundreds of unwashed men in close quarters.[10] By the time the train doors opened onto a *Midi-Pyrenees* evening in the south of France, the men who had left Paris like golden gods just ten days before entered Toulouse looking more like swarthy convicts, unshaven and exhausted. To make matters worse, the locals took them for German prisoners of war and gave them a welcome appropriate to that status. A bewildered David King recalled,

Pérignon barracks, Toulouse, France, circa 1910.

"The companies fell in and moved off smartly, in columns of four through the streets of Toulouse toward the barracks of the 183rd regiment.... To our amazement and chagrin, the column was greeted with hoots and boos, and presently apples, rotten eggs, and even dead cats."[11]

This would not be the last time that the American volunteers would suffer from a lack of cross-cultural communication.

★ ★ ★

Rising at 5:00 a.m. each morning and receiving only a steaming cup of black coffee to fill their bellies, the recruits faced days filled with drill, handling weapons, and marches of up to twenty miles. This regimen was broken only by the distribution of *soupe* at 10:30 a.m. consisting of vegetables or rice and some stewed meat. In addition, each man received a half loaf of bread, a hunk of cheese, and a half liter of sour wine called *pinard*. At 5:00 p.m. this meal was repeated.[12] And from 5:00 to 9:00 the men were free to find what trouble they might in town—however, on the regular *Légion* pay of one *sou* (approximately one penny) per day, it had to be cheap.[13]

The first night in the barracks the men slept on beds for the first time since leaving Paris, but—alas!—they had plenty of company: bed bugs had infested the straw and canvas mattresses, inflicting painful red welts on the unsuspecting newcomers with their bites. The following morning the recruits fought and won their first battle by burning the straw and boiling the canvas. But vermin (in all its various forms) would be something they could never rid themselves of completely, as both sides in this war would learn to their dismay. Their first day they received the official *Légion* uniform kit: "a heavy blue greatcoat, coarse white duck fatigue uniforms, a red *képi*, laced field shoes apparently made of iron, wool shirts, a blue sash nine feet long, two blankets, and a suit of long underwear."[14] Each man was issued an 1886 Lebel bolt-action rifle. It was an 8-shot, 8mm-caliber piece that "weighed over 9 pounds and was 51 inches long. With the long, thin, French bayonet attached, the Lebel reached the ungainly length of over 6 feet...."[15] A simple mess kit rounded out the *bleu's* gear. Emergency rations of tinned meat, biscuits, coffee, and sugar were also issued...but not be consumed. Every ten days the French government also saw fit to supply the men with *Scafarlati des Troupes*, packages of rough tobacco that Harvard grad David King dismissed as "poisonous stuff."[16] In those first days at the Pérignon barracks, the men's time was taken up largely with uninspiring *corvée* (fatigue duty) and figuring out how in the devil's name one wore a nine-foot-long sash properly. But soon the mood changed.

The arrival of a battalion of regular *légionnaires* (*anciens*) from the *2ᵉ étranger*, recently arrived from Africa, got the attention of the recruits. It was meant to. Everything about the veterans exuded professionalism and the dark mystique that surrounded them: their faces deeply bronzed by unforgiving African suns, their trim black beards, their neat appearance (not least of which was the smart manner in which they wore their nine-foot long-sashes), and above all their swagger. These men knew what they were about. This impressed the Americans.

Yet within a fairly brief period of time the *bleus* saw things somewhat differently. David King explained the cynicism that took root rather quickly: "... a battalion of bearded *Légionnaires* marched into the barracks square, stacked arms, and were divided amongst the battalions of volunteers. By nightfall they had sold the eager recruits all their spare equipment, and two days later they had it all back again."[17] Before coming to grips with the *Boche* (French slang for "German"), Seeger, King, Thaw, and the others would first have to deal with their cutthroat fellow *légionnaires* from North Africa and elsewhere. The amateur Americans were encountering a Darwinian world where the resourceful dominated and the learning curve was steep indeed.

To be fair, the injection of the professionals from the *2ᵉ étranger* had a salutary effect on the fresh recruits. They learned how to become soldiers. However, the differences between the two groups would become glaringly obvious to everyone but the most naïve. These tough, vulgar men coming from Africa simply could not comprehend the idealistic young (and often rich) men drawn to their ranks by the war with Germany. There clearly must be something wrong with them—some motive concealed. And for the recruits these impressive yet alien men were of another world beyond their experience. One of the *bleus* recalled in his memoir a conversation he had with some of the *anciens*:

> "Then why are you here?" I asked him. "Orders, of course. We're professional soldiers. We don't give a damn what we fight for! It's our job. We've nothing else in life. No families, no ideals, no loves." Others, like Rouanet who was tattooed all over with obscene pictures, considered us rank amateurs who had no right to the glorious name of *légionnaire*. To earn that, one had to live through the grueling African school of desert outposts, hunger, and thirst. They all drank heavily, talked their own colonial slang, knew the field regulations by heart, were crack marksmen, and bore up easily under prolonged marches, and had as much contempt for other regiments as for civilians.[18]

Alan Seeger, who had initially been taken with the idea of calling these men comrades-in-arms, soon formed quite a different view of them, referring to them as "the dregs of society."[19] This disdain was reciprocated by the *anciens*. The Swiss poet Blaise Cendrars, who had helped rally the foreign intellectuals in Paris to France's colors, later explained the incredulous and suspicious mindset with which the volunteers were greeted by the professional *légionnaires*: "…understanding nothing of our mentality…treating us badly, abusing us and ragging those among us who had money, that they took for the heirs of rich families, or madmen. It was completely beyond their understanding…they looked for shameful reasons, demeaning motives, and were not far from considering us criminals."[20] It was in this atmosphere of mutual antipathy and contempt that the *Légion* would have to get these men ready to fight the Germans, and quickly.

★ ★ ★

During the volunteers' stay in Rouen and their subsequent transport south to Toulouse, events were unfolding to the north that would determine the fate of France and the course of the war.

Alexander von Kluck's powerful army seemed inexorable in its advance—first across Belgium, then on into Picardy, in France. His men represented the extreme right wing of the enormous German invasion force that had attacked the defiant Belgians in early August in violation of the 1839 London Treaty that pledged Prussia—and, by extension, the German *Reich* it had created—to respect the tiny kingdom's neutrality. Germany had attacked Belgium in accordance with her army's Schlieffen Plan (named for General Count Alfred von Schlieffen, the former chief of staff of the German Army), which called for a swift and powerful blow to fall on Paris before France's ally Russia could threaten Berlin. In order to achieve this, it was decided that Germany's army must take advantage of the relatively lightly defended Belgian frontier to catch the French army off guard and then capture Paris from the west and south of the city in a giant wheel-like maneuver. What was being asked of the front-line German soldiers was nothing less than superhuman. Even with the superior numbers and firepower they could bring to bear on their opponents, the Schlieffen Plan dictated that they continually had to advance, oftentimes into intense enemy fire, over open ground. The losses were appalling. At Mons, just across the Belgian-French border, the British Expeditionary forces shot them to pieces with rifle fire but were ultimately forced to retreat. The Germans just kept coming—a zombie army of exhausted yet grimly determined men pushed to the limit of endurance and beyond. Their commander, von Kluck, was a hard man. A veteran of the Franco-Prussian War, he was resolved to finish France as a great power once and for all. The success of the Schlieffen Plan, he believed, would enable Germany to occupy France's capital and dictate a victor's peace, then move east to deal with the existential enemy, Imperial Russia.

As August turned to September, however, something curious happened. Von Kluck's army began to turn before the Plan dictated that it should do so. There were several reasons for this. First, the far right wing of the German invasion force was in jeopardy of losing contact with the German armies on its left moving more slowly toward Paris from the northeast. Second, von Kluck sensed an opportunity in pursuing a weakened French army to the southeast; its destruction would have rendered the longer route around Paris unnecessary.[21] But his men had little left. This was not the same army that had left Germany a month before.[22] The Belgians (both soldiers and irregulars) had provided far stiffer resistance than the German High Command had anticipated. The often savage reprisals that followed attacks on German soldiers by irregular forces did much to shape the image of Germany for the rest of the war. Additionally, the British Expeditionary force that had come to the support of Belgium and France had proved to be quite formidable—in the intensity of their resistance, if not in numbers. The Belgians and the British could only slow, not halt, von Kluck's advance; but, as it turned out, every hour counted. Their surprisingly stiff resistance gave Joffre time to organize the counterattack, and the Russian Army was one hour closer to Berlin in the East as it moved with unexpected

Joseph Joffre, the French commander who ordered the counterattack at the First Battle of the Marne in 1914.

rapidity to relieve pressure on its French allies.

On the French side, August was simply a blood bath. The great French armies that were to liberate Alsace and Lorraine were not only repelled but pushed back toward Paris by a German army that seemed to be everywhere at once. On September 2, the anniversary of the great French defeat at the Battle of Sedan in 1870, the government evacuated itself to the Atlantic port of Bordeaux—a decision by the socialist premier, René Viviani, that appeared both cowardly and prudent. Things did not look good.

The French Army was about to be put to the test again. Its commander, Joseph "Papa" Joffre, a large man with a bulbous red nose, white mustache, and ample belly, looked like Santa Claus without the beard, and that appearance served him well, radiating calm and confidence about the outcome of the coming struggle to defend Paris. In early September, acting on intelligence that he had received and confirmed, Joffre realized that von Kluck's turn in front of Paris, rather than from behind the city, presented him with an opportunity that might never come again. In wheeling inward to the north of Paris along the Marne River, the Germans were leaving their entire right flank exposed—while on the Allied side, Joffre's forces and those of his British ally were in good contact, concentrated in a defensive crescent to the north and east of the capital. A counterattack at this juncture would catch the Germans off balance and could potentially deliver them a crushing blow. But it was risky. As in a soccer match, if the manager throws all caution to the wind, moving his defenders to the attack, then the way is open to an easy goal for his opponents. If the attack fails, game over. On September 6, while the *bleus* were pushing brooms in Toulouse on fatigue duty, Joffre's army launched a ferocious counterattack upon the unsuspecting and exhausted Germans.

The First Battle of the Marne lasted until September 12 and resulted in a general German withdrawal to the northwest and to the east. Although Paris was saved, Joffre's was not the victory that it could have been. His troops were exhausted, too, and perhaps incapable of the vigorous and sustained pursuit that would have been necessary to knock the Germans out of the war (or at least out of France). And so the Germans dug in, on French soil. The French would have to drive them off, or give up hope of reaching any peace favorable to France. The effort to do so would define the rest of the war.

In Toulouse at the Pérignon barracks, the recruits were being pushed at a blistering pace to ready them for combat. The forced marches of ten, fifteen, twenty miles at a time were especially tough on spoiled playboys such as big, burly William "Bill" Thaw.[23] With his dark, slicked back hair, thick black Vaudevillian mustache—and tender feet—he had simply never experienced anything in his life to prepare him for this. It was much the same for many of his fellow recruits. Fighting was one thing, marching was another. The lack of any government-issued socks in their kits only exacerbated the problem. Yet they made it. The *Légion* was beginning to have its effect on them.

Besides endurance, what the army was looking to inculcate in these men was the psychology of the offense. Trenches and fixed machine gun positions were for defensive armies, and for the French Army, looking to liberate French ground, staying on the defensive was a luxury they could not indulge. The emphasis on bayonet drill was meant to instill this attacking, aggressive mindset. Half-mile sprints to sham enemy trenches with bayonets fixed became *de rigueur* for the *bleus*. Marksmanship with one's rifle was decidedly of secondary concern in this environment.[24] Physical fitness and mental fitness (and the offensive mindset) became the primary elements of the recruits' *Légion* training. Unofficially, that training also included becoming more resourceful and resilient. And as much as the newcomers often held the *anciens* in contempt, they began to take on a bit of their swagger.

This swagger was inculcated in new recruits via martial music peculiar to the *Légion*.[25] The marching song "Le Boudin" was the best known of this genre. It was first composed during the reign of Emperor Napoleon III and in subsequent decades had acquired lyrics that reflected both the composition and exploits of the *Légion*. The reference to Belgians having no *boudin* ("blood sausage") was about Belgian king Leopold's request to exempt Belgian-born *légionnaires* from having to fight in the Franco-Prussian war, while references to the battles of Camaróne in Mexico and Tuyen Quang in Tonkin reminded the *légionnaires* of their predecessors' feats of arms. The song was irreverent yet dignified, crude but ennobling. Singing it made one a *légionnaire* in spirit as well as in form:

Tiens, voilà du boudin, voilà du boudin, voilà du boudin
Pour les Alsaciens, les Suisses et les Lorrains.
Pour les Belges y en a plus.
Pour les Belges y en a plus.
Ce sont des tireurs au cul.
Pour les Belges y en a plus.
Pour les Belges y en a plus.
Ce sont des tireurs au cul.
Nous sommes des dégourdis,
Nous sommes des lascars
Des types pas ordinaires.
Nous avons souvent notre cafard,
Nous sommes des légionnaires.
Au Tonkin, la Légion immortelle
À Tuyen-Quang illustra notre drapeau,
Héros de Camerone et frères modèles
Dormez en paix dans vos tombeaux.
Nos anciens ont su mourir
Pour la gloire de la Légion.
Nous saurons bien tous périr
Suivant la tradition.
Au cours de nos campagnes lointaines,
Affrontant la fièvre et le feu,
Oublions avec nos peines,
La mort qui nous oublie si peu.
Nous la Légion.

Here you are, some blood sausage, some blood sausage, some blood sausage
For the Alsatians, the Swiss, and the Lorrains,

For the Belgians, there's none left,
For the Belgians, there's none left,
They're lazy shirkers.
For the Belgians, there's none left,
For the Belgians, there's none left,
They're lazy shirkers.
We are crafty.
We are rogues.
We are no ordinary guys.
We've often got our black moods,
For we are Légionnaires.
In Tonkin, the Immortal Légion
Honoured our flag at Tuyen Quang.
Heroes of Camarón and model brothers—
Sleep in peace in your tombs.
Our ancestors knew to die
For the glory of the Légion.
We will know to perish
According to tradition.
During our far-off campaigns,
Facing fever and fire,
Let us forget, along with our hardships,
Death, which forgets us so little.
We, the Légion.[26]

And there were moments of illumination. Alan Seeger, a young man particularly sensitive to beauty, found in the countryside nearby scenes worthy of a painting. He was moved to write of these to his mother while anticipating the call to be placed in combat. His words not only "painted" the scene for his mother but they also hinted at something else, something more profound:

> From this the panorama, spread out on three sides is incomparably fine,—yellow corn fields, vineyards, harvest fields where the workers and their teams can be seen moving about in tiny figures,—poplars, little hamlets and churchtowers, and far away to the south the blue line of the Pyrenees, the high peaks capped with snow. It makes one in love with life, it is all so peaceful and beautiful. But Nature to me is not only hills and blue skies and flowers, but the Universe, the totality of things....[27]

With his poems now behind enemy lines in Bruges, Seeger's hopes of launching a distinguished literary career must have seemed more distant than ever. But to his credit, he looked forward, not back. He was as susceptible as any of his countrymen to the various irritants that caused them to grumble about the *Légion*. But there was always that other side to Seeger—his capacity for observing and appreciating, his ability to rise above the pettiness of the now and place what he and his comrades were seeing and doing in a larger historical continuum. He was certainly no saint, but he had about him a purity of heart that defined him as a man.

Aspiring writer David King was an observant man, too. But his attention was fixed on more pedestrian concerns in camp—namely, the various ways in which the *bleus* were taken advantage of. He applied his Harvard education to determining how he might be able to equalize the scales somewhat. As in any army that has ever marched, food and drink were a focus of near daily concern on the part of the men. One repeated trick that particularly peeved them occurred during the pouring of *pinard* into their tin cups at each meal. The corporal in charge served it out from his own cup, which he dipped into a canvas bag full of the stuff. Invariably the corporal's thumb inserted into his own cup displaced that much of the intended wine—to the amount of thirty thumbs' worth.[28] As King wrote, "The only way to prevent this cheating is to watch the deal."[29] The emergency rations issued by the *Légion*, however, provided King and his comrades a way to turn the tables. Though they were not to be consumed and were carefully checked at all inspections, King and others brewed the "emergency" coffee and threw the "emergency" sugar into it. It was no small matter. One risked eight days in the stockade if caught. However, "as inspections took place in double rank it was easy to cheat. All full sacks of coffee and sugar were lent to men in the front rank, and as the officer inspected and passed on, they were flipped back to the rear rank to be inspected a second time as their turn came."[30] Brilliant! Somewhere, Harvard president Charles William Eliot had been made proud.

For all of King's cynicism, there was a lightness there as well. He seemed to both scorn and admire his new hard-boiled companions in equal measure. He recalled once witnessing the spectacle of a passel of roaring drunk *anciens* returning to barracks under the scrutinizing gaze of the sergeant-of-the-guard: "...it was an amazing sight to see some of the old-timers. They would reel up the street roaring obscene songs, at the tops of their lungs. Twenty yards before they came to the gate the songs ceased, shoulders went back, and they would march through the gate, saluting smartly like automatons. Out of sight of the guard the singing would break out

anew, as they zig-zagged across the yard and lurched up the stair-
way to their barrack room."[31]

There was still the question of which unit the Americans would
be assigned to. With the losses mounting at the Front, the French
High Command looked to the training centers for replacements.
The call went out for a combined battalion of five hundred *anciens*
and five hundred *bleus*, preferably men with some prior military
experience. The Americans saw this as their chance to get into the
fight, now. Herman Chatkoff claimed five years' service in the
Salvation Army as qualification...with a straight face. The Rockwell brothers, Thaw, and Seeger all claimed to have served in the
Mexican Revolution. David King trumped them all with his "recital
of his outstanding record at Columbia Military Institute in New
York." He failed to reveal that he was only seven years old at the
time.[32] In the end, it didn't matter. The *Légion* saw the wisdom in
keeping all the Americans at Toulouse together in Battalion C, *2*[e]
régiment de marche of the *2*[e] *étranger.*

In the *Légion*, all the commissioned officers were Frenchmen.
Non-commissioned officers, known as *sous-officiers*, were, for the
most part, not French. A number of the Americans in Battalion C
were fortunate in coming under the tutelage of an experienced
légionnaire of seventeen years, a German named Heinrich Weidemann. Weidemann was perhaps the most mysterious of the veteran
légionnaires the Americans encountered. He had joined the *Légion*
in 1898 after leaving the German Army. Most of the many Germans that had earlier enlisted in the *Légion* had been purposely
left behind in North Africa and elsewhere in 1914 rather than be
asked to cross the Mediterranean and fight their brethren. Some
left the *Légion* altogether. Why Weidemann chose to fight the

German Army isn't clear—perhaps he had suffered some wound to his honor, or his reputation, too grievous to erase other than by dying at the hands of his former comrades. No one knew for certain why he had left Germany and the German Army; this was the *Légion* and a man's past was his own.

Weidemann was profane, dismissive, demanding, and authoritarian. He also exhibited "unlimited patience with stupid recruits," according to David King.[33] In less than four weeks' time he and the other *sous-officiers* had taken unpromising material and turned it into a reasonable facsimile of a *légionnaire*. On September 27 the Americans and the other members of Battalion C were told to draw 120 rounds of ammunition and exchange their white duck trousers for the regulation *pantalons rouge* of the French Army. They now knew they were soon heading back north, towards the fighting. The question was merely "when?"

By the beginning of October the men, *anciens* and *bleus* alike, were sent north to the Front in cattle cars. The symbolism must have escaped few of them.

CHAPTER 4

CHEMIN DES DAMES

The trains from Toulouse rattled northward toward the war. This is what they had all wanted; now the inexorable journey in sealed cars made certainty of fancy. Hundreds of thousands of men had already fallen. The Americans would be entering a war zone occupied by two armies exhausted and dazed by the herculean efforts of August and September. The detritus of the fighting—abandoned equipment; bloated, unburied corpses lying in unmarked thickets; shrapnel marks scarring the iron shutters of train stations—greeted them once they disembarked at Camp-de-Mailly.

From there the *légionnaires* travelled by foot—thirty-five kilometers per day on average—to reach their final destination. This task was not eased by the fact that the *Légion* was still refusing to issue socks to the men. Instead it gave them each small squares of cheap muslin, *chausettes russes* (Russian socks), to apply to parts of the foot inside the boot. But in inexperienced hands the cloth chafed rather than protected the skin. When the inevitable blisters appeared, *sous-officier* Heinrich Weidemann showed the newcomers how to drain them by passing a needle and thread dipped in tallow through the lesion. Whatever the reason, the thread he recommended did work. The appreciative Americans were learning.

Another aspect of *Légion* life was the suspicion, bordering on hostility, that it engendered among the French themselves. The *Légion* had an unsavory reputation among the native population. Whenever they approached, local merchants would shut their stalls, shouting the warning: "*Fermez touts le portes. Voici la Légion!* (Shut your doors. It's the *Légion*!)." The reason became clear when a particularly bold (or gullible) merchant sold the Americans food and drink out of a tent while their Algerian counterparts slit the back of it and stole the man blind from behind. The Americans, suitably impressed, came up with a song to commemorate this larceny:

> We are the famous Legion
> That they talk so much about
> People lock up everything whenever we're about.
> We're noted for our pillaging,
> The nifty way we steal
> We'd pinch a baby carriage,
> And the infant, for a meal.
> As we go marching by
> And the band begins to play—Gor'blimee!
> You can hear the people shouting,

Lock all the doors, shut up the shop,
The Legion's here today.[1]

The Americans, in contrast, were generous, and had plenty of money to spend. However, their money could do little to alleviate the scourge of lice that bloated on their bodies during the march and never fully left them thereafter. David King, and others, blaming their less hygienic North African comrades, referred to the parasites as "Algerian cooties."[2] It is worth noting that a corporal who served with the Americans described *them* as the "dirtiest, lousiest, meanest soldiers we had."[3] But this itching, scratching, dirty existence was something that the men never became fully accustomed to. The inability to rid one's self of vermin could easily lead one to brood. Alan Seeger, for instance, already possessing a reputation as a pensive man, seemed to take the tiny and persistent parasites as a personal affront. Cleanliness was an unobtainable luxury.

★ ★ ★

The march north took the 1st and 2nd Regiments up the slopes of the mountain overlooking the city of Reims, where cannon fire could be heard. As Herbert Molloy Mason Jr. later described the scene, "In columns of fours the 4,000 Legionnaires, who coiled gently around the slopes and through the yellow-green Champagne vineyards, resembled, from a distance, a mammoth blue-and-red caterpillar working its way up the side of the mountain."[4] Alan Seeger remarked in a letter to his mother how curious it was that, "On this slope the grape pickers are singing merrily at their work" while "on the other the batteries are roaring. Boom! Boom!"[5]

Reims Cathedral, Champagne, bombed, 1914.

Reims's cathedral, which had been the site of the coronation of France's kings since the days of Clovis, had endured massive bombardment by German guns. History and God had mattered little; the war satisfied its own needs first, now, with little regard for what had come before. The broken cathedral stood as a monument to modern barbarism.

Interestingly, the local populace was not always friendly in this region of eastern France close by the German lines. In one village, Americans were billeted on a reluctant farm family. Their hosts' unwillingness seemed to have been warranted when one unidentified American—too tired to bother climbing down the ladder of the loft he was sleeping in—urinated, unwittingly, onto the family's invalid grandmother sleeping below. It was revealed soon after, however, that the family and most of the village were in communication with the enemy—eagerly awaiting a German counter-offensive to liberate them from the French and the

Légion. The American could now look back on that mistake with a clear conscience.

With badly cut up feet, shoulders chafing under hundred-pound packs, and a general lack of proper food, a number of the Americans chose to petition a colonel, informing him they were simply not fit to continue any further on feet they described as "marmalade." The officer, on horseback, pulled his revolver and aimed it squarely at them. The message was clear: get up and move or die.[6] Épernay, Hautveilliers, Verzy, Verzenay—the villages came and went with little incident. At Verzenay the First Regiment was ordered to deploy near the town; meanwhile their footsore comrades in the Second Regiment were greeted with the joyous sight of buses sent to ferry them the rest of the way to their destination north of the Aisne River, which they crossed on October 26 on the road to Cuiry les Chaudardes. Cuiry was the French Army's main rear staging area for the Aisne-Champagne front, then considered the "the cornerstone of the defense of Paris."[7] Forty-eight hours of rest in Cuiry, then into the front lines for the first time.

Their odyssey since leaving Toulouse, culminating in a general weariness, compounded by ignorance, made the men of the Second Regiment more vulnerable than they should have been. In the evening darkness of October 29, 1914, they trudged single file through a wooded area towards the Germans. The tree limbs tangled so thickly above them that the moon's pale rays were blotted from the ground. Here they encountered for the first time the constant companion of the front-line soldier in World War I—mud. Mud so thick it would pull the boots off one's feet. Mud "like chewing gum" with "a stench putrid and obscene."[8] Arriving on a hill facing the German lines, the *légionnaires* slipped silently into the rifle pits that had been dug by the men they were relieving—low "trenches" that were far from the formalized and at times quite elaborate trench systems to come. Dawn came, revealing a beautiful and peaceful Picardy countryside below them. Five novice *légionnaires* decided to leave their pits and stretch their cramped legs. Their red *képis* and trousers immediately caught the attention of enemy artillery observers and drew the fire of the big German "77s." Three of the bleus were killed immediately in the blast; the two survivors were grisly sights.

This was the Americans' first encounter with death in combat, but the sight would eventually become routine—one had to be hardened to it or one would lose one's ability to persevere and fight. But this mindset had to be learned. Shortly after the losses from the 77s, David King witnessed a gruesome scene that stayed with him for the rest of the war: "…a lucky shot passed clean through the loophole and burst clean inside. Our squad rushed in to help the survivors—there were none—so we set to work to clean up the mess. I was struck by the practical coolness of an old Légionnaire who was transferring a mess of blood and brains from the floor into a *képi* with the late owner's spoon."[9]

At the time of that first deployment into the front line, the two armies' defensive structures were still rudimentary. The barbed wire that would become synonymous with World War I combat had yet to be installed along most of the still-hardening Western Front. The resulting fluidity in what would come to be known as "No Man's Land" meant that covering patrols had to be sent out nightly to give warning if the Germans chose to launch a surprise attack under cover of darkness. The first time that Harvard grad and writer David King went out on patrol his commander was Edward Morlae, whose wealth of experience fighting in the Philippines and Mexico was valued by his younger comrades. But King remarked that though Morlae was a "good soldier," he could be "slightly erratic and impatient" at times[10]—and, as future events would reveal, his abusive behavior as a non-commissioned officer (Morlae was one of three American sergeants in the *Légion*) would cause problems. King himself came to be held in high regard by his comrades. Jack Bowe would have this to say of his youthful comrade: "...of uncomplaining and unflinching disposition, though small in stature, he was great in courage...I have seen him marching without a whimper when his feet were so sore that only the toes of one foot could touch the ground. He always had a cake or two of chocolate, and was willing to divide [it] with the individual who could furnish fire water."[11]

That first patrol proved to be one of the more hilarious episodes of this more often than not ghastly adventure. As the men set out towards the German lines, they perceived a dozen or more shadowy forms moving in their direction. After a brisk retreat back to their own trenches to report, the highest ranking non-commissioned officer ordered general firing, level with the ground until the enemy could be aimed at more clearly. Shots rang out in the night in front of them, and gunfire erupted all along the line. Thirty minutes later the firing stopped—when someone recognized that the "return" fire was coming at an angle formed by another *Légion* unit at the end of the line. An inspection of the battlefield revealed twelve cows that had been grazing, nine of them killed in the crossfire. The next day the lucky *légionnaires* dined on beef skewered on their bayonets, cooked over low fires.

There were other lessons to learn, too. One of the non-commissioned officers attached to David King's unit was a predatory homosexual named Pascualaggi, who bullied his targets if they rebuffed his advances. Soon after *l'affaire Vaches* (the affair of the cows), the short, thick-set Corsican led a seven-man patrol into No Man's Land. When the patrol returned some time later they carried Pascualaggi's body riddled with French bullets. They claimed they had mistaken their commander for a German outpost and fired on him. Miraculously, he survived, but the lesson was clear: respected officers who did not cross personal lines were obeyed. Officers who did could be murdered by their own men.

* * *

After their brief but eventful baptism by fire, the Second Regiment was pulled back to Cuiry for a short respite. There they found a surly native populace that clearly did not want them there except to be gouged "unmercifully from behind makeshift counters in their homes where they sold tinned jam, sweet biscuits, and vin mousseaux."[12] Matters were only made worse when the local French commander ordered the town's church steeple pulled down. It had been a useful marker for German artillery sighting their guns. The sponged Americans eagerly lent their backs to the task. Then, as November's chill replaced October's gold-tinged idyll, the Second Regiment was ordered north to Craonelle, which would be their home for the next six months.

It was a village literally divided down the middle between the German and French armies. This was the tip of the spear, the closest point at which the two ancient enemies encountered each other. Just up the road from Craonelle lay Craonne, held by the Germans, and beyond this the wooded ridge known as the Chemin des Dames or Ladies' Walk. The Aisne River flowed down to the Chemin des Dames from its source in the Ardennes Forest, its course then running parallel to it. The ridge had come by its name during the eighteenth century when King Louis XV's daughters frequently used the route to visit the Count and Countess of Narbonne-Lara. The count eventually had the road surfaced, and the name stuck long after the ladies had gone. Beyond lay the Craonne Plateau—in 1914, full of Germans, dug in for the long haul. The German commanders realized that France, to win the war, would have to drive them off French soil entirely. The Germans had the advantage, and they knew it. Craonelle was not without its own glorious military past. In 1814, while fighting what would ultimately prove to be a futile defensive war against multiple enemies, Napoleon won a notable victory at Craonelle with an army of fresh recruits. As Spanish-American War veteran Jack Bowe put it, rather grandiloquently, in his memoirs, published in 1918, "In front of Craon[ne], where, in 1814, Frank and Hun had fought for mastery, one hundred years later, the same nations battled again."

It was at Craonelle that Bowe joined the other American volunteers—having arrived in Paris too late to join those that had departed for Rouen on August 25, 1914. Once in France, however, he wasted no time enlisting and beginning his training. For a forty-five-year-old man *Légion* training was a trying endeavor; Bowe himself described it as a "fierce" and "inhuman" "survival of the fittest."[13] Frankly, it is impressive that he made it through the eight-week crash course at all. It was a measure of his commitment. He, in turn, had no reason to question the commitment of his new comrades. Commenting on his fellow Americans along the Chemin des Dames, Bowe felt that their experience was comparable to that of Washington's Army at Valley Forge in 1777–1778.[14]

As the *légionnaires* walked slowly down the hill into the wooded park enclosed by a wall, they saw the chateau for the first time. Light beamed from the giant first floor windows welcoming

Craonelle, Picardy, 1914.

them in an otherworldly silence. And then, "as if by black magic the lights went out, and the place became a gutted ruin. It had only been the moon shining through empty windows."[15] The *Chateau de Blanc Sablon* (White Sand Chateau) had been attacked in the first days of the war—all signs pointed to it having been taken suddenly. When the French armies regrouped and retook the chateau, the top floor had been entirely blown away, leaving only the skeletal mirage that now greeted the *légionnaires* descending the hill. They would be billeted there under the vaulted ceiling of the giant cellar, which had managed to avoid the general destruction. The Americans' distaste for the Germans—the *Boche*, the Hun— grew exponentially there. As they surveyed the once genteel grounds they realized the extent of the Germans' crudity and vandalism—and glimpsed hints of even more sinister behavior. David King, a man not typically given to outbursts of angry emotion, described the scene that met their eyes in the gatekeeper's lodge on the estate: "...the interior was indescribably filthy. The

Hun had evidently had one last banquet here. A long table in the main room was piled high with dirty dishes, wine glasses, and bottles, and he had left his usual trademark—excrement—on everything. In the middle of this debauch, lay a small white satin slipper. Evidently Fritz had been true to his tradition of the Kurfürstendam [the broad avenue in Berlin lined with fashionable shops and cafes—evidently King was being ironic]. Had the owner escaped?"[16]

The owner of the chateau? Or the owner of the slipper? King didn't say... but a single white satin slipper came to embody what had driven the Americans to enlist in the first place.

The fighting along the *Chemin des Dames* in the winter of 1914–1915 was an erratic, fluid war of raid and counter-raid. Neither side intended any large-scale operations in that theater until the spring thaw began. Yet neither side knew that about the other. Thus the *légionnaires*—deployed along the wall of the

In the ruins of the *Belle Époque*, 1914.

Kiffin Rockwell in the foreground (with Dennis Dowd to his immediate right) holding the line along the Chemin des Dames, 1914.

chateau park, in the bombed-out buildings on the French side of Craonelle, and in the trenches below the *Chemin des Dames*—had to be constantly at the ready to repel a massed attack by the Germans pouring down from the Craon Plateau. Having to hold low ground against enemies dug in above placed the Americans and their comrades in a decidedly vulnerable position. Added to this disadvantage was the angle of the front line to the northwest of the cha-teau, which left those inside the walls with no defilade to protect them against incoming fire. German snipers peering down their sights from the plateau had clean shots, albeit at great range. The Americans arrayed along the park wall soon learned to keep their heads down.

In the village of Craonelle itself, the *légionnaires* encountered scenes that forcefully demonstrated how quickly the initial German attack had come and how tenaciously the French had fought to repel it. Jack Bowe recalled a ghost village devoid of any civilian population—looking like something out of the ruins of Pompeii: "…many of the deserted houses were still intact, beds unmade, dishes yet upon the table, furnished, but vacant. Cattle, tied to mangers, lay dead in their stalls. In cellars where combatants had tunneled through to connect, the dead of both sides lay impaled on bayonets. One Frenchman's teeth were at another man's throat, locked in combat, even in death."[17]

The French had erected barricades to halt mad rushes by spike-helmeted Germans, and the Americans often found themselves positioned behind them. In order to discourage overly enthusiastic displays of Teutonic bravery, an enterprising officer commandeered the shotguns of the local populace for miles around and loaded them with "slugs, shot, and old nails." These proved "most effective against sudden rushes"[18] by the enemy, as one might well imagine they would. Snipers occupied ruined buildings throughout the village, picking off anyone unwary or unlucky enough to come into their sights.

It was along the chateau's park wall that the first German raiders appeared. Alan Seeger and Kiffin Rockwell had placed an old door buttressed with a ladder over a hole that had been torn in the wall by a shell. Their squad mates, with Corporal Weidemann, occupied a position along the wall further to the right. Given his long military experience, Weidemann realized how vulnerable their position was to raids. He rushed to the aid of Seeger and Rockwell when hand grenades began to be lobbed, softly hissing, over the wall. The first failed to explode—a dud. The second, however, detonated with terrific force and a "deafening roar. A squad of Germans burst through the door, catching the two *légionnaires* in the open."[19] Seeger and Rockwell turned and ran towards the woods crying *"Aux armes!"* to their startled comrades: "Capdevielle got a scratch on the scalp and the little finger on Zinn's hand was shot through."[20] Meanwhile Weidemann, running to their aid, was cut down by a German bullet and then had his head bashed in with a rifle butt.

By the time the *légionnaires* recovered and reinforcements appeared out of the chateau's cellar, the fight was over. The raiders had left the park and returned to their positions on the ridge nearby. Kiffin Rockwell, appalled at the sight of Weidemann's mangled body, described the affair as, "rather a disgrace for us all…impressed us more like a murder than warfare. The Germans had no military point to gain by doing what they did; it was done as an act of individualism and a desire to kill."[21] Despite Rockwell's outraged sense of chivalry, he was incorrect to believe that the raid had no military value. The Germans had been sent to ascertain just who their unit was up against on the other side of the line. The distinctive green Second Regiment badge cut from Weidemann's tunic told the German commanders that they were facing the *Légion*. Later, having had a chance to go through the articles they had taken from the dead man's pockets, they realized that Weidemann was a German. As David King recalled, "About an hour later we heard something new, but very old": "Down from the German lines, on the crest across the valley, came a long wolf-like howl, half human, half beast—derision, triumph, and revenge—straight back across the ages from ape-man and wolf-pack. Vetman [Weidemann] was a deserter, and war and exultation had stripped the Hun of all veneer and boasted Kultur [Germany's much-boasted-of superior culture]."[22]

For the Americans this was a pivotal moment. The abstract commitment to the fight had become something more personal—Weidemann had been the patient *ancien* who had kindly shown the *bleus* how to treat their painful blisters on the long march from Camp-de-Mailly.

Rene Phelizot, the famed big-game hunter out of Africa—and the man who had first held the stars-and-stripes aloft on that glorious August day when they all marched off to the Gare Saint-Lazare in Paris—called a meeting to plan a counter-raid. He didn't ask for official authorization. After what had happened to Weidemann, the attack simply had to be answered. Two nights later they crept up the ridge looking to bring back a live prisoner for interrogation. This was Phelizot's idea. It made a certain sense militarily, as a live prisoner could reveal far more than a dead one. Yet Phelizot was motivated by other, more personal, reasons for stalking and capturing rather than killing this "most dangerous" of game. As he confided to David King: "'You see, Dave, in the game I was in, you're killing, or spilling blood every day. If it wasn't an elephant, it was game for the boys, or just slaughtering a goat for meat. It seems to get into you, after a while, the everlasting shooting and blood; and men get what they call Blood Fever. Some of my friends got it—the natives got on your nerves so you start knocking them around with a jambok and draw blood. Then one day you lose your temper and shoot one. I felt it coming on so I quit and came home."

"The horror of it," King would explain in his memoir of the war, "was so strong that [Phelizot] could not bring himself to kill a man single handed, even in war."[23] So, bringing King with him, Phelizot "would use all his skill as a hunter to bring himself within striking range of the quarry, but once there, would risk his own life, rather than chance killing a man with a crack on the head. I told him he was crazy to try such stunts, but he only smiled...."[24] But the men returned to their own lines empty-handed from the unauthorized raid, and Weidemann's replacement raged at the Americans' lack of discipline, threatening them with charges of desertion. Each time the Americans tried to explain, he cut them off and continued his tirade. At last the *sous-officier* wound himself up to a conclusion that left an opening for David King's wit: "'So you think you are commanding this post and I count for nothing. In other words, I'm a flat-footed, lop-eared jackass, hein?' Then came my chance. Drawing myself up with dignity, I quoted, 'A soldier should never contradict a non-commissioned officer.'"

The Americans' disobedience and irreverence were frustrating for many of the career *légionnaires* who had been mixed in with them back at Toulouse. *Their Légion* was a different world altogether from this new, fresh-faced, idealistic, and for the most part well-heeled lot that they now were required to serve with. As *Légion* historian Douglas Porch has succinctly remarked, "The collision of two ideals, one patriotic and idealistic, the other professional and mercenary, was a recipe for trouble."[25]

★ ★ ★

By the time the holiday season of 1914 came within sight, it was crystal clear to all that the war would not be "over by Christmas." At this point the men had few illusions about their prospects in the months ahead. Kiffin Rockwell confided in a letter to a friend how there was "no romance in the infantry. It is only a matter of being a good laborer."[26] And indeed there was much work to do: reinforcing trenches, stringing barbed wire, digging latrines. The mundane tasks of army life in World War I knew no end. Over time, however, the lines began to take on the appearance now associated with the 1914–1918 war. The inevitable offensives would only be all the bloodier because both sides were so elaborately and effectively dug in.

Army life had its odd moments of repose—illumination even. The chateau had no roof, but it did have a piano. One of the French soldiers could "play and play well, opera and classical music," but, alas, "no ragtime!"[27] Alan Seeger, by this time doubling as a correspondent for his hometown *New York Sun*, informed the paper's readers about life on sentinel duty in Picardy:

> There is something fascinating, if one is stationed on sentry-duty immediately after arrival, in watching the dawn slowly illumine one of these new landscapes, from a position taken up under cover of darkness…left alone behind a mound of dirt, facing the north and the blank, perilous night. Slowly the mystery that it shrouds dissolves as the grey light steals over the eastern hills. Like a photograph in the washing, its high lights and shadows come gradually forth. The light splash in the foreground becomes a ruined chateau, the grey street a demolished village.[28]

American readers were thus made aware of the fact that some of their countrymen were in France serving with the Foreign Legion. They could be forgiven for not fully grasping what they were doing there. An edition of the *New York Sun* featured the headline: "MENU DE LUXE FOR FOREIGN LEGIONERS: Sardines, Buttered Toast, Vegetables, Champagne for Their Lunch."[29] It almost sounded like a picnic. Seeger's words, however, hinted at the destruction that surrounded them, no matter how beautiful a light the Picardy morning might cast on the ruins.

Though a poet, Seeger was no sentimentalist; he understood the true nature of the war he was in. But he had an instinctive eye for beauty wherever he found it. His poem "The Aisne (1914–15)" is a testament to the long months he and his comrades held the line on the tip of the spear:

> We first saw fire on the tragic slopes
> Where the flood-tide of France's early gain,
> Big with wrecked promise and abandoned hopes,
> Broke in a surf of blood along the Aisne.
> The charge her heroes left us, we assumed,
> What, dying, they conquered, we preserved,
> In the chill trenches, harried, shelled, entombed,
> Winter came down on us, but no man swerved.
> Winter came down on us. The low clouds, torn
> In the stark branches of riven pines,
> Blurred the white rockets that from dusk till morn
> Traced the wide curve of the close-grappling lines…
> There where, firm links in the unyielding chain,
> Where fell the long-planned blow and fell in vain—
> Hearts worthy of the honor and the trial,
> We helped to hold the lines along the Aisne.[30]

Trench duty was harrowing. More often than not, holding the line meant enduring probing fire from the German "77s" and then the sound of the response from the peerless French "75s" as their shells passed overhead. Cold, ill-fed, ill-clothed, bored, and scared, Seeger and his mates made what they could of it. One disturbing distraction was the fact that the trenches below the *Chateau de Blanc Sablon* were dug in front of the dead: "The *parrados* of the trenches [the banks behind trenches that provided protection from fire from the rear] were the family vaults and shelling spilled out coffins and their contents, rats and all, around the trenches."[31]

But one day an errant shell burst open a hidden treasure that the chateau's owners had had the foresight to seal in case the Germans should overrun the estate, and it was Seeger and David King who first found it. The chateau's magnificent library was illuminated by a torch as they entered like Ali Baba in the cave of the forty thieves. As *Légion* chronicler Geoffrey Bocca has described it, "The toes of their heavy *brodequins* [boots] pressed the dust into magnificent parquet floors, and they stood in the center of a great room, two dirty, unshaved Americans in mud-baked horizon-blue uniforms in one of France's great libraries."[32] The discovery of the chateau's secret library possessed aspects of both the surreal and the sublime. Once inside this cave of wonders, Seeger and King handled first editions by Jean-Jacques Rousseau, Alexandre Dumas, and Anatole France. A richly bound journal of Napoleon's campaigns—written by one of the ancestors of the Chateau's rightful occupants—particularly caught the attention of the two Harvard alums. The incongruity between the beauties of the library on the one hand and the grim business just outside could not but help but make an impression on them.

Their reverie was broken by a shout to assemble and clean a cellar, which the Germans had used as a field hospital. Its drains were clogged by excrement, bandages, and bloated corpses. According to David King, it took days to get the stink of it out of one's being.[33] The Americans found the grunt work demeaning, and for the most part, they continued to look down on the habits, hygiene, and blind obedience of their career *légionnaire* comrades (the *anciens*). There was a definite rift now. It had been exacerbated earlier by what the

Alan Seeger. Warrior-bard, New Yorker, citizen of Paris, worshipper of beauty.

Americans perceived as the lack of preparation on the part of some of the career non-commissioned officers, whom they partly blamed for the fiasco of the first German raid on the chateau. Then the rift deteriorated into something far uglier.

A coffee wagon pulled into camp, and the steaming liquid was handed out to the *légionnaires* one by one. Brooklyn native Herman Chatkoff got his coffee, drank it, and returned for more, claiming he had been missed the first time round. The *ancien* running the wagon told him he was a cheat and a liar like all Americans, and that he (the *ancien*) and one other Arab could make all the Americans eat shit. Former big game hunter René Phelizot emerged from the line and stood beside Chatkoff, and one of the cook's fellow Arabs joined him. Phelizot suggested that the four fight it out then and there, but the cook declined. His mate, however, offered to fight Phelizot one on one. Within a ring of *légionnaires*, Phelizot was beginning to get the better of his opponent—when another *ancien* intervened, swinging a heavy canteen at the American's head from behind. It connected, and he fell to the floor unconscious. A general brawl ensued.

After this incident, Phelizot was never the same. He complained of splitting headaches, but the doctor at the camp dispensary refused to send him to hospital. Later he collapsed, partially paralyzed from a fractured skull. Sent to the hospital at Fismes, his last words to his commanding officer were, *"Je suis américain!"*[34] In his clumsy, partly paralyzed hands at the moment of his death were the twisted remnants of the flag he had borne so proudly as he led his fellow volunteers on their jaunt through Paris in that now seemingly long ago golden August. David King described his fallen comrade thus: "His only fear seemed to be of himself, yet he was extraordinarily tolerant of weakness and failings in others."[35]

Jack Bowe would write, "By his untimely death, the *Légion* lost one of its strongest characters, France a fine soldier, and America a good citizen."[36] Phelizot's murderer was court-martialed, but "acquitted on the ground that he was drunk at the time."[37] Two days later, Brooklynite Chatkoff picked a fight with the Arab that degenerated into a near riot. In the midst of it, the Americans stomped him to death. David King remarked that, "When [Phelizot's murderer] went down it was all over. It is surprising how quickly hob-nailed army boots can reduce a man's head to a pulp."[38] Alan Seeger admitted afterwards that "what we did was pure violence."[39]

For a group of men motivated by the highest of ideals, fighting to defend "civilization," this was uncivilized behavior at its most savage and personal—blood revenge meted out where the law had failed to exact justice.

This episode was nearly repeated some time later when another career *légionnaire*, this one from the Balkans, took offense at a careless and dismissive remark made by Alan Seeger, who referred to him as an "imbecile." That fact that the man may well have been an imbecile certainly didn't help matters any. The ensuing match pitted Seeger boxing in an erect position according to the Marquess of Queensberry's rules, and his Balkan opponent following no rules whatsoever. After administering some punishment with his fists, Seeger went down in a heap along with his opponent when the big Serb crashed his head into Seeger's stomach. The close quarters favored the Serb, who used his powerful arms to get his thumbs close to Seeger's eye sockets, fully intending to gouge his eyes out. At the last minute, Bob Scanlon came to the rescue of the poet. "'Look, fellows,' said Scanlon, 'A fight's a fight, but mutilation is against French Army regulations.' And with his hob-nailed boot he kicked the Serb in the face and knocked him cold."[40] No one watching the fight disputed him. For his part, Seeger protested to Scanlon, "I'd have taken him." To which Scanlon responded, "But he was at your eyes. Whoever heard of a blind poet?"[41] Apparently, the husky light heavyweight had never heard of Homer. But Seeger's protests aside, Scanlon had almost certainly saved Seeger from a terrible fate. Surprisingly, in the end the "imbecile" (a *légionnaire* named Hulmaja) and the poet made up and became good friends. But Seeger learned to watch himself around him whenever he took to the bottle.

Another man Seeger and his comrades learned to watch themselves around was "old timer" Edward Morlae, who, along with Charles Sweeny and Edgar Bouligny, was one of three Americans who had gained a sergeant's chevrons. Unfortunately, he often used them to bully and deride his countrymen. Described as "[j]ealous, aggressive, and ill-natured," Morlae accused both Jack Casey and Alan Seeger, on separate occasions, of spying for the enemy—the

Baby-faced David King holding the line along the Chemin des Dames, with Fred Zinn in the foreground.

former because he had accidentally set fire to some straw in a trench, and the latter because he had a habit of wandering off alone. The charges were ludicrous, and eventually dropped, but the rancor lingered. According to Irving Werstein, Seeger's trench mate Egyptian Rif Baer even offered to slit their sergeant's throat.[42] Fred Zinn of Battle Creek, Michigan, was another target of Morlae's vindictiveness, as was Kiffin Rockwell. But in Rockwell, Morlae had provoked the wrong man. He wrote his brother Paul, in the hospital after he had developed a crippling case of inflammatory rheumatism after being wounded in the right shoulder,[43] a letter that illustrated how serious the feeling against Morlae had become: "He takes every opportunity to insult the Americans in front of superior officers, so as to try and curry favor with them. He and I are always at swords' points and I have told him that some

day we will both be back in America. The first thing I will do when
we are back there is to beat the hell out of him. None of us has any
use for him. But you know how it is in the French Army. A sergeant
has it over a private. I have even been thinking of changing my
company because I might lose my temper some time and kill the
blackguard...."[44]

Paul Rockwell was at least free of this festering internecine
conflict, even if he couldn't lift a rifle anymore. He was just one in
what would become a steady attrition of the volunteers' ranks as
the weeks and months wore on. It was the fate of Edward Mandell
Stone, however, that showed all of the Americans that they were
not somehow immune to what had befallen so many of their French
comrades and German foes.

Young, accomplished, and handsome, the Chicago-born Stone
had become a machine gunner in the *Légion*. It was quite a departure from his days at Harvard and later in the U.S. diplomatic
corps, where he had served in Buenos Aires, Argentina. The day
after Kiffin Rockwell had written his brother Paul about Edward
Morlae, the Germans began shelling the French trenches with
greater intensity than usual. Stone, worried that this might be the
signal for a general assault, stood by his gun instead of seeking
cover in a dugout. A piece of shrapnel penetrated his side and
lodged itself in one of his lungs. He lingered for twelve painful days
before succumbing to his wound—the first American to fall in
World War I.[45]

Up from the *Légion*'s training *dépôts* came new recruits to
replace those lost or in hospital. And so the winter of 1914–1915
went on. No glorious advances, no desperate stands, only raid and
counter-raid taking their toll on everyone's nerves. And the cold

taking no sides, but affecting all. Yet spring would come—did come—and with it movement.

CHAPTER 5

SANS PEUR SANS PITIÉ

لا خوف لا شفقة

The Foreign Legion fighting in France was initially divided into two separate regiments: the *1ᵉʳ Régiment étranger* (1st Regiment) and the *2ᵉ Régiment étranger* (2nd Regiment). The Americans serving along the Chemin des Dames in the winter of 1914–1915 were incorporated into the latter. Not all of the American volunteers of 1914, however, were with the *2ᵉ étranger*. For a variety of reasons, smaller numbers of American volunteers had been mustered into the *1ᵉʳ étranger*. Within this regiment, two *régiments des marche* (the Second and the Third companies) had Americans in them. The Second Company of the *1ᵉʳ étranger* included among its ranks Kenneth Weeks of Boston, Paul Pavelka of Madison, Connecticut, Russell Kelly and Jack Cordonnier of New York, Frank Musgrave of San Antonio, Lawrence Scanlan of Cedarhurst, Long Island, and Jack Janz of Philadelphia.

Weeks was one of the more interesting volunteers of 1914. An aspiring architect who had studied at MIT and the École des Beaux Arts in Paris, he had turned to writing in the years immediately before the war, publishing a number of books. Like Alan Seeger, he had fully embraced Paris, and France as a whole. Kenneth Weeks was "old money." He could trace his lineage back to ancestors aboard the *Mayflower* in 1620. He was also generous, sharing the comforts his considerable fortune made possible with his comrades.[1] Like so many of the volunteers of 1914, he saw the war in highly idealistic terms. Writing to his mother after enlisting in August, he explained to her that "In defending France I hope to defend you."[2]

Paul Pavelka, on the other hand, seems to have been drawn simply by the possibility of a great adventure. Nicknamed "Sailor" or "Skipper" by his comrades, Pavelka had left home at age fourteen; he had "been cook in a sheep-camp in the West, a cowboy, an assistant nurse in a San Francisco hospital. Then he had taken to sea, and sailed on all the oceans. With a small band of comrades he had once walked across South America.... He had been in Australia and the South Sea Isles" and was living at a sailors' home in New York when the war started.[3] After working his way across the Atlantic on a horse transport, he enlisted in the *Légion* at the port of La Rochelle in November 1914. With his enlistment papers signed, he was given five francs and a railway ticket to the main *Légion* depot in Lyon.[4] Russell Kelly, formerly a cadet at the Virginia Military Institute, and electrical engineering student Lawrence Scanlan met Pavelka in Lyon, where the three received their training before being sent to the trenches. Kelly's letters home to his father revealed a young man taken with France and the camaraderie of life in the *Légion*. He was particularly impressed with the bread in France, which he described as "excellent," asserting that "no bread in the States can equal it."[5]

Tulane University graduate Frank Musgrave was practicing law in Texas. Jack Janz, like Pavelka, was a seaman. Both also found their way across the Atlantic and into the *Légion* in 1914 and would serve with the Second Company of the 1st Regiment.

In March of 1915, having reached the limit of what he would take from abusive sergeant Edward Morlae, Kiffin Rockwell requested a transfer from the *2ᵉ Régiment étranger* to the *1ᵉʳ étranger*. With his request approved, Rockwell joined Weeks, Pavelka, and the other Americans of the Second Company of the *1ᵉʳ étranger* in early April 1915. He found his new mates much to his liking and was pleasantly surprised to find a fellow VMI man, Kelly, among their number.

Initially put into the lines near Verzenay, they experienced the filth, the rats, the boredom—and baseball. Paul Pavelka, demonstrating his resourceful nature, made a baseball out of the "business end of a cartridge" around which he "wound worsted and thread alternately" and covered with leather he stitched together from a leather puttee.[6] In a war zone the Americans entertained the rest of their comrades in the Second Company by playing the game they had played as boys on the other side of the Atlantic. The crowd looked on curiously until Long Islander Lawrence Scanlan hit a mighty home run into a nearby canal, putting an end to Pavelka's ball—and the game.

Within weeks the Americans were headed for the Arras sector in Artois. Something big was afoot. France was preparing to drive the German invaders from its soil. The effort would be unprecedented in size and scope. Russell Kelly sensed something was imminent as they departed Verzenay, but the New Yorker admitted that what exactly it was was "a puzzle to all."[7]

* * *

The Second Company of the *1er étranger* was one of a number of distinct units that collectively formed the *Division Marocaine*. Along with the heterogeneous *légionnaires*, there were units of Algerian and Tunisian *tirailleur* (light infantry recruited from France's colonial possessions), Senegalese, and, of course, Moroccans in its ranks. It was as part of this unit that American volunteers found themselves relocated to a staging area in the village of Bethonsart in Artois. The country north of the city of Arras was primarily farmland, with an imposing ridge commanding the view in all directions. This land would see some of the most intense fighting of the entire war, and it would bear the scars. German veteran and author Ernst Jünger described what he saw there:

> Ripped haversacks, broken rifles, scraps of cloth, counterpointed grotesquely with children's toys, shell fuses, deep craters from explosions, bottles, harvest implements, shredded books, battered household gear, holes whose gaping darkness betrayed the presence of basements, where the bodies of the unlucky inhabitants of the houses were gnawed by the particularly assiduous swarms of rats; a little espaliered peach tree despoiled of its sustaining wall, and spreading its arms pitifully; in the cattle byres and stables and barns the bones of livestock still dangling from their chains; trenches dug through the ravaged gardens, in among sprouting bulbs

of onion, wormwood, rhubarb, narcissus, buried under weeds; on the neighboring fields grain barns, through whose roofs the grain was already sprouting; all that, with half-buried communication trench through it, and all suffused with the smell of burning and decay.[8]

The Division Marocaine was given the task of leading the attack on the German positions in this haunted and depopulated landscape. There had already been serious fighting in this sector in the fall of 1914, when the Germans seized the ridge and the Allies tried, unsuccessfully, to drive them off in the First Battle of Artois. The hamlet of La Targette was their first objective; then on to seize Vimy Ridge three kilometers away. The French High Command had confidence in the Division's ability to carry this off; it was already becoming renowned for its uncanny dash and ferociousness when attacking—when defending, well, that was another matter, but that's not what they were being ordered to do. The Division Marocaine's offensive ethos was captured in its motto, *Sans Peur, Sans Pitié*, which means "No Fear, No Pity."

Rockwell and his new comrades were swept up in the anticipation for the attack they all knew was coming soon. From Bethonsart they moved into reserve trenches just behind the front line at a place named Berthonval Farm. Here "they made acquaintance with the sticky red mud of Artois."[9] For six days they waited, not without their own individual fears certainly, but collectively restless, eager, like thoroughbreds, to be allowed to run. Shortly before the attack the *légionnaires* decided to shave off their winter beards. Kiffin Rockwell had acquired the nickname throughout both regiments of the *Légion* of *le Grand avec la barbe* ("the tall fellow with the beard") for his impressive facial hair.[10] Now they would all face battle clean-shaven. The unit's French officers also recognized the moment for what it was and "put on their best uniforms, with all their medals, and wore fresh white gloves, as if going to dress parade."[11] They would make conspicuous targets for German gunners.

After an initial postponement, the attack was on for the morning of May 9, 1915. There was a deafening artillery bombardment intended to soften up the German defenses but in reality only warned them of the imminent offensive. Having gotten almost no sleep the night before, the Division Marocaine and its contingent of *légionnaires* went "over the top" across the fertile red soil of Artois. This was the last major engagement in which the French Army went into battle wearing their famed *pantalons rouge* (with blue overalls over the bright red trousers) and simple cloth *képis*. The Division poured out of the front-line trenches, "with their bayonets glittering against the sun, and advancing on the Boches" without "a sign of hesitation."[12] As the Americans' captain shouted *En avant!* the men moved forward into the front-line trench—then out into "No Man's Land" in support of their comrades. The first wave was taking enormous casualties as the gunfire from strong German positions was brought to bear on their bodies. The *légionnaires* ran toward the enemy, then dropped to the ground when the fire became too hot, only to raise themselves and run another twenty-five meters or so before again dropping to the ground and then once again renewing the advance. Rockwell described the experience to his brother Paul in a letter:

> To think of the fear or the horror of the thing was impossible. All I could think of was what a wonderful advance it was, and how everyone was going up against that

stream of lead as if he loved it. I kept that up for five hours. By then we had advanced three or four kilometers, but were badly cut up and also mixed up with men from other regiments, mostly Algerian *tirailleurs*. Most of our officers had fallen, including the colonel, and three commandants.[13]

Part of the reason for the high casualty rate was that the larger village of Neuville St. Vaast, off to the *légionnaires'* right, was still held by German units, exposing them to murderous fire on their flank. Until one could come to grips with the enemy in hand-to-hand combat there was little one could do about it except keep running, dropping to the ground, then getting up and running again. One of the things that modern readers commonly fail to grasp about World War I is the distance that often had to be crossed between the trenches and attackers' objectives. This is partly a result of famous films such as *All Quiet on the Western Front* and *Paths of Glory* that depict bloody attacks across relatively short distances through "No Man's Land"—about a couple football fields in length. But what the Division Marocaine was being ordered to do was advance over three kilometers under heavy fire—the last portion of which was uphill—and then take and hold a long, imposing ridge.

Today the spot where Rockwell and his comrades went over the top is a narrow country lane. There is no trace of Berthonval Farm, but there is a tree where the lane meets a path into the fields in the direction of La Targette. From this vantage point one can see La Targette close by, with Neuville St. Vaast off to its right, and then the ridge some distance beyond. Viewed from this angle, what the French High Command expected the Division Marocaine to

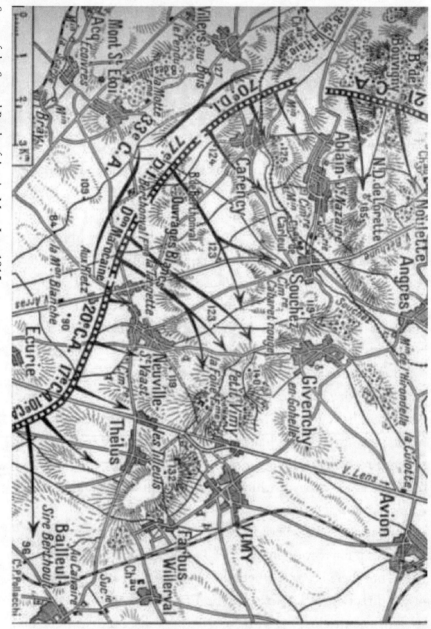

Scene of the Second Battle of Artois, May–June 1915.

accomplish under such intense fire seems nearly superhuman. Yet Colonel Pein, the *1ᵉʳ étranger*'s commanding officer, remarked, "My men will charge without their packs, in order to run better. If their clothes bother them they will go stark naked, but they will jump upon Hill 140 [the code name for the northwestern spur of Vimy Ridge]."[14]

The advance continued. A German attempt to infiltrate the *légionnaires'* rear in the Ouvrages Blancs was snuffed out by Colonel Pein and a handful of men, but the colonel fell mortally wounded from enemy fire. Machine guns were cutting wide swaths in the onrushing troops—known to soldiers as "daisy cutters," they fired up to a dozen bullets per second, greatly eroding (though not eliminating) the decisive nature of individual bravery in determining a battle's outcome. To a certain extent the machine gun represented the real "weapon of mass destruction" in twentieth-century warfare, when one considers the losses inflicted from its muzzle—or, as Rudyard Kipling once described it, its "reeking tube." There was simply no way around it; on a World War I battlefield one had to advance under machine gun fire, period. The Division Marocaine was absolutely relentless, however, and gradually, as the fine spring day progressed, each objective was realized. Kiffin Rockwell and Paul Pavelka found themselves pinned down by enemy fire with a second lieutenant from their company when a messenger arrived informing the officer that both the captain and first lieutenant were dead and that he now must assume command. He ordered the men to advance, "en avant," single file towards a machine gun position that had momentarily been quieted. Rockwell looked at "Skipper" Pavelka and told him "we might as well get it over with at once," and the two Americans jumped up and started running.[15]

After about twenty meters, Rockwell was hit by a bullet in the thigh and fell to the ground. Pavelka stopped, reached for his first aid pack, and tried to help his comrade, but Rockwell waved him off. The bullet in his thigh had "gone through the fleshy part, without touching the bone"[16] "leaving a neat, bluish hole,"[17] and thus posed no immediate threat to his life. As Pavelka continued the attack, Rockwell found a shell hole, and shared it for a time with a dying fellow soldier: "He wanted water, but I had none and could get none for him. That was the cry going up everywhere, for water. I stayed there until he died."[18]

Making his way back through No Man's Land to the French lines, Rockwell wouldn't have known that the Division Marocaine had reached the ridge, driven the Germans off a portion of it and were now waiting for reinforcements to exploit the breathtaking gap they had driven into the German line. Even the High Command had been caught by surprise. Whatever the pre-attack rhetoric may have been, the truth was that the generals hadn't anticipated such gains, so rapidly. Thus the reinforcements never arrived, and in the ensuing German counterattack the Division was forced to relinquish much of what had been gained so dearly. As Herbert Molloy Mason Jr. would explain, "The field was a charnel house of the dead and the dying. Of the 4,000 men of the 1st Regiment who had gone against the enemy, only 1,700 escaped death or wounds.... The First Battle of Artois ended after forty-eight hours with more than 100,000 casualties.... After murderous losses, what was left of the French Divisions pulled back...keeping only 10,000 yards of riddled earth. The cost, at ten men per yard, was frightful...."[19]

★ ★ ★

For Kiffin Rockwell, the journey to the rear became an odyssey of sorts that tested his endurance more than the attack itself. In World War I, a wounded soldier had as great a chance of dying from infection as from the wound itself. Thus a seemingly "perfect" wound that would get one a nice bed surrounded by pretty, adoring nurses and a long convalescence could become life threatening if not treated quickly. After stumbling out of the shell hole he had shared with a dead man, Rockwell tried to rejoin his comrades but was warned against it. In the event of a German counterattack, as immobile as he was he almost certainly would have been made prisoner or bayonetted. So he began to slowly make his way back through No Man's Land, moving at a crawl, snake-like towards the French lines. What he saw was a pitiful sight: some of the dead looked peaceful, as if asleep, while others, "sprawled in grotesque attitudes," obviously had died in great pain. Those still alive and screaming in agony, beyond help, begged for a bullet to the head to put them out of their misery.[20] Rockwell, who had left his rifle back in the shell hole, demurred. He shared a haystack with other wounded men the first night. But he realized he was essentially on his own. Only the most grievously injured were being brought back by stretcher bearers. Walking with the aid of a stick, Rockwell managed to get two or three kilometers more to a farm where he spent a second night with his wounds undressed. Finally, on the third day since being shot, he received an evacuation card and boarded a crowded train bound for a hospital in Rennes. In a letter to his brother Paul, he remarked, "I went four days without any attention to my wound (there were so many more badly wounded than I that I did not have the heart to ask)."[21] But he was lucky. The chance of gangrene setting in during those four days had been quite high, but he had escaped it. At this point Rockwell seemed to be living something of a charmed life—participating in a great battle like his Confederate forebears, cheating death, getting the perfect wound, avoiding infection, and receiving the royal treatment in a hospital far from the trenches. His fellow Americans had also been lucky in the attack of May 9. None of them had been killed, though sailor Jack Janz was wounded twice—first, when advancing, by a bullet to the shoulder; then, returning to the rear, by a shell casing that went deep into his hip. He remarked later that he "got it coming and going."[22] Jack Cordonnier of New York was "hit over the heart by a bullet" which subsequently struck a rib and "tore a nasty hole downward."[23] Texan Frank Musgrave was also injured when he had a hard fall into a deep German trench during the attack, dislocating his shoulder: "Finding a doctor who was following the wave of assault, he had the shoulder pulled back into place, and rejoined his comrades in the charge."[24] Kenneth Weeks and the other Americans had also come through, but it was only a temporary reprieve. The French High Command determined to give it another try the following month. The date was set for June 16, and the Division Marocaine was again called upon to spearhead the attack on the forbidding ridge. An honor, no doubt—but one that everyone knew would be accompanied by severe losses.

★ ★ ★

The failure to exploit the dramatic gains of May 9 and the subsequent attack of June 16 on the very same sector of the German line were indicative of a pathology that would become all but systemic in the Allied High Command throughout the war—the stubborn insistence that an objective that might have been achieved but had not been could still be won, with just a greater effort.

One of the men given responsibility for carrying out the new attack was General Charles Mangin. Mangin had been one of the French Empire's greatest warriors in the years before 1914. Fearless, aggressive, imperious, with just a hint of the prissiness of the martinet, Mangin gloried in the attack and in provoking the enemy: "In 1915, he moved into a requisitioned chateau near Neuville-Saint-Vaast, the population was left goggle-eyed by the sight of twenty soldiers working for half a day unpacking furniture and rugs and tableware.... Mangin had more cars at his disposal than Joffre, most luxurious among them a captured Opel, not military gray, but of a highly polished bright red. German airmen could spot it on the roads and signal its whereabouts to their artillery. But Mangin relished this mark of the enemy's special attention."[25]

Few battlefield commanders in World War I were more attached to the idea of the offensive or had more faith in French courage and French steel (that is, bayonets). His presence added a new element.

On the afternoon of June 16, 1915, the Division Marocaine—or what was left of it, reinforced by new recruits from the depot in Lyon—led the assault on the Cabaret Rouge, the nearby village of Souchez, and Hill 119. "Skipper" Pavelka recalled a mad dash for the German trenches immediately in front of them, only to find that they had been relinquished without a fight. The Germans, anticipating another attack, had simply withdrawn to a second line of trenches further back. Braving a storm of bullets and shells, the Division Marocaine gradually made its way to this second line. Pavelka described the scene in the middle of the battle: "As I reached the edge of the trench, I noticed the gray caps of the Bavarians, and almost instantly I felt a stinging pain through my left leg.

Kenneth Weeks. Architect, author, Bostonian, *légionnaire*.

A Bavarian had stabbed me with his bayonet; he then threw up his hands and yelled 'Kamerad,' but I blew his brains out. I dropped just in front of the trench.... The next was a mix-up of howling and hurrahing for tirailleurs, the Zouaves, and the Légion were all piling in on them. It was soon over, the Germans getting out and running for their lives to the rear, without arms and nobody stopping them."[26]

Pavelka lay bleeding and wounded in the trench as his comrades stormed Hill 119 just as they had stormed Hill 140 the month before. From his vantage point they were readily distinguishable by the pieces of white cloth that had been pinned to the back of their tunics. They carried no packs during the assault and thus were easy to pinpoint from the rear with binoculars. The observers who had been placed in tree tops and on roofs to relay their position to the artillery had been killed early in the battle, however, and thus many of the advancing troops were killed by their own side's guns[27] (the same thing had happened on May 9, as it would be many other times during the war—to both the Germans and the Allies). In a hail of German *and* French shell fire, the *légionnaires* and *tirailleurs* held onto the ridge, waiting for reinforcements. Engineering student

Lawrence Scanlan was struck by German bullets in the thigh and ankle and would lie on the battlefield for over two days before being discovered by stretcher bearers. (Scanlan would be the first American awarded the *Croix de Guerre*. As a result of his wounds, his injured leg was six inches shorter than his uninjured leg.)

Below the ridge in the heavily fortified area known as the Cabaret Rouge, the Germans, hidden away in tunnels known by the soldiers as the "labyrinth," waited as the advancing army swept over them, then emerged in its rear. In a tactic not dissimilar to that used by the Japanese against U.S. Marines at Iwo Jima in World War II, the Germans were employing the tactic of a "defense in depth," in which an attack would be contested on the front lines, but actually broken only once it had already passed them. In order to deal with this threat "two men in each squad in the *Légion* were given long knives and bags of grenades, and instructed to clear out every shelter where foes might be lurking. Kenneth Weeks was one of the men entrusted with this dangerous mission."[28] The hand-to-hand fighting in the "labyrinth" has been described as "some of the fiercest ever known."[29] Weeks was never seen alive again. His remains were later identified when the French Army moved towards Souchez in November 1915. He was posthumously awarded the *Croix de Guerre* for his actions on June 16.

Meanwhile the Division Marocaine atop Hill 119 was subjected to not one but a series of German counterattacks. They doggedly held their position until they were relieved by a French unit the following day. Down in the Cabaret Rouge some of the Division's units had penetrated deep into the German lines, but as a result were vulnerable both to attack from the rear and to counterattack from the front. At dawn on June 17, Tulane graduate and Texas lawyer Frank Musgrave found himself in one of these advanced positions facing counterattack, but the French field artillery, the "75's," were brought to bear on the German assault and the Division Marocaine held the ground. Other units, however, were surrounded or overrun and never heard from again. New Yorker Russell Kelly, wounded in the thigh, was among those listed "missing." Like Weeks, he would not be seen alive again. He was one of the youngest of the American volunteers to fall. Later on there were rumors that Kelly had survived and was in hiding or that he had been taken prisoner. His father, a prominent lawyer, pursued all of these stories; what father wouldn't? But in the end they all came to naught. To a certain degree the same could be said of the French plans in Artois. Much of the ridge still lay in German hands, and no decisive breakthrough had been achieved. The effort had been tremendous, but without air support and armor (neither of which would be used to great effect until 1918) or timely—and massive—reinforcements to exploit the breaches, it had been doomed from the start. Kiffin Rockwell, Jack Cordonnier, Jack Janz, Lawrence Scanlan, and Paul Pavelka lay wounded. Kenneth Weeks and Russell Kelly lay dead. The American contribution to this great battle had been small, but what it lacked quantitatively it more than made up for qualitatively.

★ ★ ★

One of the ironies of World War I was the fact that the Allies—England, France, and even little Belgium—insisted they were fighting for democratic values in Europe, while abroad these very countries possessed enormous empires where they lorded over large populations of primarily people of color. These subject peoples, to a considerable degree, gave the lie to the cause the original American volunteers felt they were fighting for. The *Légion* itself had waged wars of near extermination against Algerian resistance fighters and the followers of independent-minded Moroccan chieftains in the decades before the war. Yet, in Artois in 1915, these very peoples not only fought for France against her enemies; they were sent in first, and thus suffered disproportionately high casualties. But the Division Marocaine saw this as an honor, and they were right. Charles Mangin and other officers who had served in North Africa knew the fighting quality of these men. If an incredibly tough job had to be done, these were the soldiers to entrust it to. So then what did they achieve? Victory in the war did not loosen France's grip on its African colonies. Thus one is forced to reach the conclusion that they did it to achieve respect and glory. They succeeded. And the *légionnaires*, not only on their own merits but by association with the North African troops, shared in those achievements.

The memorial at Vimy Ridge.

Today Vimy Ridge is the site of one of the most impressive memorials from the Great War. Set back from the road that runs along the ridge, commanding the horizon, is a giant white limestone structure of great power. Multitudes of Canadian tourists visit it each year. It commemorates the sacrifices made by the Canadian Army in finally capturing the ridge from the Germans in 1917. But often missed, on just the other side of the ridge road, is a more modest monument, set slightly back. The inscription on the monument, *Aux Morts de la Division Marocaine A la Mémoire [In memory of the dead of the Moroccan Division]* is flanked by two stylized cypress trees, traditional symbols of mourning in the Mediterranean. In the middle is the Division Marocaine 's motto— *Sans Peur Sans Pitié* —in French and Arabic, with a Muslim crescent beneath. They left many dead on this ridge, and on the fields below.

Affixed to the monument's base are a number of plaques commemorating the part played by various nationalities in the battle on the French side. Swedes, Greeks, Jews, Czechoslovaks, Armenians—the plaques provide a lasting testament to the cosmopolitan character of the *Légion* volunteers of 1914 and the international appeal of France's cause in the struggle. Alan Seeger, in Champagne with the *2ᵉ Régiment étranger* at the time, heard of the sacrifices made by his countrymen in Artois. He was moved to include a stanza about what had happened there in his *Ode in Memory of the American Volunteers Fallen for France*:

> Be they remembered here with each reviving spring,
> Not only in May, when life is loveliest,
> Around Neuville-Saint-Vaast, and the disputed crest
> Of Vimy, they, superb, unfaltering,

In that fine onslaught that no force could halt,
Parted impetuous to their first assault;
But that they brought fresh hearts and springlike too
To that high mission, and 'tis meet to strew
With twigs of lilac and spring's earliest rose
The Cenotaph of those
Who in the cause that history most endears
Fell in the sunny morn and flower of their young years.[30]

CHAPTER 6

ESCADRILLE AMERICAINE

O n May 13, 1915, Kiffin Rockwell awoke in a peaceful world he had not known for many months. Since leaving Paris in August, 1914, he had not slept in a proper bed, with clean sheets. For months he hadn't been out of earshot of machine gun and artillery fire. The quiet of Brittany presented a stark contrast. Now, in the officers' ward of the military hospital in Rennes, he was afforded "every convenience,"[1] and a "pretty blond Alsatian"[2] presented a welcome distraction. But true to his nature he grew restless as the weeks passed and his leg healed. His thoughts were never far from his comrades in Artois. Rockwell's idealism proved unshakeable, even as he heard news from the Front confirming that the *légionnaires'* gallant attack had all been for nothing. In a letter to a French acquaintance, the Vicomte de Peloux, he tried to explain his feelings about the sacrifices being made by the foreign volunteers and their French officers: "I don't want you to think that I am cold-blooded, without feeling, but the horror of it all is overshadowed by the feeling of pride, and admiration I have for them all. This life does not hold such great value in my eyes as it does in some people's, and I feel that those men that died that day, died having made a success of their lives in their own little way, doing something for posterity, and their characters are their souls which will live and be passed down from generation to generation. So, is not that success? And what more can a man ask for in life than success?"[3]

It wasn't the result—the failure of the offensive, in this instance—but the gesture, the act itself, that mattered most. Kiffin Rockwell was where he wanted to be. Well, perhaps not while he was in hospital. But France in 1915 was made for great deeds. As his leg became less stiff and the weather grew warmer, Kiffin Rockwell wanted to get out. Paris beckoned.

★ ★ ★

Ah, Paris! The previous summer, in scenes of hopeful pageantry, the city of light had sent its best sons off to fight. But as the death toll grew and the infirm and disfigured returned, the city became subdued. The cultural and artistic life of Paris quieted. Black was the color that best captured the prevailing mood—black, the color of austerity, which permitted the people to feel a sense of solidarity with their army. But this mood did not last. Tentatively at first, but then more confidently, the old Paris reasserted itself. This was natural. There was now a realization that the war would be a prolonged affair. The death tolls in 1915 were no less staggering than in 1914, but one could gradually become numb to them.

Paris had been under threat of bombardment by German aircraft and within range of the Germans' heaviest guns in 1914, but it would not again be in imminent danger of actually falling to the Germans until near the end of the war, in 1918. Thus the city, and the home front in general, would become increasingly disconnected from the soldiers in the trenches. Paris changed its mourning dress and began slowly to get back to the business of living, creating, making money. To be fair, this Paris was not the Paris of the time before the war; but it was not the Paris of the early part of the war either.

Since being invalided out of the *Légion*, Kiffin's brother Paul had established himself in the capital city. He had tried to be reinstated but alas, to no avail. A soldier who couldn't carry his own pack or fire his rifle simply wasn't wanted. So instead he made himself as useful as he could to his brother and their fellow countrymen fighting in the *Légion*. He put them in contact with members of the American expatriate community, as well as sympathetic Parisians—which meant a small loan here, a drink there, a hot bath when on leave, communications with home. These friends would also reach out to loved ones with the news of casualties. Eventually Paul landed a job as a war correspondent for the *Chicago Daily News* and with the Information Section of the French Army. He made connections, got to know Paris, and became a familiar figure in the American expatriate community. He became engaged to a lovely French girl who was the daughter of aristocratic parents. One can imagine how excited he was to welcome his brother into the life he had made for himself in Paris when in late June Kiffin Rockwell left hospital and was generously granted one month's convalescence. The two brothers were reunited in the greatest city in Europe.

At this time, Kenneth Weeks's final fate was still uncertain, and his mother, Alice Weeks, was in Paris looking for news of her son. As Kiffin Rockwell had known and served with Weeks, it was unsurprising that his mother sought some solace from him—the two men were of about the same age and shared an unalloyed idealism about the struggle they were involved in. Kiffin was always keenly sensitive to the widows accompanied by small children and grieving mothers in black that he encountered.[4] In fighting the Germans he may well have created more widows and grieving mothers himself. But they were in Germany. His concern was France.

"Skipper" Pavelka, recovering from his bayonet wound in the foot, joined Kiffin for a brief sojourn in Paris. Rockwell certainly had a sense of himself as a "gentleman," and tended to draw a line between himself and others as a result. To his credit, however, he embraced Pavelka, the professional roustabout, like a brother. Rockwell justified the exception he made in Pavelka's case in a letter to Paul, writing that while Pavelka's "family didn't amount to anything, he has the sentiments of a gentleman."[5] His recognition of Pavelka's worth showed that Kiffin's elitism—for that's what it most certainly was—was based not so much on who one's parents were or where one had attended college but rather on one's character and actions. Kiffin Rockwell could be very judgmental, and his friendship was not easily attained. But once it was, it was pure gold. The Rockwell brothers were always willing to send Pavelka a few francs and to look out for his interests with their Paris connections—considerations that Pavelka, a common seaman from nowhere in particular, could never have relied on otherwise.

Besides Alice Weeks and Paul Pavelka, Kiffin Rockwell also encountered another old comrade from the *2ᵉ étranger* with whom he had served along the Chemin des Dames, William Thaw of Pittsburgh. "Bill" Thaw was finally where he had wanted to be from the beginning of the war—in aviation. He was in Paris on temporary leave from Escadrille C (Squadron C for Caudron, the make of the airplanes they flew) 42—and he made quite an impression on Rockwell in his dark blue French aviator's uniform with red and silver pilots' wings attached to the collar of his tunic. The experiences Thaw shared with Rockwell over a bottle opened up an entirely new realm of possibilities for the Carolinian.[6] Kiffin had already learned from "Skipper" Pavelka that the *1ᵉʳ étranger*, as he knew it, was being reorganized, and likely consolidated with other *Légion* units. Therefore, a return to his old unit was unrealistic. Then what? Transferring into the "aviation," as it was called at the time, seemed to present a fresh and exciting start. As his leave drew near, Rockwell made up his mind. He would take to the air.

Bill Thaw was one of the few Americans who joined the French aviation service because he genuinely loved to fly. His exploits before the war—dropping out of Yale to pursue his passion for flight, the East River bridges stunt in 1913, and his trans-Atlantic quest to convince the French government to purchase the device he and his brother had designed—all spoke to this. Thaw was an aviator. Yet, his initial request to be permitted to fly for France was politely declined, and he had joined the *Légion* instead. Thaw understood what was at stake in 1914, and he was not about to let his disappointment over not being able to fly get in the way of doing the right thing, as he saw it. As a member of the *2ᵉ étranger*, he shared his fellow volunteers' experiences from Rouen and Toulouse through Champagne and Picardy to Craonelle and the Chemin des Dames. But he knew he wasn't cut out to be a soldier. The marching alone was murder on his feet. But he was graded a "marksman"

and took part in the notorious *l'affaire Vaches*.[7] Thaw belonged.
He was one of the old guard. Then one day in November 1914
Thaw, cold and miserable, looked up from his post in the trenches
and saw two airplanes dueling in the skies above. There was something mesmerizing about these two fragile machines "darting at
one another in graceful maneuvers."[8] Thaw and his comrades on
the ground watched, speechless. But Thaw knew what it felt like
to be up there. And in that instant, he made up his mind to wangle
a transfer to the "aviation." At the first opportunity he set off in
the snow with two of his countrymen, Bert Hall and James Bach,
in tow for the nearest French aerodrome. Felix Brocard, an officer
there, was aware of Thaw's reputation as a pilot and promised to
see what he could do. The irony of it was that Hall and Bach were
transferred shortly thereafter, but inexplicably Thaw was not.
Brocard soon gained command of his own squadron, and Thaw
again asked for a transfer. This time it was arranged, to Brocard's
Escadrille D (Squadron "D" for Deperdussin, again named after
the particular make of airplane the squadron flew) 6, the first unit
for which Thaw would fly, though not as a pilot—but as an
observer and machine gunner in the two-seat monoplanes.[9]

Thaw may have had a difficult time joining the French air
service at least partly because so many young French soldiers were
eager to do the same. There was also a sense that one first had to
see combat as an infantryman or cavalryman before gaining the
privilege to fly for France. There was undoubtedly danger in flying
so high above the ground, but there was a certain glamour attached
to it as well. Many young Frenchmen envisioned themselves at the
controls, high above it all, with all eyes turned upwards in wonder
and admiration. Thaw was different. He loved the reality, not the
idea, of flying—an important distinction that one cannot ignore

when one considers his record as a wartime pilot. He was the consummate professional. His first forays as an observer-gunner in 1915 would serve as an education in just how rapidly the war in the air had evolved since August 1914.

★ ★ ★

When the war began, aviation was seen as a potentially useful but unproven tool by many, and as little more than a toy by some. A pilot's most obvious utility was his ability to observe the movements of the enemy. The airplane, with its freedom of movement and greater range, was a significant upgrade from the tethered observation balloons employed in the U.S. Civil War and Franco-Prussian War, for instance. Balloons would still play an important role throughout the World War I in spotting for artillery, but even the relatively primitive airplanes available in August 1914 could provide details impossible for balloons to obtain. Of course, neither side was particularly pleased with having its movements exposed so nakedly to the enemy, and thus the first air combat ensued—first with pistols, rifles, even grappling hooks, then, more seriously, with machine guns mounted on the planes themselves. This was what Bill Thaw was doing in Escadrille D. 6.

His old unit, the *2ᵉ étranger*, had an early lesson in the importance of airpower soon after entering the combat zone, as described by Herbert Molloy Mason Jr.: "All that day, they slammed picks into the hard ground, tearing up the earth.... By late afternoon the trench was deep enough to stand in. At five the *légionnaires* were told to quit work for the day and stand by for hot food. They put their jackets and greatcoats back on and sat on the cold trench floor to wait for the soup *corvée* to come up from the field kitchens that had been installed 300 yards down the reverse slope in a patch of woods.... The sound of a droning engine jerked their attention upward, where a lone German airplane flew overhead. The plane slowly circled the woods for a few minutes, then flew back across the lines. Its pilot dropped a map on which were marked the coordinates of the wood. A few minutes later the sound of incoming 77s (German artillery) filled the air again and the earth shook with the detonation of dozens of 25-pound rounds of high explosive. When the shelling stopped, the kitchen was scattered over half an acre of landscape. Fourteen men lay dead and another thirty were badly wounded. There was no hot food that night, nor on any night thereafter. The new kitchen was set up two miles to the rear in the middle of a swamp."[10]

Soon both sides in the war were rapidly constructing large numbers of various types of aircraft to observe, to protect their observers and attack those of the enemy, and—finally—to bomb enemy targets. Perhaps the greatest advance in this early period was in the mounting of machine guns in the front of the plane above the single propeller engines, allowing the *pilotes de chasse* ("pursuit squadron pilots") in their single-seat aircraft to aim their planes at the enemy and fire. The planes (or "machines" as they then referred to them), in essence, became their guns. There was the problem, however, of the propeller whirring away a few feet from the pilot's face. How to fire the gun without having bullets hit and damage the propeller? One answer was to mount the gun atop the top wing of a biplane. This arrangement was far from ideal, particularly because the pilot had to reload the machine gun above his head while flying the plane, sometimes even during air combat itself. Nonetheless, this method was used by the French air force in its *groupes de chasse* for a period during the war. The other solution was to synchronize the firing of the bullets with the revolutions of the propeller. In fact, a designer named Franz Schneider working for the French aeronautical company, Nieuport, patented an interrupter gear in 1913 that would achieve just this. But it was not a seamless design, and some bullets still hit the propeller blades with all too dangerous consequences.

The French *pilote de chasse* Roland Garros used a modified version of this device designed by the Morane-Saulnier company on his airplane featuring deflector blades attached to the rear of the propeller to "deflect" bullets that didn't fire through the blades. It was an imperfect modification, but Garros enjoyed success with it, bringing down three German aircraft in April 1915 alone. Garros was an interesting figure. Born on the French island of Réunion in the Indian Ocean, he became fixated on flight as a student in Paris. This was the age of the great Louis Blériot, of English Channel fame, and Garros looked to join him in the skies over Europe. In 1911 he competed in both the Paris-Madrid and Paris-London-Paris air races, and then in 1913, the same year that Bill Thaw piloted his hydroplane beneath the bridges of the East River, Garros became the first person to fly across the Mediterranean Sea, piloting his plane from the south of France to Tunisia. It was a remarkable achievement for its time. Garros shared much in common with Thaw. Both were true aviators; in the sense that word once held—they belonged to an elite of the skies. Their enlistment in the French *Service Aéronautique* was merely a practical way for them to use their skills in defense of France and her values and ideals. The war didn't make them fly. They would have been flying no matter what.

As much as Garros is known for his aeronautical exploits both in peace and war, perhaps the most significant consequence of his

ROLAND GARROS   Né le 6 Octobre 1888, à Saint-Denis (Réunion)   ⒷⒹ

Roland Garros. French racing pilot, aviation pioneer, war hero.

career in aviation was from the forced landing of his plane—
whether from mechanical failure or enemy fire has never been
conclusively determined—behind German lines on April 18, 1915.
Garros attempted to destroy his "machine" before it fell onto
enemy hands but failed, and the German military authorities recognized the significance of the gun mounted just behind the propeller, with its synchronization gear and deflector blades. This gave
an urgency to their appeal to designer Anthony Fokker to develop
something similar for the German air force. Fokker, in fact, was
already working on just such a device, so the timing couldn't have
been better for Germany's pilots nor worse for Allied pilots.

　　William Thaw's early service in the French air force largely
coincided with what would come to be known in the press as the
"Fokker Scourge." That was the name for the period, beginning
in the summer of 1915 and lasting well into 1916, during which
Germany enjoyed a clear technological superiority in aviation.

Thaw knew that he had to keep his wits about him or he would die.

Bill Thaw belonged in the pilot's seat, and after a month in Brocard's squadron he convinced his superiors to allow him to demonstrate his skills. He was ordered to St. Cyr and told to take a Caudron G2 up in the air, maneuver it, and land it to the satisfaction of the assembled flight instructors. As Herbert Molloy Mason Jr. would recount, "He later admitted he was scared witless for the first few minutes of flight, since he had never taken off from anything except salt water and had never seen a G2 except at a distance. After ten minutes Thaw brought the Caudron down for a smooth landing on the grass...."[11] The instructors were suitably impressed—the Caudron G2 was a notoriously ungainly craft that was being phased out by the army. Bill Thaw now had his pilot's wings, and after advanced combat training he was in the air, and at the controls of a G3 in Squadron C 42 based in Nancy. He was the first of the American volunteers of 1914 to fly against the Germans. And though others would follow on the path he took, he would also be the last of the American volunteers of 1914 to fly against them.

Bert Hall and James Bach, who had followed Thaw through the snow to the aerodrome back in November 1914, had been assigned to flight school and thus had a longer route to becoming pilots. Aside from possibly Edward Morlae, Hall was probably the most infamous of the American volunteers of 1914. No one really seemed to know where Hall came from, only that he was an American driving a taxicab in Paris when the war broke out. He claimed then, and later, to have served as a pilot in the Balkan Wars, but this fantasy was exposed early on in his training when he attempted to bluff his way into the skies at the controls of a Blériot monoplane. He crashed it into a hangar and was sent to flight school at Pau, at the foot of the Pyrenees. The French authorities didn't seem to know what to make of Hall. His shady background contrasted with his obvious sang froid. So the authorities chose to keep him around, but always with an especially watchful eye on his activities. Some even thought he was a German spy.[12]

James Bach's experience at flight school was far less remarkable, and by the early summer of 1915 he was piloting a French-built aircraft in Squadron MS (Morane-Saulnier) 38. On one of his first missions he transported a saboteur behind enemy lines to blow a bridge on the Belgian frontier between Hirson and Mézières. A squadron mate was tasked with bringing along the saboteur's partner. They made a rough landing, and only Bach was able to regain the skies after the demolition team ran for the woods. Bach went back for his fellow pilot and then taxied along the rough ground for take-off. But his propeller hit a tree stump—now they were both stuck behind enemy lines. At a nearby farmhouse they stumbled into a passel of Germans and soon found themselves facing a military tribunal, accused of espionage. The bridge had indeed been blown, but it could not be conclusively proven that they had any connection to the act, as neither of the saboteurs was ever apprehended. A long internment in a German prisoner of war camp followed. Thus Bach became the first American POW of World War I, a distinction he, no doubt, would have preferred not to have held.[13] Besides Thaw, Hall, and Bach, one other American was by this time serving in the *Service Aéronautique*. His name was Norman Prince, and his story was different in certain fundamental respects from those of his fellow American airmen.

★ ★ ★

Like a number of the American volunteers of 1914, Norman Prince came from a wealthy background and had a sentimental attachment to France, after having spent time there with his family. That said, he was not a volunteer of 1914; he arrived in France in early 1915. Prince had grown up living the life of a country squire on Massachusetts's North Shore—riding, hunting, playing polo. He was spoiled and willful, and inclined to be reckless. In 1915 he was twenty-eight years old, a Harvard graduate with a law degree and an interest in flying. He was also an elitist. One almost can't help but think of the character Tom Buchanan from F. Scott Fitzgerald's novel *The Great Gatsby* when reading about Prince. He had openly disobeyed his father to go to France, but he was, after all, *twenty-eight years old*. He had no interest in joining his countrymen in the trenches with *la Légion Étrangère*. Before embarking for France, Norman Prince had made up his mind to serve as a pilot, and to do so in an all-American unit. Within his willful mind lay the seeds of what would one day become the famous "Lafayette Escadrille."

Prince would have an extremely capable collaborator in this endeavor in the form of the American expatriate Dr. Edmund Gros. Though initially Prince was frustrated in his efforts to convince the French government of the efficacy of his idea, he was nothing if not persistent. He set himself up in style at the elegant *Hotel d'Orsay* and became a regular visitor to the nearby War Ministry. Two other would-be American pilots, Elliot Cowdin and Frazier Curtis, joined him in his scheme, and along with Prince enlisted in the *Service Aéronautique* in the hope of forming the nucleus for the unit they envisioned. All three managed to join the French air force without going through the process of first joining the Foreign Legion, a testament to the power of money and influential

Dr. Edmund Gros.

connections—including one William K. Vanderbilt. Curtis crapped out at flight school but returned to Paris to become an advocate for Prince's idea of an all-American squadron. It was there that he met Dr. Gros, who had been an influential fixture of the American expatriate set in Paris for many years. Identifying strongly with France's cause in 1914, Gros set about enlisting the aid of his wealthy countrymen to fund an all-American volunteer ambulance field service. He proved himself to be ideally suited to raising money and recruiting young American gentlemen to serve in France under his nominal leadership. Dr. Gros affected a military bearing, wearing a uniform of his own design with a certain degree of *élan*.[14] He was also a snob and a bigot of the first order.

Gros, like Prince, saw the possibilities of aviation as a means of enlisting more Americans in the cause of France—and in a frankly high profile manner. His vision, however, was not restricted to a small all-American squadron. He preferred to form a corps of American volunteer pilots to be placed in French squadrons in large numbers. Ultimately he came round to Prince's idea without fully abandoning his own. The turning point in the realization of the Americans' ambitions proved to be a letter from Jarousse de Sillac of the French Foreign Ministry, with whom Prince had gained an audience, to Colonel Paul Victor Bouttieaux of the War Ministry. The gist of the letter was that Prince's ambitions should be encouraged, but not for military reasons *per se*, at least not in the short run:

> It appears to me that there might be great advantages in creating an American squadron. The United States would be proud of the fact that certain of her young men, acting as did Lafayette, have come to fight for France and civilization. The resulting sentiment of enthusiasm could have but one effect: to turn the Americans in the direction of the Allies.[15]

This hopeful and astute observation on the part of de Sillac gave Norman Prince and Edmund Gros a powerful practical argument for forming an all-American squadron. Of course the very same argument was made about the Americans serving in *la Légion Étrangère*. The Americans' contributions in the trenches were arguably inconsequential in the larger scheme of things. But if their example and sacrifice inspired their countrymen to call for intervention on the Allied side, then their contribution would be significant indeed—perhaps it would decide the war. But still there was something qualitatively different about combat in the skies, as opposed to combat in the trenches. If the overarching aim was to help get America into the war, then the focus on aviation made sense from the standpoint of cultivating the press. It was still a novelty, and as the war progressed the concept of "aces"—five confirmed enemy aircraft shot down entitled an Allied pilot to that distinction; eight in the German air force—flying for famous squadrons high above the trenches was exciting. The war in the air was also much easier for the average person to grasp than the bloody stalemate on the Western Front, and the even bloodier attempts to break that stalemate, such as at Artois in 1915. With Thaw flying for Squadron C 42 and Prince and Cowdin completing their flight training at Pau and then flying bombers for Squadron VB (VB for Voisin Bombardment) 108, the nucleus just needed to be brought together. This took time, far more than the impatient Norman Prince wanted, in fact. But in December 1915 the three American pilots were granted leave to return to America to celebrate Christmas with loved ones. There was also the unspoken intention that their very presence might stir the pot in the press and gin up American support for France. It was a calculated move, one that not unsurprisingly provoked a strong reaction from the German embassy. If America was neutral, why would it allow U.S. citizens to fight for France? Since most American aviators had enlisted in the *Légion* first and only then become pilots, their service to France was seen as within the spirit of the law. From the German perspective, though, the fact that Americans were serving in the *Légion* was bad enough, and this very public visit by American pilots serving in regular French air units, two of whom had never even first been *légionnaires* (Prince and Cowdin had powerful connnections—Vanderbilt, for example—and had managed to avoid service in the *Légion*, going straight into aviation), was a flagrant contravention of neutrality.

According to one story, Germany's American ambassador Count von Bernstorff just happened to meet Bill Thaw at the men's barbershop in the Ritz-Carlton hotel in New York. They knew each other from social functions before the war, and the Count was cordial enough initially. But he insisted on telling the American aviator that he and his fellow pilots should not be flying for France. Thaw met the admonition with stony silence and then, his shave finished, turned to the count with a curt reply: "Excellency, war is hell."[16] This story may be apocryphal, yet the fact that it had any currency speaks volumes about the effect the visit had on relations between the two countries. But before the scrutiny became too intense, the three pilots were ensconced aboard a steamship making the return journey to Europe. Herbert Molloy Mason Jr., in his excellent book on the Lafayette Escadrille, gave this assessment of the impact of the visit: "It is difficult to ascertain the full impact at the Ministry of War and upon G.Q.G. [the general headquarters of the French Army] of the tumult created by the appearance of the three volunteer airmen in neutral America, but the facts are clear enough. Shortly after the pilots returned to France, Hirschauer was replaced by Colonel Henri Jacques Regnier, and on March 14 Regnier informed de Sillac and Gros that G.Q.G. had formally approved the plan of grouping American pilots in one squadron."[17]

By early September 1915 Kiffin Rockwell had received news of his transfer to the flight school at Avord—realizing his ambition of joining the *Service Aéronautique*.[18] It was here, in the "aviation," that Rockwell seemed to find his true home. Soon after his arrival he wrote to his mother that it was "the life of a gentleman" and that he was "surrounded by gentlemen,"[19]—reassuring words for a mother to hear, but also perhaps an honest admission of his own elitist tendencies. His instructor at Avord was a friend of the artist Jack Casey, Kiffin's old comrade in the *2ᵉ étranger*. He felt great pride in becoming a pilot, and had a smart-looking uniform custom-made by a tailor in the nearby city of Bourges. Rockwell took to his training with great enthusiasm and seriousness, as his letters to his French friend, the Vicomte de Peloux, to his "Aunt" Alice Weeks—mother of the missing *légionnaire* Kenneth Weeks, whose body would not be found until November 1915—and to his brother Paul demonstrate. A letter he wrote Paul on September 27, 1915, included two items of significance in light of Rockwell's own future:

> The last flying we have had at all was Friday morning and it was an unlucky morning, as we had three men killed and one badly injured. Two of the deaths were very horrible. It was one of the instructors in a Morane aeroplane and a mechanic. They started out to the end of the field to an accident. On the way a puff of wind caught the aeroplane and almost upset it, then something went wrong and it shot straight up in the air, then fell. The instructor and the mechanic were imprisoned in the wreckage and there was an explosion and the whole mass went up in flames, and they were burned alive with all the men watching but unable to do a thing....
>
> An American named Chapman, from the 3eme de Marche arrived here this morning and seems to be a very fine fellow indeed....[20]

After the difficult interview with his father in England at the start of the war, Harvard graduate and aspiring architect Victor Chapman had arrived back in Paris in early September 1914, just missing being part of the original contingent of American volunteers that marched off to the Gare Saint-Lazare on August 25. He and a number of the other volunteers that late summer and fall were instead mustered into the *1er étranger*'s *3eme régiment de marche* (Third Company). Of all of the units that the volunteers of 1914 served in, the *3eme de Marche* was perhaps the most unusual. Initially the unit was designated the "Marching Regiment of the Entrenched Camp of Paris." And, in fact, the unit was originally stationed in the metropolitan area at the Caserne de Reuilly.[21] The unit's instructors were initially Paris firemen. This was a result of the odd (at least to American conceptions) arrangement whereby the city's firemen were officially members of the French military. The Third had a number of Americans in addition to Chapman, but in its early incarnation it was perhaps best characterized by its contingent of so-called street "apaches"—the assorted flotsam and jetsam of the city's foreign-born population that was forced to enlist by the police, or be sent to jail. Needless to say, this state of affairs did not make for a unit that was in any way, shape, or form ready for front-line duty anytime soon. So, in contrast to the unit Kiffin Rockwell had initially served in, the Third's training period was extended for a number of months. It was not until December that they went into the trenches of the Somme sector of the Allied line.

Chapman loved the physical labor that *Légion* life imposed on recruits. The gentle giant would do twice the work of his comrades with a smile. The Americans with whom he served were a fairly diverse lot. Eugene Jacob was a middle-aged butcher from Woonsocket, Rhode Island; Christopher Charles was an eighteen-year-old mechanic from Brooklyn; John G. Hopper was a mining engineer from San Francisco; diminutive William E. Dugan was the son of a shoe manufacturer from Rochester; John Brown was an African-American musician "picking a banjo in a Montmartre orchestra when the war started";[22] Walter K. Appleton was the son of a New York publishing magnate. And there were other American volunteers. Some fell by the wayside on account of desertion or illness; some from enemy bullets or shells.

There were also new arrivals from the depot at Lyon, like the Bostonian, Henry Weston Farnsworth. Farnsworth, like a significant number of the American volunteers, had attended Harvard. In fact, by late 1916, an article in the *Princeton Union* claimed that over four hundred Harvard men were then serving abroad in some capacity; and that nineteen of them had been killed.[23] Farnsworth had left school his sophomore year to travel the world, taking whatever work he could find to fund his travels. And after returning to Harvard to complete his degree, Farnsworth found wanderlust calling to him again. He spent time in the Balkans, Russia, and Paris and went to Mexico to cover the civil war there for the *Providence Journal*. When news of the war in Europe broke out he was still in Mexico. Finally making his way to France, he enlisted in the *Légion* on New Year's Day, 1915. Why? In his own words, "Nothing can over-express the quiet fortitude of the French people." Their German enemies, he believed, were "frothing at the mouth" and "Mad with envy."[24]

Another notable addition to the Third Marching Regiment's American contingent was Dr. David Wheeler of Buffalo. Wheeler had initially come with his wife to volunteer in the French military hospitals—she serving as a nurse; he as a doctor.[25] But the forty-two-year-old graduate of Columbia University's College of Physicians and Surgeons decided to kill Germans, not just help heal Frenchman. He would prove to be an intrepid soldier.

Their first winter in the trenches was cruel. Through it all, Victor Chapman demonstrated great energy, selflessness, and physical hardiness. On one occasion he was shot in the arm but, after ascertaining that the bullet hadn't struck bone, refused to be invalided back to a field hospital. On another occasion he and a comrade, under heavy enemy machine fire, dug Rhode Island butcher Eugene Jacob out of the earth in which he had been buried alive by an exploding shell. In saving a life, was Chapman still compensating in some way for the life of his brother whom he had been unable to save? Perhaps the most poignant story regarding Chapman involved a close friend who had been shot: "Picking him up as if he were a child, Victor carried Kohn to the aid station. It was the only time anyone had ever seen the big American with tears in his eyes. The medical officer took one look at Kohn and shook his head. 'Save him, sir,' Victor sobbed. The doctor could only continue shaking his head."[26]

When one stops to consider Chapman's predispositions, it is difficult not to come to the conclusion that he may well have been better suited to the ambulance field service than the *Légion*. He was fearless. He was a mountain of strength. But a killer? He grew disillusioned with life in the trenches, with its daily monotonies punctuated by seemingly random and meaningless death. And there was the ugliness, inescapable ugliness. He was an artist, after all. Chapman's uncle William Astor Chanler, acquainted with Norman Prince and his ambitious plans for an all-American squadron, suggested Chapman apply for transfer to the *Service Aéronautique*. His application was approved in August 1915, and on September 27 he arrived at Avord. Chapman was a near-perfect candidate to become a pilot—personally fearless and acutely sensitive to the beauty of the skies and the world seen from high above.

The French military's flight schools followed a curriculum for aspiring pilots that was unusual, to say the least. The emphasis was on learning how to imitate birds. The first bird they were taught to imitate was a penguin—in outdated 1909 Blériot airplanes, with literally clipped wings. These were extremely sensitive and ungainly craft, "moths that fluttered across the field making a terrific racket but never getting off the ground."[27] The idea was simply to get used to the feel of a plane, operate its controls, and see how it responded. They were brought along slowly, gaining steadily in skill and confidence. In a letter to his brother Paul, Rockwell explained, "Altogether, I have between twelve and fourteen hours (not sure exactly) of actual work in the five weeks I have been here. Yet when I go up I shoot straight up into the air anywhere from 1,000 to 2,000 meters high and I make fancy descents, showing perfect control..."[28]

Rockwell and Chapman were quick learners, and as they evolved from penguins to birds of flight their friendship grew into something like the closeness of brothers. Kiffin's relationship with his brother Paul was close, but ultimately based on blood and shared heritage. His friendship with Chapman was based on something more: "They shared a mystical belief in the rightness of their cause—'the greatest struggle between right and wrong in the history of the world,' one of their companions phrased it."[29]

At Avord Kiffin Rockwell also encountered the enigmatic Bert Hall again. After his first ill-conceived attempt to bluff his way out of having to attend flight school, Hall had turned out to be a competent pilot. He served briefly at Avord as an instructor but was keen on being included in Norman Prince's proposed all-American squadron. Chapman wasn't altogether sure what to make of him. He seemed to have no ideals.[30] (It is interesting to note that of the first American pilots only Thaw, Prince, and Cowdin were sent to the U.S. to cultivate sympathy for France's cause. Perhaps Hall wasn't seen as a gentleman, the sort the authorities wanted talking to reporters.)

Kiffin Rockwell was initially assigned to fly Maurice Farman biplanes, protecting Paris from zeppelin raids. His task was primarily reconnaissance. Chapman would follow him flying the "wheezy old Farmans."[31]

William Thaw, for his part, had earned a commission in the *Service Aéronautique* by early 1916, becoming a lieutenant. With the French government now committed to forming an all-American squadron, Thaw reached out to Georges Thénault, his fellow officer in Squadron C 42, to broach the idea of Thénault's taking command of the new entity, and his response was enthusiastic. Thénault brought along an ex-cavalryman named Alfred de Laage de Meux, as his second-in-command, and on March 21, 1916, the *Escadrille Americaine* was officially authorized by the *Service Aéronautique*. They were to be based at Luxeuil-les-Bains and would deploy within a month.

CHAPTER 7

CHAMPAGNE

With the sweet wine of France that concentrates

The sunshine and the beauty of the world,

Drink sometimes, you whose footsteps yet may tread

The undisturbed, delightful paths of Earth,

To those whose blood, in pious duty shed,

Hallows the soil where that same wine had birth.[1]

Champagne is known the world over; opening a bottle means celebration, christenings, general gaiety. And as any good Frenchmen can tell you, real champagne is produced only in a certain region of his country. All other vintages are imposters. Planted in the chalky white soil of Champagne are the vineyards that produce the most famous wine in the world. All of the American volunteers of 1914 would spend at least some of their Légion service in Champagne. They would come to know its chalky soil intimately—they would all dig in it, live in it, and many would die in it.

The Americans could not help but be affected by the region's natural beauty and fertility. As new recruit Russell Kelly of the Second Company of the *1ᵉʳ étranger* remarked in 1915 near Bouzy in Champagne, "the weather is mild.... Ploughing is almost finished and planting will soon begin. From the outskirts of this place

Suippes, Champagne, France.

to the summit of the mountain [Reims Mountain] (about three miles) the ground rises in a gentle slope covered by vineyards. It is a great wine country and from the heights a wonderful view is obtained of this extensive and fertile valley."[2] Kelly and the Second Company of the *1er étranger* had been sent to Artois in April 1915 and were replaced in Champagne by the Second Company of the *2e étranger*, which had been pulled back from the Chemin des Dames. The long winter along the Aisne had been a trying experience for the men, and the change in both season and scenery had a salutary effect. Alan Seeger remarked cheerily in his diary, "Beautiful spring weather. Glad to be in Champagne."[3] And it was at this time that West Pointer Charles Sweeney became the first American volunteer of 1914 to receive a commission in the French Army.[4] When the Americans in the *2e étranger*, Kiffin Rockwell's old regiment, heard news of the *1er étranger*'s actions in the Artois Offensive and Rockwell's stint in hospital, there was both concern over his wound—but also a touch of envy over how he had acquired it. To take part in such a grand assault was what they had signed up for. There had been no such opportunities in the Chemin des Dames. Alan Seeger in particular yearned to "go into the furnace," as he confided in his journal.[5] He would be frustrated in achieving that desire—for a few more months anyway.

In addition to the brighter mood engendered by a Champagne spring and Sweeney's promotion, there was one other cause for celebration during this period. The *New York Sun*'s Paris correspondent M. B. Grundy initiated a petition among his fellow journalists—Hedin of the *Brooklyn Eagle*, Mower of the *Chicago Daily News*, Roberts of the Associated Press, and Williams of the *New York Times*—to obtain a leave for the American volunteers for the Fourth of July holiday.[6] Destination: Paris. Success! The success of the petition was greeted with pure joy among the Americans in the *2e étranger*. Alan Seeger recalled, "On the evening of July 3rd the sergeant came quite unexpectedly to get the names of all Americans wanting permission of 48 hours in Paris! We could hardly believe such good fortune possible.... We fairly danced for joy. To see Paris again after almost a year's absence!...Next day after breakfast in the village we marched—thirty-two of us in all—to the railway station of Moulin-de-Courmont, on the line from Fismes to Reims, where we got on the train at two o'clock and left. Arrived at Noisy-le-Sec at nine and continued to the Gare de l'Est on another train. Joy to walk in the streets of Paris again."[7]

The journey west started in a sunny mood with French fried potatoes "à la Sweeney" and wine for breakfast. Racecar driver Bob Soubiron "[h]ad the time of his life down on the footboard of the coach. He was determined not to miss the green fields, the lovely flowers and smiles of the girls, as they wished the Americans 'Bon Voyage.'"[8]

But when they reached the capital, the joy the Americans felt was tempered by their encounter with a city different from the one they had left behind:

> On the platform at Paris.... A petite Parisienne stepped up to Sweeney, saying: "Pardon, Monsieur, you come from near Rheims; did you see anyone from the 97th Regiment on the train?" The 97th had been badly cut up. Sweeney remembered that. In an instant his face changed. He smiled back at the girl and answered: "No, there were no French permissionaires; only Americans were on the train."[9]

Alan Seeger noted the absence of men in Paris, at least able-bodied men. He observed, "A great many wounded soldiers on *congé de convalescence*, almost all wearing the old dark blue capote and red trousers."[10] But the somber reminders of the front they had just come from did not entirely alter the Americans' good humor at being let out in Paris for forty-eight hours. Bob Scanlon headed for his old haunts in Montmartre, inquiring after a girl named Susie in Pigalle. Others sought out French patrons they were in touch with, by all accounts splendid hosts. Dennis Dowd of New York had an interesting experience at the Palais d'Orsay. Invited by a French patron to a banquet being given by the American Chamber of Commerce, he would later recount his experience: "There was just one table of us soldiers of the Legion and two long tables of men from the American Ambulance. The Frenchmen were glad to see us—the Ambulance men did not seem glad at all. 'How is that,' said an American visitor, speaking to a well-dressed, manicured doctor, 'are there many Americans in the legion?' 'I don't know.' 'Well, aren't there a good many of our boys there?' 'There may be, but, of course, WE don't know them.'"[11]

Dowd had encountered Dr. Edmund Gros, who was putting on a party for the young gentlemen ambulance drivers of his field service—a party the *légionnaires* had, essentially, crashed. The awkwardness of the ambulance men's being seated near veterans who were straight from the trenches and—given the short notice they had had of their leave—probably still looked like it, can readily be imagined. Those whom Gros had intended to be fêted as heroes knew, or likely at least suspected, who the genuine heroes were there that night. Dr. Gros's discomfort at their arrival and at their enthusiastic reception by grateful French guests must have spoiled his evening. But still the champagne flowed. It was the Fourth of July after all.

★ ★ ★

With conflicted feelings, and in some cases with sore heads, the Americans returned to the war. Trench duty in Champagne was shortly replaced by an unexplained journey southeast to Alsace, in the lee of the Vosges Mountains. Looking at the mountains, aspiring architect and artist Victor Chapman was reminded of the Camden Hills in Maine.[12] This interlude was one of the most pleasant experiences of the entire war for the American volunteers and for the *Légion* more generally. With the losses sustained in the battle at Artois and the departure of large contingents of Russians, Italians, Greeks, and Belgians to their home countries, it was decided that the *2eme* and the *3eme régiments des marche* were to be consolidated into one company. This meant that for the first time all of the units containing American volunteers would be in relatively close proximity to one another. The Harvard boys were all able to sit at a café and enjoy each other's company over a coffee or a bottle. Victor Chapman, Alan Seeger, David King, and Henry Farnsworth were all a long way from the Charles River. But even as close as they were to Germany in this part of Eastern France, the war seemed distant too. As Alan Seeger confided in his journal soon after arriving in Alsace, "in general one feels far removed from the theatre of war."[13] David King put it more pithily: "For a month we were in clover."[14] Seeger found the full-figured Alsatian girls pretty. This part of Alsace had not experienced invasion and occupation by the German army, something that made itself felt in the seeming normality of life in the local towns and villages. There was plenty of drill and a lot of spit and polish, but the overwhelming sense was one of ease and small comforts to be had for a few francs. Seeger seemed to enjoy this time in provincial Alsace even more than he had his visit to his beloved Paris earlier in the summer. He wrote "there is always plenty of time on each side of the morning and evening meal to rest, read, or loaf. This we do—King and I usually—in the cafés of the village. There is the 'Cheval Blanc' across the street, but pleasantest of all is the Café de la Gare, on account of the pretty *gosse* [young girl] that serves one there. I am reading Trietschke's 'Lectures on Politics' that Chapman lent me, and the daily papers...."[15]

This life was not hard to get used to. But they all knew it wouldn't last. There was a sense that they were being readied for something big, something on the scale of the Artois Offensive, perhaps even more ambitious. The fact that not only the *Légion* but the entire Division Marocaine was billeted in nearby villages suggested something was in the works. The men became restless—good food and drink, drill, then more of the same led them to become edgy; and brawls became common in the bistros. David King and boxer Bob Scanlon were enjoying a drink when an Italian *légionnaire* burst in and raced out the other side in fear for his life, soon followed by a giant Algerian and a Russian of similar size, both "stark raving mad with cheap liquor." They asked after the Italian and received an unsatisfactory response, "Whereupon they each grabbed two empty bottles by the neck, broke the bottoms off" and began slashing about at anyone within reach. David King recounted what happened next: "Bob's reaction was immediate. 'Look here boy! Ah seen this befo'. You do like me.' And he promptly ducked under the table. I bumped heads with him in my eagerness to imitate. As soon as the roisterers swept by, we were out and up; wrenched a leg apiece from the table, and stole after them. Bob crowned one and I the other, and then the guard came."[16]

But the French Army knew how to get these men in line, and to lift their morale onto a higher plane. Harvard grads Henry Farnsworth, Alan Seeger, and David King all described being woken at 2:00 a.m. and ordered to march to an unspecified destination across the Vosges. From their billets in villages and hamlets scattered throughout the Alsatian countryside, the men of the Division Marocaine converged on a rectangular field in the morning sun, twenty-five thousand strong. Farnsworth, the former Mexican Civil War correspondent for the *Providence Journal*, was moved to write:

> ...about dawn the sun came out and, as is usual with the Legion, everybody cheered up, and at 7 a.m. we arrived at the parade ground.... Two regiments of Zouaves from Africa were already drawn up. We formed

beside them, and then came the two tirailleurs regiments, their colors with them, then the second Étrangère, two thousand strong, and finally a squadron of Chasseurs d'Afrique. We all stacked arms and lay about on the grass till 8:30. Suddenly the Zouave bugles crashed out sounding the "Garde à vous," and in two minutes the division was lined up, every man stiff as a board—and all the time the bugles ringing angrily from up the line, and the short staccato trumpets of the chasseurs answering from the other extremity. The ringing stopped suddenly and the voices of the colonels crying "Bayonettes aux canons" sounded thin and long drawn out and were drowned by the flashing rattle of the bayonets going on—a moment of perfect silence, and then the slow, courtly-sounding of the "Général! Général! Qui passe!" broken by the occasional crash as regiment after regiment presented arms.... It was all very glorious to see and hear, and to wind up the chasseurs went by at the gallop—going off to their quarters.[17]

Seeger was moved as well, particularly when he recognized the general riding down the line reviewing the troops as the famous Hubert Lyautey—hero of the *légionnaires*, legend to the North Africans. Lyautey was both a conqueror who had been involved in fierce fighting in Madagascar and Morocco and a builder who is perhaps better known as an exemplar of *civilistrise*, or France's civilizing mission. Seeger wrote, "He rides along the ranks and raises his hat as he passes the *porte-drapeau* of the *Tirailleurs*, who dips the flag at the same time."[18] Even the hard-boiled David King confessed "most of us had a choky feeling" describing a "flash of white steel in the sunlight" a "wheat field of bayonets" and then Lyautey tearing "along at full gallop with the figure and élan of a young cavalry officer."[19] This is what the men of the *Légion*—a majority of whom, unlike the volunteers of 1914, were career soldiers—thirsted for. The pageantry of serving with a self-consciously elite unit filled them with a common pride. And that pride was their *raison d'être*. The American volunteers could not resist this powerful emotion. These men whom they had often looked down upon were infusing them with their own values. "A day like this made up for a lot," King admitted.[20]

The hike back across the Vosges was a long one, but these men were fit, and it made little impression. They arrived at their billets in the afternoon. Seeger looked forward to meeting Farnsworth and Chapman for dinner the following evening in the village of Plancher-des-Mines. In the bistro that night were groups of *légionnaires* from the *1er étranger* that had taken part in the great attacks in Artois at Neuville St. Vaast and Vimy Ridge. The *2e étranger* had not, of course, been there, and Seeger felt this keenly: "[T]he *camaraderie* of the soldiers whose bond is that of great exploits achieved in common was of a sort which does not exist among us, and which I envied."[21] Seeger seemed to long for a great battle, in the open, with all at stake—a Marathon or a Gettysburg in which he could play a part. The distinction between democracy and slavery, as in those earlier battles, however, was not so clearly defined to him as it was to some of his fellow volunteers of 1914 such as Rockwell, Bowe, and King. Seeger confided to his diary during his time in Alsace that, "The German contribution to civilization is too large, and German ideals too generally in accord with my own, to allow me to join in the chorus of hate against a people whom I frankly admire. It was only that the France, and especially the

Paris, that I love should not cease to be the glory and the beauty that they are that I engaged. For that cause I am willing to stick to the end."[22] As this idyllic summer wound to its close, the Division Marocaine would return to Champagne, and Alan Seeger would have his Marathon.

*   *   *

The French High Command launched two major offensives in 1915. The first, in Artois, had failed to achieve its larger objectives. But much had been learned. If used properly, these lessons might lead to a different outcome in future attacks. The second offensive was planned for September, in the open country to the east of Reims, while a simultaneous effort would be made against the Germans in Artois. (France's British allies referred to this as the Battle of Loos.) This made good strategic sense. The giant salient in the German lines that ran approximately from Arras to Reims appeared vulnerable if breakthroughs could be achieved. And the German Army would most likely have to withdraw back across the Belgian frontier if its communications centers on the Douai Plain were seized and the crucial Mezières-Hirson railway cut. In 1915 the Allies enjoyed a manpower advantage over the Germans on the Western Front, and the accepted wisdom shared by Joffre and other French general was that it could be used to simply overwhelm the invaders,[23] *if* the men in the trenches were given proper artillery and cavalry support—artillery to pound the German trenches in advance of the French attack, cavalry to exploit the massive breakthroughs that were anticipated. The feeling among the *légionnaires* in Alsace that they were being primed for something big was prescient. If not fattened for the kill, they certainly were a rested and restless bunch in the peak of fighting trim. They would need to be.

On September 15 the *Légion* detrained at St.-Hilaire. They were all there, together for the first time, in Champagne, all of the American volunteers of 1914. All, that is, minus those killed, convalescing from wounds, or transferred to the "aviation." (Victor Chapman had received news of his transfer in August shortly after he had dined with his ex-Harvard mates Alan Seeger and Henry Farnsworth. Kiffin Rockwell would transfer soon after, joining William Thaw and Bert Hall. James Bach was in a prisoner-of-war camp.) Something David King saw on the road to the town of Suippes made him realize that this offensive was something the like of which he had yet to experience in the war: "The road was blocked with regiments. I had never seen so many men." He continued, "Our hopes ran high—it was the big offensive—open warfare— Berlin! Still the blue columns rolled on—picked men, shock troops—the lance head of the army."[24] Gone were the rakish cloth *képis*, replaced by the new "Adrian" helmets designed to protect soldiers' heads from shrapnel, if not necessarily bullets. By this time new sky-blue-colored uniforms had also been adopted by the French Army. The one exception were the khaki uniforms of colonial units such as those in the Division Marocaine.

The artillery was moved up *en masse*, the 75s ready to do their deadly work. Even six divisions of cavalry waited anxiously to take part in the attack that they hoped would win the war. Both the *1er étranger* and *2e étranger* were marched up to the front lines each night, picks and shovels in hand, to expand and reinforce the existing network of trenches and *boyeaux* (smaller connecting ditches— literally "intestines"). On September 22 the French artillery began what would be a massive three-day bombardment of the German

positions on a crest north of Souain, known to the locals as Navarin Farm, and an adjacent wooded area at the base of the Butte
Souain. There was no attempt made at surprising the Germans.
German aircraft (both balloons and airplanes) had a clear view of
the massive French build-up in the area. Two mighty armies were
about to go toe-to-toe in the chalky white soil of Champagne. If
not for a miserable rain that fell just before the attack, the ground
was ideal for a set piece battle: long rolling fields broken by gently
undulating hills with only a wooded hill, the *Bois de Sabot* or
"wooden shoe," altering the landscape. This French Army was,
perhaps, the best supplied force that France ever sent into battle.
There was no shortage of food, drink, cartridges, shoes, blankets,
bullets, or knives.[25] The anticipation built through the rainy night
of September 24 and 25, until the men assembled in the *tranchées
de départ* and waited for the order to go "over the top." The first
wave of colonial troops would be supported by the *2e étranger* in
the second wave. At 9:10 a.m. the order came. Alan Seeger confided
to his diary, "I have been waiting for this moment for more than a
year. It will be the greatest moment in my life. I shall take good
care to live up to it."[26] He nudged his sled toward the snowy slope,
and sped down the hill…

"Amid the most infernal roar of every kind of firearms and
through an atmosphere heavy with dust and smoke, we marched
up," recounted Alan Seeger in a letter to his mother.[27] The German
artillery had zeroed in on the French front-line trenches and
wreaked carnage. Beside Alan Seeger, forty-eight-year-old John
Bowe, father of four, steadied himself: "dead were lying so thick
soldiers walked on upturned faces grazed by hob-nailed shoes.… At
one corner leaning against two corpses lay a young soldier, smooth
shaven, curly-hair, mustache trimmed, his face settling into the

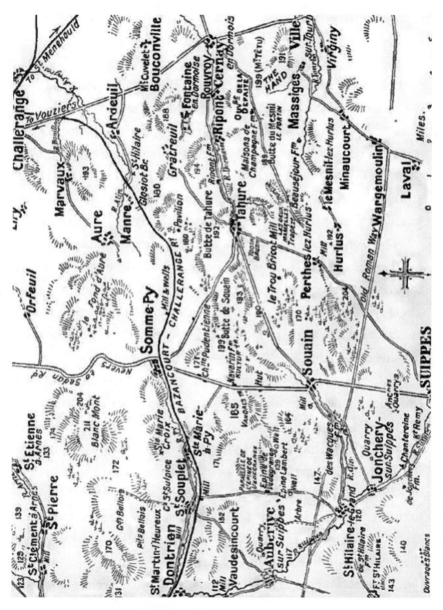

Scene of Battle, Champagne, September–October 1915.

soft, creamy whiteness of death, a smile on his lips. My mind flashed over to Madam Tussaud's wax figure exhibition in London."[28] Then it was time: "The man alongside puts on his bayonet as the order is passed down the line to go over on command. The officers snap out: 'Five minutes, three minutes, one minute, En Avant!'"[29] Through the smoke could be seen the *tirailleurs* advancing up the long hill towards the Germans' front-line trenches. And then they were in them. The word went round among the 2e *étranger* to come up in support of the North Africans and they followed them up the long hill at a quick walk.

The *légionnaires* passed the wounded and the dead and large numbers of German prisoners. The French artillery had devastated the German front line. The barbed wire in front of the trench had largely been obliterated as well, making the going easier there than anticipated. The artillery was brought out into the open to support the advance from No Man's Land, "a magnificent spectacle." Then, to Alan Seeger's wonder and delight, "Squadrons of cavalry came up. Suddenly the long, unpicturesque *guerre de tranchées* was at an end and the field really presented the aspect of the familiar battle pictures—the battalions in manoeuvre, the officers, superbly indifferent to danger, galloping about on their chargers."[30]

But this was merely the preliminary of the battle that the Germans expected to fight. As at Artois, their defense-in-depth relied far more heavily on the second line of trenches, the pre-sighting of their own front-line trenches as targets for their artillery, and the well-timed counterattack. In fact, on this day, the *légionnaires* had drawn by far the more difficult assignment. They would have to advance towards the second line, bristling with machine guns and rifles, supported by the Germans' deadly artillery (the 77s and 105s); hold the captured front-line trench, or what was left of it, under a hail of artillery fire; and then somehow break through into the German rear. It would prove to be an impossible task.

David King moved quickly, pausing briefly at the German front-line trench, where he saw that "Nothing was left but a series of mounds and holes with half buried men, machine guns, and barbed wire entanglements."[31] Then on into the inferno: "A shell burst just above us.... The Corporal on my right buried his face in his hands squeaking like a snared rabbit...weeping in such a high falsetto we thought he was fooling, but when we pulled his hands down from his face we found it split open like a ripe melon."[32] Lieutenant Charles Sweeney fell with a bullet through the chest. Taken back to a field hospital, he refused last rites and clung tenaciously to life. He would be the first American decorated with both the *Croix de Guerre* and the Legion of Honor medal.[33]

The chaos of war presented itself to John Bowe in all its surreal qualities: "Germans running, equipment strewn everywhere, black bread, cigars.... Broken caissons, dead horses...Trenches full of dead, legs, arms and heads sticking out."[34] Navarin Farm was within sight, but not yet within reach. The intensity of fire from the German fortifications there was such that the *légionnaires* were ordered to simply lie down and withstand the shelling as best they could for two hours before attempting to advance further towards the crest. Those hours could age a man years...if he lived. In perhaps his finest poem, Alan Seeger recounted the anxiety and fatalism that being under shell fire in Champagne engendered:

> A shell surprised our post one day
> And killed a comrade at my side.
> My heart was sick to see the way
> He suffered as he died.

I dug about the place he fell,
And found, no bigger than my thumb,
A fragment of the splintered shell
In warm aluminum.

I melted it, and made a mould,
And poured it in the opening,
And worked it, when the cast was cold,
Into a shapely ring.

And when my ring was smooth and bright.
Holding it on a rounded stick,
For seal, I bade a Turco write
Maktoob in Arabic.

Maktoob! "'Tis written!"...So they think,
These children of the desert, who
From its immense expanses drink
Some of its grandeur too.

Within the book of Destiny,
Whose leaves are time, whose cover, space,
The day when you shall cease to be,
The hour, the mode, the place,

Are marked, they say; and you shall not
By taking thought or using wit
Alter that certain fate one jot,
Postpone or conjure it.

Learn to drive fear, then, from your heart.

If you must perish, know, O man,
'Tis an inevitable part
Of the predestined plan.

And, seeing that through the ebon door
Once only you may pass, and meet
Of those that have gone through before
The mighty, the élite—

Guard that not bowed nor blanched with fear
You enter, but serene, erect,
As you would wish most to appear
To those you most respect.

So die as though your funeral
Ushered you through the doors that led
Into a stately banquet hall
Where heroes banqueted;

And it shall all depend therein
Whether you come as slave or lord,
If they acclaim you as their kin
Or spurn you from their board.

So, when the order comes: "Attack!"
And the assaulting wave deploys,
And the heart trembles to look back
On life and all its joys;

Or in a ditch that they seem near
To find, and round your shallow trough

Drop the big shells that you can hear
Coming a half mile off;

When, not to hear, some try to talk,
And some to clean their guns, or sing,
And some dig deeper in the chalk
I look upon my ring:

And nerves relax that were most tense,
And Death comes whistling down unheard,
As I consider all the sense
Held in that mystic word.

And it brings, quieting like balm
My heart whose flutterings have ceased,
The resignation and the calm
And wisdom of the East.[35]

They waited. They had no choice. As Seeger later observed, "German second line defenses...proved to be so formidable that all further advance without a preliminary artillery preparation was out of the question."[36] Finally, the French 75s began to blast the German positions at Navarin Farm. John Bowe had been gassed in the initial attack. Fortunately for Bowe it was not a fatal dose, and he pushed forward with the rest, "Over the top again. A backward glimpse.... I noticed the Legionnaires running, chin forward, bayonet fixed, greatly bunched, and thought the Germans could not miss hitting so many men."[37] The artist Jack Casey fell, painfully wounded. Edgar Bouligny was hit in the groin by a shell splinter as he cleared out a German machine gun nest with hand

grenades.[38] At dusk, David King and his comrades found themselves dug in in an advanced position two hundred yards back of
Navarin Farm:

> The battalion on the right had taken the Ferme de Nava-
> rin but our gunners didn't know it and our barrage stuck
> fast, just in front of the farm. The German barrage was
> some twenty yards back of the farm, so the battalion was
> boxed. Fritz discovered their predicament first and short-
> ened his range.... Meantime, we were consolidating our
> position on the ridge. The Germans turned everything
> they had on us—shrapnel, marmites (H-E shell), aerial
> torpedoes, and machine guns. It was raining hard by
> now—it always rained when the allies attacked.... About
> midnight chaos broke out in the Ferme de Navarin. Wild
> firing, then the panic-stricken bleating of the battalion
> holding it, guttural German cheers, and clear-cut com-
> mands of French officers trying to rally their men (it was
> a line battalion made up entirely of the young class of
> 1916). The Boches had counterattacked and the kids had
> scattered and broken. Suddenly a bugle cut clear and
> calm through all the noise and confusion—first the reg-
> imental call of the Legion, then the rally. The German
> shouting stopped. There was a half-hearted cheer from
> the young troops. The Legion went mad. Every man
> sprang to his feet and whipped out his bayonet. The
> bugle began again—clear and inviting it sounded the
> charge. This was too much! Low growls ran down the
> line—We started forward with the long swinging pas de
> charge. The officers ran out in front, beating us back

with the flat of their swords. "Stay where you are! Don't fire! We must wait till they are driven back to us and then counter attack." Discipline held—the Legion subsided and waited with grim expectancy. Now the bugler had passed to the double time of the charge! The kids pulled themselves together and fairly hustled the Germans out of the farm.[39]

That night was a long one, as the rain and the shells continued to fall and hunger began to gnaw at the *légionnaires*. John Bowe discovered a piece of hardtack. He stuck it in the water collected at the bottom of his shell hole and dined.[40] Edward Morlae was luckier than most. Buried alive by a German shell, he avoided an awful fate only because of the quick thinking and bravery of his fellow Americans. David King, Dennis Dowd, Bob Soubiron, and Fred Zinn risked withering enemy fire to dig him out and revive his unconscious body. Considering how petty, deceptive, and mean-spirited his conduct had been toward many of his countrymen fighting in France, it's a wonder they didn't leave him to die.[41]

★ ★ ★

For the Americans in the *1er étranger*, the opening attack on September 25 was a time of waiting and watching, with German shells keeping them company in the front-line trenches. They had been held in reserve with an eye towards a coordinated attack against the nettlesome Bois de Sabot on the right flank of their comrades at Navarin Farm.

The members of the old Third Company of the *1er étranger*, which had now been absorbed into the *2eme regiment de marche*, had never taken part in an action of anything like this magnitude, but the few remaining American volunteers from the original Second Company of the *1ᵉʳ étranger* knew what to expect when their unit's number was called. Veterans of the Artois offensive such as Texan Frank Musgrave and "Skipper" Paul Pavelka—who, after the German bayonet through his leg in the original Artois campaign and before rejoining his unit in time for the Champagne offensive, had enjoyed a not altogether unpleasant convalescence teaching English to girls at a French boarding school—had no illusions about glorious bayonet charges. When pressed by his uninitiated comrades, Musgrave was blunt about their prospects: "If you have ever seen the Chicago slaughterhouses you have already seen something like the carnage you will witness here."[42] Described as "long-limbed" and "raw-boned," Frank Musgrave was as "[o]riginal as they make them, even in original states,"[43] and by this time he had gained a reputation as a lucky *légionnaire*. Dislocated shoulder notwithstanding, he had emerged from both the May 9 and June 16, 1915, attacks in Artois with nary a scratch. Henry Farnsworth, Dr. David Wheeler, Christopher Charles, and the other members of the old Third Company hoped some of "Lucky" Frank's aura would attach itself to them when on September 28 they moved up into position adjacent the *2ᵉ étranger*.

The Germans were well-concealed in the pines and undergrowth, and patrols were sent out to ascertain their position. Frank Musgrave, true to his moniker, was the only man in his patrol to come back alive. When asked where his sergeant was, Musgrave grimly replied, "Hung up on the Boches' barbed wire, along with my corporal and other comrades."[44] They had stumbled into the wire and had been met with point-blank machine gun fire. But now that they knew where the Germans were, the attack was launched.

The German fortifications in the Bois de Sabot were no less formidable than those at Navarin Farm. The *tirailleurs* had been first to attack—and had been simply cut to pieces. David King and the other members of the *2ᵉ étranger* first had to cross the field where the German front lines had been on the first day of battle in order to get into position to join the *1ᵉʳ étranger* in the attack. The German artillery opened up on them with devastating effect. King recalled, "Horrible apparitions crawled out of shell holes as we went by. A thing with no face—only four caverns in a red mask, where eyes, nose and mouth had been—mooed and gibbered at us as it heard the clink of accoutrements passing. Some strong-minded humanitarian put a bullet into it as we filed by."[45] The Bois de Sabot was "like a scene from the underworld—ghostly columns picking their way through shell-torn trees in the smoke and fog of high explosives."[46] The *1ᵉʳ étranger* charged the fortifications and their bodies absorbed the full force of the bullets, shells, and shrapnel being hurled at them. "Men pitched forward into graves freshly dug by bursting shells, to be immediately covered deep with earth by a fresh explosion. A veritable death-trap seemed to have been laid for the Legion, but each man who went down fell facing forward. At points in the line the stream of lead was so thick that falling men were turned over and over and rolled along the ground like dead leaves before a late autumn wind."[47]

The *legionnaires*' officers, primarily Frenchmen, led from the front and paid the price. Three were killed as they reached the barbed wire, urging their men on. As Paul Rockwell remarked, "Not an officer who went into the attack came back whole."[48] Henry Farnsworth had his spine broken by a bullet. Another one, to the throat, killed him. A small memorial to the Harvard graduate, world traveler, and Mexican Civil War correspondent is located near where he fell. This piece of land is now part of a French military base, and is off limits to the public.

Jeweller's engraver Charles Trinkard was hit twice in the shoulder: "[T]he first struck just over the heart, but was deflected upward by a safety razor he carried in his breast pocket, and tore a nasty wound upward."[49] The young Brooklyn mechanic Christopher Charles was hit. The African-American banjo player John Brown was blown so high into the air by an exploding shell that the fall left him paralyzed. Dr. David Wheeler had one of his calves ripped away. After binding up his wound, he did what he could for his suffering comrades with the medical kit he always brought with him. He then carried a stricken comrade on his back as he crawled to the field dressing station in the rear. The good doctor eventually made his way to the hospital at Neuilly, where his wife, a nurse, welcomed him.[50] His bravery, skill, and selflessness in the attack on the Bois de Sabot on September 28 stand as one of the greatest acts of heroism exhibited by any American in the entire war. For this Wheeler was awarded the *Croix de Guerre*.

The charge of the *1er étranger* was broken. The attack failed. The ferocity of the Division Marocaine's assault, however, allowed other units to outflank the wood—and then take it from behind two days later. But the *Légion* in France never recovered from this battle. Of two companies of two-hundred and fifty men each in the *1er étranger* that took part in the charge, only thirty-one were fit to answer roll call the next day. The only officer left standing was the adjutant.[51]

In the coming weeks, as September rolled into October, the French High Command continued to insist on further offensives, as it had in Artois in the spring. Only when his commanders made it clear that additional attacks could not be sustained did Joffre call

Monument de la Ferme de Navarin, *Aux Morts des Armées de Champagne.*

off the offensive, which had been a magnificent failure, in terms of achieving its larger objectives. But no one that had witnessed the bravery of the French Army in seizing Navarin Farm and the Bois de Sabot could ever label those men, the living and the dead, failures. In the end, the Germans "lost 140,000 killed and wounded and 25,000 prisoners—by another account 80,000 and 41,000 respectively. The French lost 135,000 and 290,000 were wounded in the Artois-Champagne battles."[52] Thousands of horses also were killed in the futile cavalry charge towards the crest in pursuit of the retreating Germans, a sacrifice to the French generals' unwillingness to let go of the past. The Swiss poet Blaise Cendrars, who had spoken so eloquently in those heated days of late July and early

August 1914, in the Paris cafés in support of France, fought here and lost his right hand. Invalided out of the army, he had to learn to write new verses with his left. Today a giant monument commands the plain on the site where Navarin Farm once stood. Below the monument lie the bones of numberless unidentified soldiers, mingled forever where they were killed. The remnants of trenches and barbed wire can still be seen: a haunting reminder of what happened there.

For the American volunteers of 1914 the Battle of Champagne was a turning point. The first reaction to what had occurred was the need to find out who had survived, who was wounded, and where they had been taken. As *Légion* historian Geoffrey Bocca explained, "Always, among these American boys, as the charge was over and the action ended, there was a reaching out as for children in the dark, to touch each other, and make sure they were not alone in this hell of death."[53] The *2ᵉ étranger* had been held back from the direct frontal assault in the Bois de Sabot when their commanding officer saw that the barbed wire was still untouched. This prudent decision likely saved the lives of a number of Americans.[54] But the bleeding remnants of the *1ᵉʳ étranger* could not be put back together again. For Victor Chapman and Kiffin Rockwell, undergoing their training for the aviation, the news from Champagne was, of course, of supreme interest. There was concern over who among their former comrades had fallen. There was also envy that they had missed this great battle; guilt perhaps, too, at not having been with their trench mates? In a letter to his father, Victor Chapman described his feelings as he witnessed Kiffin Rockwell's reaction to a letter he himself had received as the battle was raging in Champagne: "At this moment I have mixed feelings of pride, envy, and sorrow, for he has just received a postal from a friend who has returned to the Regiment. They were given a banner, and three days ago were up where the big advance took place. On account of their reputation and the general understanding that they were reserved for attack, the regiment must have been in the very thick of it, and has enormous losses. Even Rockwell is chafing because he changed too soon. 'There is nothing like it, you float across the field, you drop, you rise again. The sack, the 325 extra rounds, the gun—have no weight. And a ball in the head and it's all over,—*no pain.*'"[55]

Word of the *légionnaires*' fate reached the public slowly, and miscommunication was not out of the ordinary. Alan Seeger, for instance, was falsely reported dead in his hometown *New York Tribune.*"[56] One can only imagine the joy his family must have felt when they received his postcard confirming that he was still with the living, and unhurt. He reassured them with these words: "I am writing you in a little café amid the best of comrades. You must take heart thinking of me as always content and really happy as I have never been before and as perhaps I will never be after."[57] Seeger did, however, recognize the serious nature of the strategic defeat that had been inflicted on the French (by the Germans? by the French themselves?) in Champagne and Artois: "This check...makes the present hour a rather grave one for us. Yet it cannot be said to be worse than certain moments that arrived even much later in the course of the Civil War, when things looked as critical for the North, though in the end of a similar *guerre d'usure* they pulled out victorious." He continued, "This affair only deepened my admiration for, my loyalty to, the French. If we did not succeed, it was not the fault of the French soldier. He is a better man, man for man, than the German."[58]

But not every American volunteer was moved to recommit himself to the fight for civilization. After his near-death experience at Navarin Farm, Edward Morlae seized the first opportunity that presented itself to head for the Spanish frontier, using his American passport to return to the U.S. via a third country. Back home, this deserter—detested by most of his fellow American volunteers— postured as a war hero, and slandered the *Légion*.[59]

In France, the *Légion* was forced to face logistical realities. To continue fighting on the Western Front as a unit was now very much in doubt. Too many officers and men had fallen in the 1915 attacks. Being a part of the Division Marocaine almost guaranteed an unsustainably high casualty rate among the *légionnaires*. The French High Command gave serious consideration to returning the remaining *légionnaires* to Africa. In this uncertain atmosphere, the surviving Americans were given the opportunity to transfer to a line regiment in the regular French Army, the 170th. Service with this unit came with the promise of being used only in the attack— no dreary, interminable trench duty.

For a number of the volunteers of 1914, the offer was simply too attractive to pass up, especially taking into consideration the uncertainty surrounding the future of the *Légion* in France. In the end, most transferred—among them David King, John Bowe, "Lucky" Frank Musgrave (who received the *Croix de Guerre* for his exploits in Artois and at the Bois de Sabot in 1915), Paul Pavelka, Bob Soubiron, Dennis Dowd, William Dugan, and Eugene Jacob. Another transfer was a black ex-boxer and musician named Eugene Bullard from Columbus, Georgia,[60] who joined his fellow boxer Bob Scanlon in the new regiment. Alan Seeger, Jack Casey, and Edgar Bouligny chose to remain in the *Légion*. It had become their home, in a sense, and they could not leave it. Ultimately, the

French High Command chose to consolidate the *1ᵉʳ étranger* with the *2ᵉ étranger* to form one unit: the *Regiment de Marche de la Légion Étrangère*. It would fight until the end of the war in 1918, three long years away...

CHAPTER 8

VERDUN

France's failures to expel the Germans in 1915 were matched by Russia's failures on the Eastern Front. Ever since the twin debacles of the battles of Tannenberg and the Masurian Lakes in 1914, Russia's giant ill-equipped army had been on the defensive against the smaller but better-equipped German Army. In 1915 their losses only mounted, with the fighting shifting from Poland (now lost to Russia) into the Czar's possessions on the Baltic Sea. Even St. Petersburg—the capital, whose name was officially changed to the more Slavic "Petrograd" during the war—began to look vulnerable. The Russian Army was no longer in a position to seriously threaten Berlin.

As a result, the German High Command felt it could afford the luxury of looking west again in 1916, and possibly dealing France the knockout blow it had narrowly missed landing in 1914. The

Erich von Falkenhayn, architect of the German offensive against Verdun.

architect of Germany's plan was General Erich von Falkenhayn. Much has been written about von Falkenhayn's assault, with historians debating it for decades. Confusingly, von Falkenhayn gave different versions of his ultimate strategic objective in official communiqués, offhand remarks, and in his memoirs. But the common understanding (if not consensus) is that he planned to force France to fight a battle of attrition on a hitherto unimaginable scale, in order to bleed it white. To accomplish this end, he had to attack a location of such significance to the French that they would do anything rather than see it fall to the Germans. He chose to attack a small city on the Meuse River called Verdun.

Verdun was located in the part of Lorraine which had not been ceded to Germany in 1871. The city itself had ancient roots. Founded by the Gauls and conquered by the Romans, it became an important center in the Frankish Empire. In 843 AD, Charlemagne's vast domains were divided amongst his grandsons by the Treaty of Verdun. By its terms, the territories to the west were given to his grandson Charles the Bald; those to the east, to Charles's brother Louis the German; and a central kingdom extending from the North Sea to the Mediterranean, to the third and eldest brother, Lothar. The name "Lorraine," in fact, is derived from "Lotharingia," the kingdom of Lothar. Charles's kingdom became the progenitor of France, and Louis's kingdom became the progenitor of the German nation. The land between the two future nation-states was contested soon after Lothar's death, and it remained contested through the centuries. This partitioning of Charlemagne's empire was a fateful division for Europe; before 1914, France and Germany had already fought many wars as a result of it.

Verdun and its commanding heights were officially ceded to France as a result of the Treaty of Westphalia in 1648, and soon afterwards the noted French military engineer the Marquis de Vauban drew up plans for extensive fortifications around the city. These were expanded and enhanced following France's humiliating 1870 defeat in the Franco-Prussian War. Verdun, in fact, had been the last French fortress facing the German frontier to surrender. Von Falkenhayn's prediction about the French High Command's response to an attack on Verdun was correct. As the ancient Chinese philosopher of war Sun Tzu had commented in his famous sixth-century BC work, *The Art of War*, "If asked how to cope with a great host of the enemy in orderly array and on the point of marching to the attack, I should say: 'Begin by seizing something which your opponent holds dear; then he will be amenable to your will.'" The attack on Verdun would draw France into a war of attrition. But that war would also, inevitably, bleed Germany's forces white as well. Thus the attack would require the marshaling of Germany's full economic might and logistical mastery, its capacity to sustain a battle of attrition longer than its opponent, and its superior will in order to force the eventual collapse not only of

France's army but also of its entire political system. Thus Verdun would break France. Or so von Falkenhayn believed.

* * *

The Americans who would be thrown into the maelstrom that Verdun would become had no inkling of what lay ahead—except that they now would be serving in a regular French line unit that had gained a fierce reputation. If there was going to be a fight to the finish, they would assuredly take part in it. The 170th Regiment was known more commonly by its nickname: *les Hirondelles de la Mort*, the "Swallows of Death." Spanish-American War veteran John Bowe had heard of their exploits and was effusive in his praise of the 170th: "Time and again have its members been complimented by General Joffre.... Never were they called upon when they failed to make good. They have rushed into near extermination and come out alive. Anointed with success, they fear nothing."[1] The bar could not have been set higher for the new American members of the *Hirondelles*.

Their first days in the regiment came with a humorous twist of sorts. The volunteers were marched thirty-five kilometers to the rear to join the 170th, which was recuperating after sustaining severe losses in the Champagne Offensive. Then, the Americans were promptly marched thirty-five kilometers back to the front-line trenches they had just left, where the 170th relieved the *Légion*! So much for only being used for the attack. Their post was located in a German headquarters captured in the recent battle. Next to the headquarters was a graveyard full of German dead. Once the German artillery got wind of the French occupying the position, they gave it hell. As John Bowe explained, "They shot up those dead

Germans—the atmosphere grew pungent—the stench permeated every corner. It settled heavy in the lungs. It was impossible to get away from it."[2] Then it was time to eat. As French historian Georges Blond would comment, "Civilians may pronounce the words 'war' and 'battlefield,' but the most important single feature, of which they are totally ignorant, is the sickly-sweet stench of the dead."[3]

Trench duty was the defining experience of the war for most of the men who served in it. By the end of 1915 the trenches had begun to take on the look of permanence. For the Americans of the 170th it had to be disheartening to be stuck in a trench, with the cold coming on, and the German guns zeroed in on one's position. And always, there were the dead. David King recalled a post where "we sat, slept, even ate, sitting on corpses." Once he lost his balance momentarily and grabbed the parapet above "to save myself from falling and was almost sick as I felt a face come away under my hand. For days everything I ate or touched smelled of putrid flesh."[4]

It was inevitable that the Americans would sustain casualties in this very active frontline post. New Yorker Dennis Dowd was wounded by shrapnel in the hand; Bob Soubiron was hit by a shell splinter in the knee; Frank Musgrave was gassed; "Skipper" Pavelka cut his hands badly on barbed wire.[5] John Bowe remembered looking at "shrapnel burst overhead" then a ball "embedded itself in my forehead."[6] Bob Scanlon stared incredulously at Bowe, "You lucky fool. You lay rolled up warm in those Boche blankets all morning, while I was up trying to find a place to heat the coffee. Now, you will go south, where it is warm, and I shall have to stay here and freeze."[7] David King was buried alive by a shell. The sudden, smothering blackness, the lack of oxygen, the desperation, then being pulled clear—it was all too much for him, and shaking like a baby King was on the verge of a breakdown when his sergeant lit into him for sitting there when others were still buried. King grabbed a pick in his unsteady hands, then—realizing it could kill the men he was trying to save—he switched to a shovel and started digging. King later recognized that the sergeant had saved him by not allowing him to "sit down and think over my narrow escape and work myself up into a state of shell shock.... He took control of my mind before I had time to realize the shock, and directed it along normal channels."[8] But King was never the same after this episode. The blast had inflicted a severe concussion and left him without the use of his right eye. Saying nothing about the injury, he learned to shoot from his left shoulder.

Winter came early. The Americans' French comrades seemed to take it with an uncommon degree of stoicism. In the 170th, the war was less of an abstraction or an ideal; it was very personal. Many of the *Hirondelles* "were from the part of France occupied by the Germans," and "did not even have the consolation and encouragement of letters and news from their loved ones."[9] These men were fighting to liberate their homes and families. What was a little cold? Who knew what those they had left behind had endured...or were enduring?

★ ★ ★

One of the great ironies of the Battle of Verdun—and of the supreme sacrifice that the French Army made to hold the Germans at bay there—was that the French High Command had ordered the city's defenses reduced to skeletal garrisons in the weeks leading up to the battle. Why? By early 1916, the accepted wisdom was that fixed fortifications were all but obsolete. The fall of the great fortresses of Liège and Namur in Belgium and of Maubeuge in France early in the war had led to a reorientation in military thinking. Why place all of those men and artillery pieces in a single fixed spot that could easily become a trap? Verdun was also undermanned because the area around it had been one of the more quiet sectors of the Western Front for some time and General Joffre needed men for the great offensive that he planned to launch in 1916 along the Somme River. For these reasons when the Germans launched *their* great offensive of 1916 in Lorraine, the French were outnumbered, massively outgunned, and unprepared. To be fair, the German Army could not build up its forces to the degree that it did east of Verdun without drawing the attention of French aviators and spies. It was clear in the days leading up to the attack that something big was up—yet little was done to reinforce the French garrisons. Either Joffre believed this was a feint intended to draw his attention away from the Somme sector or he was simply blind to the threat posed by the Germans. If so, it would seem to have been a willful blindness, as his own commanders at Verdun, sensing what faced them, were asking for reinforcements.

Texan Frank Musgrave was one of the few soldiers sent to Verdun as reinforcements in mid-February. "Lucky" Frank had spent two months in hospital recovering from being gassed in Champagne. But when he was deemed "fit for duty" he wasn't returned to the 170th. Instead he found himself with orders to report to the 44th line regiment stationed in the village of Vaux, five kilometers in front of Verdun. This placed him front and center for the largest artillery bombardment in history up to that time. On the morning of February 21, 1916, *Unternehmen Gericht* ("Operation Judgment") was launched when over eight hundred

German guns opened up on the French trenches and fortifications around Verdun. Many of these guns dwarfed the 77s and 105s the Germans had used with such deadly precision in Champagne. Some of them were 420s, which was like someone firing a car at you. The pounding could be heard, or felt, hundreds of kilometers away. According to Musgrave, the artillery bombardments at Artois and Champagne were "mere child's play" compared to this.[10] The front-line trenches essentially ceased to exist; then the guns lengthened their range to reach the French rear and halt any reinforcements being rushed up to fill the gaps. It wasn't until the afternoon that German infantry emerged and, finding little resistance, occupied what had been the French front lines. Musgrave, and what was left of the 44th, dug in below the fortress of Vaux. For five days they hung on, the last forty-eight hours without food or water. Finally, on February 26, "their ammunition exhausted," they surrendered to the Germans.[11] "Lucky" Frank would spend the rest of the war in a prisoner-of-war camp.

His former comrades in the *Hirondelles* were in Champagne when the attack commenced. They had just been immunized against typhoid fever and were in a sorry state when the orders came: *"Allons là haut! Tous le monde en bas! Faites les sacs. On part à six heures"* ("Come on, everybody on deck! Make up the sacks. We leave at six.").[12] It was clear something big was up as they piled into waiting automobiles to be chauffeured east in style (of a sort), toward the sound of the distant guns. David King recalled the *Hirondelles* singing ribald songs in the early morning light, "We passed peasant girls in *sabots* coming from the bakery with the family loaves clasped under their arms, yawning as they walked—they scarcely looked up, however, as the troops thundered by."[13] How different from 1914. The girls might have paid these men more mind if they had known they were about to help save France from collapse, defeat, and humiliation.

It began to snow, the roads grew treacherous, and the men of the 170th were ordered out, shouldered their packs, and got under way, "a blue-grey column...shuffling precariously along the icy road."[14] A new recruit had joined them—Jack Janz of Philadelphia, the sailor twice wounded at Artois the previous spring. While convalescing, he had received word that his good mate Frank Musgrave was now in the 170th, so he had signed on to join him.[15] Unfortunately for him, Musgrave was already in the furnace of Verdun with the 44th. Janz would never see his friend again.

The final part of their journey took them over the Voie Sacrée, the "Sacred Way," as it would come to be known: the only access into the city from Bar-le-Duc, to the west. The Germans were never able to cut this link to the outside, though they certainly tried. Hundreds of thousands of French soldiers would eventually make this same journey, on this same road. For many it was a one-way trip. As the *Hirondelles* drew nearer to Verdun and its environs, they witnessed the human flotsam being driven from their homes by the German guns heading in the other direction. This aspect of the war was something the Americans had heard plenty about, but had not witnessed firsthand, at least on this scale. With the exception of those earliest days at Rouen, when the men of what would become the Second Company of the *2ᵉ étranger* saw refugees fleeing von Kluck's invading army, this was a novelty.

One of the untold, or at least under-told, stories of World War I is that of the refugees—civilians driven from their homes in terror with nowhere to go, with little or no money, their few remaining possessions trundled along in a wheelbarrow or an old hand-cart. What became of these people? Writer David King's description of what he saw coming out of Verdun, as he and his comrades marched in, etches itself in one's mind:

> Suddenly, freakish shapes loom up on the road ahead. They crowd to one side as the column slouches by: old men in queer heterogeneous apparel—women pushing baby carriages, piled high with household possessions over and above the wailing occupant. Terror-stricken, dumb, they drift by like startled ghosts; their wide eyes scarcely see the troops. Women, half pushed, half dragged along, calling for killed or missing babies.
>
> Lost children struggling to keep up with forced, uneven steps, moaning pitifully for dead parents! "Where do you come from? What's going on?" we shout in passing. But the only answer is a murmur—"the big shells— oh, the big shells!"[16]

And so they entered Verdun. Or rather, they entered the fortified area of Verdun which encompassed some twenty-two separate fortifications and nearby villages, as well as the city itself. After a nineteen-hour forced march over icy roads, the 170th reached Fort de la Sartelle, just to the west of the city proper. There they were greeted by shells from the long-range German guns and bombs dropped by the German aircraft that seemed to dominate the skies. Held in reserve for one week, the *Hirondelles* were soon called upon to defend the fortress of Vaux, which David King, upon first sight, described as "a huge dark mound."[17] Vaux and its twin Douaumont commanded the gateway to Verdun. Today, from the tops of the ruins of these forts one can enjoy a limitless vista to the east on a clear day. It seems as if one could see all the way into

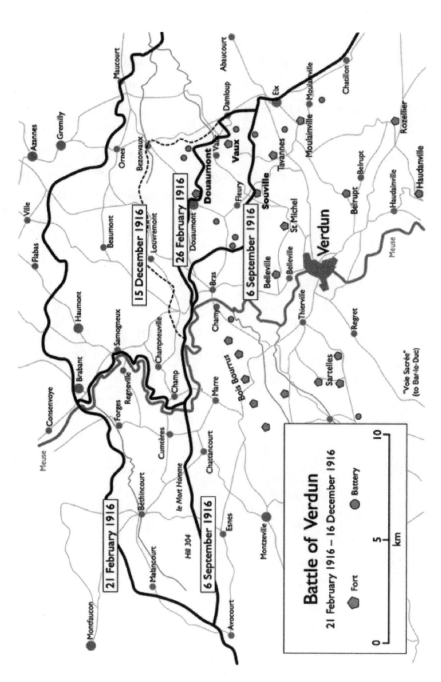

Scene of battle, Verdun, February–December 1916.

Germany. Only the horizon presents limitations, like at sea. It is immediately understandable why these forts mattered—they commanded the high ground from which any invasion coming from Germany itself could be stopped. And yet Douaumont had fallen in shockingly easy fashion to the surprised Germans; what was perhaps the most important fortress in France had been garrisoned by a mere one hundred middle-aged "territorials," the approximate equivalent of the National Guard in the United States. Douaumont's fall finally awakened Joffre and the French High Command to the seriousness of what confronted them along the Meuse. Vaux could not suffer the same ignominious fate. The 170th was there to ensure that it did not.

In March of 1916 the 170th regiment relieved Fort Vaux's previous defenders. It was not a pretty sight. It seemed there were more wounded than able-bodied soldiers emerging from the fortress. David King was particularly disturbed by what he termed the "basket cases" being brought to the rear: "Why they don't put them out painlessly, then and there, is beyond civilized intelligence. Mere trunks, both arms and legs shot off, some of them blind as well, what possible use can they have for life, except that horrible instinct to live? Yet they must be carried for miles, go through torture in hospital, and drag out lives of helpless hell, to satisfy a squeamish sentimentality we call humanity."[18]

The *Hirondelles* had little time to reflect on their situation before the German guns opened up on them, both on front-line positions dug in below the fort in the village where Frank Musgrave had been taken prisoner, and on the fort itself. The barrage was unlike anything the Americans—or anyone else in the 170th—had experienced. Jack Janz, who had hoped to find word of Musgrave in Vaux, was hit by a shell and simply disappeared. According to a later account, "not enough of his body was found for a burial."[19] This was not at all unusual at Verdun. The violence and frequency of the bombardments with large-caliber artillery pieces literally obliterated many men. Often they were simply listed as "lost." This classification implies a degree of doubt over their fate. The reality in World War I, and in particular at the Battle of Verdun, was that there was no doubt over their fate, simply the lack of a body.

The shelling grew even more intense. Then came the shout up the line: "*Attention! Ils vont donner!*" (Here they come!) And a "solid green-grey mass of men rolled up over the rise in front."[20] This is it! The brave German soldiers stand nearly shoulder to shoulder as they move as one towards the 170th, with Fort Vaux the prize. This time it is the French machine guns that mow down the advancing men. But more come on, as the fallen are quickly replaced by those just behind them. Closer, closer, then—"My God, where are the 75s!"—finally, the French artillery smashes bloody holes in the dense German formation. David King described what the whistle of those French shells at that moment meant to Vaux's defenders: "the most cheering sound in the world, that continuous roll—like drums—the sharp, spiteful crack."[21] The Germans wavered, rallied, and attacked six more times. But by the end of the day they had taken the measure of the 170th and wanted no more of them. The Germans would not try to seize the fort in a *coup de main* again until June.

The aftermath was both grisly and glorious. One detachment of defenders stationed in a bombproof shelter sustained a hit from a shell fired by a German 380. David King described it: "Of the two hundred and fifty men, only six survive, and the walls are plastered with blood, brains, and bits of smoking uniform."[22] American Ferdinand Capdevielle, the New York fencing master's

son, received a promotion for his part in the defense of the fort.
This was a great honor for a foreigner, as the 170th was a regular
French regiment of the line. Joffre summed up the stand made
by Vaux's defenders and their counterparts elsewhere along the
French line: "Germany...had not reckoned with you.... Of you
it will be said: they barred to the Germans the way to Verdun."[23]
And yet the shelling continued. The Germans pounded Vaux
mercilessly. The *Hirondelles*, holed up inside, could only wonder
at the fort's ability to withstand it. There was just no let-up. In
a letter to a friend, King observed, "Allah knows how long this
old band box will hold together. We laugh and munch army
biscuits and smoke, but there is cold death in the eye of every
man...."[24]

He wrote in his journal, "The inside of the casement looks like
Goya's picture of a madhouse. No room to lie down and no benches
to sit on.... Here and there a smoky kerosene lamp lit up a group
of faces, hollow-eyed, gaunt. We had to relight the lamps continually as the concussion of direct hits blew them out. Periodically, the
silence in the room was broken by a shout from the man nearest
the door: 'Sentinel's killed! Send up another!'"[25]

The air, what there was of it, was foul. Mercifully it was cold
in the grim confines of the fort. Otherwise the corpses of unburied dead placed in one of the rear chambers would have begun to
decompose more quickly, adding their foulness to the already
unbearable atmosphere. The men held on, making occasional
sorties to reinforce the front-line trenches below. The effect that
this continual shelling with heavy guns had on the nerves can well
be imagined. World War I seemed to indicate that human beings
were not built to withstand the destructive power of the terrible
machines they themselves invented. The men of the 170th were

like so many ants scrambling over an anthill. The artillery pieces were, in comparison, giants capable of crushing them with ease in an instant. The war seemed to highlight the increasingly inconsequential nature of humans on a modern battlefield: small, vulnerable figures in an alien landscape. The English painter Paul Nash, a veteran of the fighting in Flanders, perhaps best captured this in his painting "The Menin Road." The soldiers that fought at Verdun in 1916 may not have served in Flanders, but they certainly would have recognized the images Nash created. They had lived them.

The 170th was rotated out of the Vaux garrison a few days after the battle. The Germans would eventually capture Vaux on June 7, but not without first engaging in vicious hand-to-hand combat in the smoke-filled corridors of the fort. In what historian Georges Blond would memorably describe as "one group of rats, threatened by another,"[26] the French used hand grenades and a machine gun in the narrow passageways to the end. In a final act of defiance, explosions blew bloody clouds, and bullets ricocheted off the concrete walls. For the attackers it was much as their commander, Lieutenant Ranckow, had said it would be: "An iron cross or a wooden cross, one or the other."[27] After its capture by the Germans, the French would, in their turn, pour men into multiple attempts to recapture the fort. All failed. Few spots on the face of the earth (with the possible exception of its twin, Fort Douaumont), were ever the object of such intense, sustained warfare as Fort Vaux. Finally, on November 2, 1916, a French patrol entered Fort Vaux without encountering opposition. The Germans had simply abandoned it.

* * *

The cratered and pitted ruins of Fort Vaux, Verdun, France.

The 170th now shifted to the attack—the mode of warfare they were most suited for. When the American volunteers had chosen to transfer, they knew this was what they would be expected to do; otherwise they would be held in reserve to rest. What they didn't know was that, once thrown into the attack, it was policy that they would not be withdrawn until they had had lost three-quarters of their effectives.[28] Their orders were to seize the village of Fleury, then move onto Fort Douaumont and recapture it. *"En avant!"* Over the top and into the village—or what was left of it. The German artillery laid down a murderous barrage; and the attack on Douaumont was abandoned for the night.

The 170th went into battle without having eaten for two days. Unlike the *Légion*, where soup kitchens were brought right up to the trenches, the regular French Army's kitchens were well in the rear. David King convinced some of his comrades to go get the food themselves and bring it back up to the line. Boxer Bob Scanlon grumbled as he and King trudged through the mud on the four-hour trek to the soup kitchens. "What's the matter now, Bob?" King asked. To which Scanlon replied, "Hungry yesterday. Hungry today. Hungry the day before. Don't care how soon my military experience terminates."[29] By the time they returned, the stew was nothing but cold grease. And the man carrying the canvas buckets of coffee was hit just as he re-entered the trenches, spilling it all into the putrid Lorraine dirt. Now thirst gripped the men. The Germans counterattacked and were driven back by a unit of *chasseurs* that arrived as reinforcements. The 170th held the village of Fleury, but the Douaumont was as distant as if it had been the moon. It was at this moment that David King reached the bottom:

> All we could think of was our thirst. I waded into a shell
> hole and drank greedily from the green-scummed water.
> A rocket flared up what I had taken for a log, lying in
> the pool, was a corpse! I didn't give a damn....[30]

The 170th would serve in the Verdun sector throughout the spring of 1916 before what remained of it was transferred to the Somme in July. Of the various actions in which the regiment played a part at this time, it was in the Bois de Caillette on May 1, 1916, that it earned the greatest distinction. The Bois de Caillette was a wooded ravine approximately mid-way between Vaux and Douaumont. Beyond it lay Fort de Souville, and beyond that the great prize itself—the city of Verdun. The Germans made a great effort in this direction. Flame-throwers were now being used with terrible effect by the attacking forces. "Butcher" Charles Mangin, the general who would acquire his bloody sobriquet at Verdun, ordered a counterattack. Mangin understood the strategic nature of the

wood and how critical it was to drive the Germans from it immediately. Ferdinand Capdevielle, who would be awarded the *Croix
de Guerre* for his actions in the Bois de Caillette, would describe
the beginning of the assault: "It was the hardest fighting of all. We
marched to the firing line in the dark, picking our way by the dead
bodies lining the route.... After a stay in a poorly made open
trench, we were ordered to charge the Germans. The boys were
glad to be in action, and covered the distance between them and
the Boches in a hurry. Some of us had trench knives. Charles Hoffecker practically decapitated four Huns before he was struck by
shell fragments and gravely wounded."[31]

The American volunteers of 1914 acquitted themselves with
tremendous *élan* in the Bois de Caillette—and paid a price. Hoffecker never returned to San Francisco. He died from his wounds.
William Dugan, the shoe manufacturer's son from Rochester, New
York, was also wounded by shell fragments, in his arms and shoulder; boxer Bob Scanlon had a hole torn through his left hand by a
shell casing. David King was injured by shrapnel in his spine and
partly paralyzed, but a French doctor removed the shrapnel, and
he regained the use of all of his limbs.[32] Along with Capdevielle,
Dugan and Rhode Island butcher Eugene Jacob received the *Croix
de Guerre*. Dugan had helped storm a German trench and then
had taken a number of prisoners. Jacob was cited for his uncommon *sang-froid* and leadership under fire and promoted.[33] The
Germans quit the wood.

But the larger Battle of Verdun, fought over a wide sector, raged
on for another seven months. The total death toll (killed and "missing") would eventually exceed half a million,[34] a figure that does
not include the equal or greater numbers of those wounded in the
fighting, many of whom were incapacitated for life, nor the

civilians killed or maimed in the initial German bombardment. Von Falkenhayn's strategy had brought on a battle of attrition, but it was Germany that would decide it had had enough. All of the ground that their troops had taken at great sacrifice was reconquered by the French before Christmas 1916, including Fort Douaumont—the Division Marocaine led the assault that finally captured it in October of that year—which by the end had become a symbol out of all proportion to its military significance. When one considers the great swings in the battle during the nine months that it was fought, it's difficult to point to one stand, one attack, one counterattack and say definitively that *this* turned the tide of the battle as a whole. It can seem that it was all a pointless waste, in which the suffering and gallantry of individuals and their units amounted to nothing in the larger scheme of things. But when one looks more closely at Verdun, the importance of every last action in attaining the cumulative result of a great French victory—and it was a great victory—only becomes more apparent, not just at Vaux or in the Bois de Caillette, but in countless, nameless, desperate combats. Thus the tiny American contributions at Verdun were not insignificant. They were all important. Take one contribution away here, or one there, and that could have made the difference; Germany might have finally broken through. If Verdun as a whole indeed represented "waste," it was on the German side, not the French. The hundreds of thousands of French mothers who lost their sons at least knew they had died defending their homes, defending *them*. The hundreds of thousands of German mothers knew only that their sons had died in a battle that the German High Command had ordered, then abandoned.

The 170th was withdrawn from the fighting in the late spring, and enjoyed a brief respite of six weeks in a trench in a quiet sector of the line. Besides the rats and the shells it was almost idyllic, at least in comparison to what they had just been through. David King waxed rhapsodic: "Between bombardments came the calls of thrushes and finches—once I heard a lark.... Days of quiet reading, bathing in the canal, endless games of 'Manille' [a French card game that uses a thirty-two-card deck] and symphonies on cigar box fiddles."[35]

The Americans' experience at Verdun was over. The battle in which they had taken part would come to be seen by historians as the defining battle, if not the decisive battle, of World War I. French historian Marc Ferro's assessment of the battle is worth noting:

> There was an extreme promiscuity of life and death on the battlefield—its salients, strong points, parapets and fox-holes often themselves composed of dead flesh. Troops coming up to relieve the soldiers were often overwhelmed at the horror of Verdun: they saw an implacable fate before them, of digging a grave to stay alive, and then supporting its defence with their corpses.... The army at the time counted over 330 infantry battalions, not counting chasseurs, and 259 of them went through Verdun whereas only 109 underwent the Somme. These scarcely known figures are important in so far as they show how France saw Verdun as the great test, a purely French affair, since there were only three of four colonial battalions in it and no British. Verdun, fought with unequal strength, was almost a victory of the race.[36]

Ferro's fellow Frenchman Georges Blond shared Ferro's views, but saw the stand in a larger strategic and historical context, as well:

> Why not let the Germans take Verdun, in the expectation of dislodging them as soon as the Allied armies were the stronger? Strategically, this was a viable idea.... Yet the Germans could not be allowed to take and hold Verdun, even for a single month, a single week. For France and the whole world the name had become a symbol. The capture of Verdun would not mean the loss of the war from a strategic point of view, but it might bring on, first, a serious loss of morale, then a demand for a change in government, perhaps even a revolution. This was what happened a little later in Russia.... And at the same time it might cause the United States to reverse its stand, to decide to bargain with Germany. The factor of "Verdun" could not be isolated and stripped of its wider significance.[37]

Perhaps the most telling assessment of Verdun came from von Falkenhayn's successor, Paul von Hindenburg. He remarked, in retrospect, "The battles which were fought in this region exhausted our strength as does a wound which will not heal."[38]

CHAPTER 9

KNIGHTS OF THE AIR

A s David King, Bob Scanlon, Ferdinand Capdevielle, William Dugan and the other Americans in the 170th fought for their lives on the ground at Verdun, a desperate struggle was taking place in the skies above them. The French High Command was determined to overturn the overwhelming air superiority enjoyed by the Germans at the outset of the battle. The orders went out to clear the skies of Germans, and the small experimental squadron of American pilots led by Frenchmen Georges Thénault and Alfred de Laage de Meux would take part in this struggle. Flying the Nieuport no. 11 biplane, better known as the "Bébé" for its diminutive size, the American unit became something of a cross between a legitimate *groupe de chasse* (pursuit squadron) and a flying publicity stunt.

The "Bébé," the Nieuport no. 11.

★ ★ ★

The members of Squadron N 124 of the *Service Aéronautique* first assembled in April 1916 at an aerodrome outside of Luxeuil-les-Bains. The village was located west of the Vosges and south of Verdun in a quiet sector far removed from the front lines. Officially they were assigned to this locale as fighter escorts for a nearby bomber base, but that was more on paper than reality. It was believed that this interlude would allow the squadron to learn how to function as a unit and thus not embarrass themselves or their supporters once they entered combat over Verdun. There was simply too much riding on the success or failure of this endeavor to leave it to chance.

The original seven pilots included four of the volunteers of 1914: Kiffin Rockwell, Ivy leaguers William Thaw and Victor Chapman, and mystery man Bert Hall. They were joined by

Norman Prince—the Massachusetts North Shore country squire—
fellow blueblood Elliot Cowdin, and James McConnell, who had
served with Dr. Edmund Gros's Ambulance Field Service prior to
enlisting in the *Service Aéronautique* and earning his pilot's wings.
There were only five planes for the nine members of the squadron,
however: brand-spanking-new Nieuport 11s, fresh from the fac-
tory.[1] All of the pilots had served with French squadrons in various
sectors in 1915 and early 1916—primarily piloting slower-moving
aircraft involved in observing enemy preparations or bombing
enemy positions. Now they would have the chance to fly the single
seat fighters as *pilotes de chasse*. It was a difficult and dangerous
job. It was also a glamorous one. With the possible exception of
William Thaw, the Americans were all affected by this. How could
they not be? By 1916 the exploits of pilots such as the German
Oswald Boelcke and the Frenchmen Charles Nungesser and
Georges Guynemer had made them matinee idols. The press loved
them, and the militaries were happy to create heroes for the public
to adulate. In a war that had become incomprehensible to most civilians, these dashing men dueling high above France reminded them
of the medieval knights that they had read about as children. The
Americans embraced the part.

    Luxeuil-les-Bains had an atmosphere of Eden-like unreality. The
surrounding countryside on the western slope of the Vosges was
some of the prettiest in France. Victor Chapman was already familiar with the region after having hiked a number of peaks there in the
summer of 1915. The town itself was the site of a spa, its population
a little less than three thousand inhabitants in 1916, most of whom
were women.[2] Thénault's "young eagles" lived well. The historian
Herbert Molloy Mason Jr. has described their time there as an idyll:
"The pilots moved into a small stone villa adjoining the Roman

From left to right, James McConnell, Victor Chapman, and Kiffin Rockwell at the Hôtel Pomme d'Or, 1916.

baths. Each had a private room with a feather bed and a window overlooking the hills beyond. Five minutes' walk down the shaded cobblestoned street brought them to the dining room of the Hôtel Pomme d'Or.... For all its great quantity and indisputable quality, a meal at the Pomme d'Or never cost more than four francs—less than one American dollar."[3]

The squadron's first flight was a sortie over the German lines near Mulhouse on the Swiss border on May 13, 1916. It was a beautiful spring day. The Nieuports, painted in a camouflage design of green and brown—or an odd cream color, with the distinctive French *cocarde* of red, white, and blue concentric circles on their wings—"crow-hopped" over the airfield, then growled into the skies. The "Bébé" was France's answer to the "Fokker Scourge" that had menaced France since mid-1915. The plane's powerful rotary engine spun with its propeller, creating a highly responsive machine, particularly when making tight turns to the right.[4] This enhanced maneuverability came with a price, however. When flying the "Bébé," one needed to pay constant attention to it. A moment's lapse in attention could lead to dangerous consequences. Thus the plane was both a joy and at the same time extremely stressful to fly. Fitted midway atop the top wing was a Lewis machine gun that fired forty-seven rounds of bullets. With the pilot's finger pressing the trigger continuously this meant approximately a five-second burst of fire.[5] After that the French pilot would have to stand up, remove the empty can, and replace it, all the while minding the plane's controls (sometimes with his knees). For comparison's sake, German planes, with their synchronized guns, could fire a thousand rounds before having to reload.[6] This was a distinct disadvantage, yet the "Bébé" was so superior in both speed and maneuverability that a patient and skillful pilot could all but eliminate the Germans' edge.

Thénault had selected Thaw, Rockwell, Chapman, and McConnell to join him in the squadron's inaugural patrol. The plan was to fly in a V-shaped formation, with the more experienced Thénault and Thaw flying behind and slightly above their fellow pilots. Rockwell would take the lead, at the point of the V. Once airborne, they circled above the meadow and got into formation, heading east. All went smoothly—until at seven thousand feet they encountered clouds and lost James McConnell, who headed off course toward the snow-topped Alps to the south. Fortunately, Thénault spotted his wayward sheep and dove to shepherd him back to the flock. Being so high above the earth in these rickety planes (little more than string and canvas and a powerful engine) was exhilarating. Never mind the deafening noise of the engine and the high-pitched whine of the bracing wires, the overpowering smell of castor oil—much like French fries, and castor oil is a powerful laxative, so that breathing its fumes in the sky might lead to a decidedly unromantic result for a pilot—and the bone-numbing cold as they climbed higher, it was exhilarating. There is something elemental about flying in an open cockpit aircraft that speaks to the inner Icarus in all human beings. The closed cockpits and pressurized cabins of later decades have provided more comfort for pilots and passengers alike, but something of the thrill of flight has been lost. For the five men headed east that morning toward the Rhine, shining silver in the distance, the thrill was all there was.

At thirteen thousand feet the five planes crossed No Man's Land over Mulhouse and encountered German antiaircraft fire from the "Archies," guns that seldom proved lethal, but shells bursting in the air could play havoc with a pilot's nerves as their concussions jostled the fragile aircraft. Kiffin Rockwell, true to form, chose to make a game of piloting his plane through the puffs of black smoke created by the bursting shells. Chapman and McConnell joined him, "shredding the smoke in swirling tendrils with their propellers."[7] Then Rockwell dove gracefully towards the German airbase at Habsheim, casting "his plane around in whirling acrobatics, challenging the Germans. But no Germans came, and, low on fuel, the Nieuports turned for home...."[8]

And so the *Escadrille Americaine* passed its first test with flying colors. No combat, but no serious mishaps either. That same day Norman Prince and Elliot Cowdin returned from Paris with a reporter and a film crew to document their activities for audiences back home. The French bomber crews in their Maurice Farmans and the Americans in their Nieuports put on an impromptu aerial display for the cameras. Rockwell and Bert Hall groused afterward that they had some royalties coming for risking their necks in maneuvers so close to the ground.[9] The anecdote is telling because there was an element of show business about what they were doing, even as deadly earnest as they were. This romantic venture had the potential to stir hearts on the other side of the Atlantic—though perhaps not President Woodrow Wilson's—and generate more sympathy for the fight France was waging. It would have been impossible for camera crews to accurately document what had occurred at Navarin Farm or the Bois de Caillette, for instance. But this...this was simple. That was the beauty of it from a public relations standpoint. Even the Germans were aware of Thénault's "young eagles." They were keen to test them, and best them—to send a message of their own.

To no one's surprise, it was Kiffin Rockwell who drew first blood in combat against the Germans. The aerodrome at Luxeuil-les-Bains had been bombed by the Germans soon after the squadron's first *sortie*. His fighting blood up, Kiffin climbed into his Nieuport and headed east, alone, toward the German lines: nothing. (The French air force emphasized individual initiative, and thus pilots such as Kiffin Rockwell were often encouraged by their commanders to patrol on their own, in between their established schedules of regular patrols, if they wished to do so.) Engine trouble forced him homeward. Then, inside the French lines he saw it, about two thousand feet below him—an LVG biplane with the distinctive black crosses painted on its wings. He dove, forgetting his engine trouble, and the Bébé responded. Closing with his intended victim, Rockwell saw "a stream of lead spouting at him" from the gunner located in the rear of the reconnaissance aircraft.[10] Rockwell recounted what happened next in an excited letter written to his brother Paul that very day: "...my machine was hit, but

I didn't pay attention to that and kept going straight for him, until I got within twenty-five or thirty meters of him. Then, just as I was afraid of running into him, I fired four or five shots then swerved my machine to the right to keep from running into him. As I did that, I saw the mitrailleur fall back dead on the pilot, the mitrailleuse fall from its position and point straight up in the air, the pilot fell to one side of the machine as if he were done for also. The machine itself fell first to one side, then dived vertically towards the ground with a lot of smoke coming out of the rear."[11]

Rockwell's victory was confirmed by a French forward observation post. They telephoned the news to the aerodrome before he landed, and he received a rousing welcome. Like the knights he had read about as a boy, he had felled a worthy opponent in single combat: an opponent who just as easily could have killed him. To congratulate him, his jealous but beamingly proud brother sent him an eighty-year-old bottle of Bourbon, as Herbert Molloy Mason Jr. describes, "a treasure almost beyond price in France. After some debate, it was decided to ration the liquid gold one drink at a time to a pilot whenever he had a confirmed kill. Rockwell drained his two ounces and the bottle was put away. 'All Luxeuil,' commented McConnell, 'smiled on Kiffin—especially the girls.'"[12]

Within days of Rockwell's triumph, Squadron N 124 flew north to the aerodrome at Behonne, twenty miles from the Verdun battlefront. In a letter he wrote to his cousin soon after arriving, Victor Chapman described what he saw from above as a "smoldering inferno": "The landscape—one wasted surface of brown powdered earth, where hills, valleys, forest, and villages all merged in phantoms—were boiling with puffs of black smoke."[13]

★ ★ ★

The war in the air had reached a new level of intensity by this time as well. The crews of the big guns on both sides relied heavily on airborne reconnaissance to learn where to fire their shells with the greatest effect. Both tethered balloons and observation aircraft were absolutely vital. They were extremely vulnerable, however, to enemy fighters. Thus, protecting one's own observers was an important duty for the squadron's *pilotes de chasse*. No other mission for the pilots had as much direct bearing on the fighting on the ground as this, compared to which the World War I aerial "dogfights" that have captured the imagination of so many over the years, in and of themselves, were not important—except insofar as they allowed one side or the other to continue observing the opponent's dispositions unmolested. Far too much attention has been paid through the years to the one-on-one duels between individual pilots. It's thrilling to read about these encounters, which often possessed qualities reminiscent of the code of chivalry. But their importance to what was occurring below was nearly zero. Shooting down a reconnaissance plane or even an ungainly observation balloon, or "sausage," had far more military value to the soldiers in the trenches—and it was not nearly as easy to shoot them down as one might think at first glance. They were heavily protected by anti-aircraft guns and their own protective fighter planes. They also could be lowered very quickly.

The squadron's first confirmed kill over Verdun came about in just such a reconnaissance-aircraft-focused exchange. Bert Hall was escorting a French observation plane above Fort Douaumont on May 20, 1916. With him were Thénault, Thaw, Prince, and Rockwell. Hall spied a German Aviatik headed across the French

The *pilotes de chasse* of N 124, spring 1916. From left to right, Kiffin Rockwell, Georges Thénault, Norman Prince, Alfred de Laage de Meux, Elliott Cowdin, Bert Hall, James McConnell, and Victor Chapman.

lines and decided to leave the others to pursue it. The Aviatik was a two-seater reconnaissance biplane, with a machine gun mounted in the rear. This was the type of aircraft that could cause enormous havoc with the information it gleaned during its flight. The German pilot, realizing too late he was being pursued, made for home. Hall caught him at twelve thousand feet and closed for the kill. The German machine gun bullets grazed his right wing, but a short burst from his Lewis gun finished the pilot, and the plane spiraled to earth.[14] The ex–Paris taxi driver had shown himself to be a capable pilot with strong nerves. But as time would tell, he was a leopard that would never altogether lose his spots.

The pilots headed back to base, then to their quarters at a villa near Bar-le-Duc. Their surroundings made an unsettling contrast with what they had just witnessed below at Douaumont. Kiffin

Rockwell wrote to his mother, "We are very nicely quartered here, having a very nice villa to live in, a cook also, so that we don't have to go out for our meals. We are certainly living an incongruous life. We live like princes when not working. An auto comes and takes us up to the field; we climb into our machines (which the mechanics have taken care of), they fasten us up snugly, and put the motor en route, away we go for two or three hours, to prowl through the air...."[15]

This privileged existence masked a chilling reality. The average life expectancy of a World War I era pilot was approximately two weeks from the time he entered active duty.[16] The men on the ground knew. They had seen too many pilots fall into the trenches or No Man's Land and meet grisly ends in broken or burned aircraft. According to French historian Georges Blond there was surprisingly little rancor on the part of the infantry toward their pampered comrades in the skies above: "Flyers...were not looked down upon as cowards. They could be seen being shot down in combat too often for that...and there was a romantic aura about them besides. They were commonly imagined to spend their time between missions drinking and whoring, but this actually gave their mud-stained comrades on the ground a vicarious satisfaction."[17]

On May 24, 1916, the *Escadrille Americaine* experienced the most momentous day of its brief life to that point. Bill Thaw and Kiffin Rockwell took to the skies in the early morning hours on the dawn patrol. High above Verdun, they spotted an Aviatik with a Fokker monoplane escort below them. The pilots used hand signals to communicate which of the two planes each would pursue: Thaw chose the Fokker; Rockwell the Aviatik. They dove. The Fokker's pilot was unaware of the danger he faced. Thaw fired a burst from his Lewis gun, and it was all over in a matter of seconds. "The poor Boche didn't even see me," he commented.[18] Thaw's first kill felt more like murder than combat. Rockwell's prey eluded him and fled back over the German lines. They returned, refueled, and joined Thénault, second-in-command, Alfred de Laage de Meux, and Victor Chapman for the regular morning patrol.

Leading the patrol towards the battlefront in a V formation, Thénault saw a large formation of a dozen or more German observation planes below, well within the German lines. Before take-off, he had reminded his "young eagles" not to attack unless he signaled. The Germans were far away, and far too numerous. He demurred. Then, just below him, he saw a Nieuport dive for the Germans, with the others following. Thénault chased after them, sick with worry that this could be the end of them all. His squadron was heading into a hornets' nest. The Germans went into a circular formation, with each covering the others' rear. Victor Chapman's plane was getting cut up by bullets, and then his arm was hit. Kiffin Rockwell's "windshield flew apart. Bits of glass and steel ripped into his face. And blood covered his goggles. He could scarcely see, his face searing with pain."[19] The two pilots broke off and flew back to Behonne, where they encountered a none-too-happy Georges Thénault and Alfred de Laage de Meux. What had they been thinking? If that flight of observation planes had been escorted, as was the norm, by accompanying Fokkers hiding in the sun up at high altitude, none of them likely would have made it back alive. And where was Thaw? Anxious hours passed until a phone call confirmed Thaw had landed his "blood-spattered plane" safely behind the French lines. Like Chapman, he had run into an "aerial porcupine," had his plane shot up, and been hit in the arm. Over his objections he was taken to a Paris hospital to mend.[20]

That eventful day also saw the arrival of a new pilot: Raoul Lufberry, who was destined to become the *Escadrille Americaine's* greatest ace. Lufberry had lived an eclectic and interesting life. His claim to membership in this all-American unit was through his American father, a man whom he had never met. He was raised by his French grandmother after his mother died. Much like René Phelizot and "Skipper" Pavelka, Lufberry had left home young and never looked back. His travels had taken him to his father's homeland, as well as to the Philippines (where he served a stint in the U.S. Army), Japan, China, and India. It was in Asia that he became involved in aviation, signing on with a French pilot named Marc Pourpe, who performed air shows for audiences that had never seen such wonders. Nineteen-fourteen found Lufberry back in France with Pourpe, looking for a replacement for the Blériot he had been flying. The war intervened, and Pourpe volunteered for the *Service Aéronautique*, bringing Lufberry along as his mechanic. The arrangement ended with Pourpe's death in December 1914. Soon afterwards, Lufberry requested a transfer to flight school. His progress was anything but meteoric, but he was a good learner, methodical in his approach, and professional in his demeanor. At thirty-one years of age, Lufberry immediately became the senior member of N 124. His would be a steadying influence that would be much needed in the weeks and months ahead.

★ ★ ★

Victor Chapman saw it all with an artist's eye. He had the force of his convictions to drive him in combat, but Chapman never seemed to entirely tune out the beauty all around him. In a letter to his father dated June 1, 1916, he described flying as "much too romantic to be modern war with all its horrors. There is something so unreal and fairy like about it, which ought to be told and described by Poets...."[21] Or painters. Chapman described the skies to his father, "full of those very thick fuzzy clouds like imaginary froth of gods or genii.... At 3000 metres one floated secure through a purple sea of mist." Earlier that same day, Chapman had been out on patrol with Norman Prince. They encountered two German aircraft over Douaumont, but their attack was in Chapman's own words, "badly executed."[22] The skirmish did not prove deadly. Continuing his patrol, he had returned to the aerodrome at Behonne to find sorrowful news awaited him: German planes had bombed the base and the nearby town of Bar-le-Duc. Their fellow pilots were safe, but over forty civilians, including ten school children, had been killed in the raid. Chapman and the others blamed themselves for the destruction—mistakenly assuming that it was a message from the Germans to the darlings of the American press: "...this is what comes of getting notoriety. There were disgusting notices about us in the papers two days ago—even yesterday, I am ashamed to be seen in town today if our presence here has again caused death...to innocent people."[23]

Kiffin Rockwell seconded his friend's feelings: "I thought I was going to be killed by the bombs, which was a very disgusting feeling; as it is, they got a great number of women and children.... P.S. For heaven's sake, let's try and shut down on the publicity about the Escadrille!"[24]

But the publicity was the whole point—to use the popularity of the *Escadrille Americaine* to aggravate and provoke the Germans and inspire and persuade the Americans back home. The pilots felt a little better about what had transpired after they learned that other towns to the west of Verdun had also been hit.[25] As

Chapman admitted soon thereafter, it was "a bit of self-importance to say the Boche came here for us."[26]

The escadrille continued to grow. Thaw was still in a Paris hospital but by mid-June the squadron had grown to fifteen members: there were a number of Americans from the Ambulance Field Service, no doubt encouraged to enlist by Dr. Gros, as well as another Frenchman with American roots named Didier Masson. This made Chapman, Hall, Rockwell, Prince, and Cowdin practically seasoned veterans of air warfare—something they, no doubt, would have found quite amusing. Part of the reason for this expansion of N 124 was a general policy on the part of the French High Command to counter the large numbers of German planes by enlarging existing French squadrons. As historian Edward Jablonski points out, "The fighting had become desperate, deadly and massive"[27] by mid-1916. There were no "routine" patrols. Only inclement weather gave respite from the nerve-jangling realities of air combat. Elliott Cowdin, for one, was slowly falling to pieces.

Victor Chapman, on the other hand, seemed unfazed by the intensity of the air war, and grew restless on those days he couldn't get into the fight. On June 17, 1916, he joined a patrol with Thénault, De Laage, and a young Texan new to the squadron named Clyde Balsley. As he had done previously, Thénault gave explicit instructions not to break formation and only to attack on his signal. But Chapman disobeyed Thénault and made a bid for a German bomber on the other side of the Meuse. To his chagrin, it flew out of range. Then, instead of flying back to Behonne to face the wrath of his commanding officer, Chapman landed at a nearby French aerodrome, refueled, and went back towards the Meuse looking for the bomber. Perhaps Chapman had the ten dead school children in Bar-le-Duc in his thoughts. Whatever the case, he failed to locate the bomber. He did locate five Fokkers, however, and, in an act that can only be described as foolhardy or suicidal, he dove on them. He fired a burst of bullets at the nearest Fokker, only to find it had vanished. In fact, it had looped behind him and was now firing on his tail. Trying desperately to shake his pursuer, Chapman felt a sharp pain: "a slug had passed through the fuselage…and coursed through his helmet, making a four-inch cut in his scalp. Instantly his goggles were covered with blood."[28] And then, a small miracle: the Fokker disappeared. There is circumstantial evidence that Chapman had narrowly missed becoming a victim of the great German ace Oswald Boelcke. The German described a similar engagement at this time in which his guns jammed and he was forced to disengage.[29] If this were true, then Victor Chapman was indeed flying under a lucky star that day. Flipping back his goggles, he managed to land his damaged craft

Victor Chapman. Artist, *légionnaire, pilote de chasse.*

at a nearby French airfield. His head swathed in bandages like some grotesque turban,[30] Chapman insisted on going up again that same day on afternoon patrol! Thénault nixed that but did agree not to send Chapman to join Thaw in hospital. And with a new Nieuport, Chapman was back in action within days. Described as "considerate, kind, and so courageous that all admired and liked him," people (including Thénault) found it "impossible to be angry with him."[31] And so he was still flying, and not back in Paris convalescing as he probably should have been.

On June 18 young Texan Clyde Balsley was grievously wounded in an exchange of fire with German planes, and forced to crashland his Nieuport in No Man's Land. Four French soldiers risked their own lives to extract him from the wreck. He was removed to the hospital at Vadelaincourt, hovering initially between life and death. When Victor Chapman heard of Balsley's predicament, he flew directly to the hospital and asked the partially paralyzed pilot if there was anything he could do for him. Denied water due to wounds in his stomach that had not yet healed, Balsley could only suck on a wet rag to relieve his thirst. Chapman asked the attending doctor if his friend could suck on oranges instead. The answer was "yes," but he seriously doubted any could be found in Verdun. Chapman promised Balsley he would get him some oranges, he just needed to hang on.[32]

Somehow Chapman, who certainly was not without resources, obtained the fruit, and along with some chocolate and a few newspapers, he assembled a care package of sorts for his wounded comrade. On June 23, 1916, Chapman loaded his goods into his Nieuport intending to fly by the hospital at the end of his patrol. He was the last to take off from the airfield at Behonne, flying slightly behind and above the other planes in the formation. They passed over the festering wound of Douaumont and sighted a pair of German reconnaissance craft below. Thénault signaled for the attack and dove, but before he could fire, an equal number of Fokkers appeared to wreak havoc with his plans. They had been waiting at high altitude, and descended on the Nieuports from out of the sun, a favorite tactic of German pilots. It was effective. Thénault knew the game was up and called off the attack—the speedier Nieuports handily outdistancing their pursuers, all except for Chapman's plane. It wasn't until they had returned to base that Thénault fully realized something was amiss. They waited through the afternoon for Chapman's plane to appear. The telephone rang. It was the pilot of a Maurice Farman. He and his observer had witnessed what had transpired. Chapman, following from behind, had seen his fellow pilots ambushed by the Fokkers and in an act of reckless courage had thrown himself at the Germans in a bid to save his comrades. As the last into the mêlée, he was last out. He didn't make it. Caught in a "withering cross fire," he had likely been killed instantly, his plane descending nearly vertically in a headlong ten-thousand-foot dive feet into the ground.[33]

Though his close friend Kiffin Rockwell claimed that Chapman must have killed a number of the enemy in the numerous engagements he saw him fight in the air, the truth is, as far as can be ascertained with any certainty, Chapman never killed a single one. He never shot down a plane or took a prisoner. Yet he was perhaps the truest personification of a knight of the air. Not a Lancelot—but a Percival, certainly. He embodied so many of the qualities that were the best of his generation—or of any other. And his death touched the squadron in the deepest sense. There would be victories and ribald amusements ahead for the *Escadrille Americane*, but something of the light, something pure, had died with Victor

Chapman. They all knew it. Elliott Cowdin bought a sack of oranges for Clyde Balsley delivered them in person; and then resigned, his war finished. Balsley, continuing to hover between life and death, eventually pulled through, returning to America a cripple for life. He would always remember Victor Chapman. It was Kiffin Rockwell, however, who was the most affected by Chapman's death. In a letter to his brother, Paul, he struggled to articulate the emotions that gripped him: "I feel very blue tonight. Victor was killed this afternoon.... If possible, try not to let anything get in the papers in America, until his parents are notified, which we are in train to do. After that, I would like to see every paper in the world pay a tribute to him. There is no question but that Victor had more courage than all the rest of us put together...as I say, he and I roomed together and flew very much together, so I rather feel it, as I had grown to like him very much. I am afraid it is going to rain tomorrow...."[34]

He closed with a vow: "Prince and I are going to fly about ten hours, and will do our best to kill one or two Germans for him."[35] This cold-blooded pledge betrayed a side of Kiffin Rockwell that made him a somewhat scary figure—rigid, fearless, filled with hate for Germany and all that he believed it stood for. Once described by a French admirer has having "something of the falcon on his face,"[36] Rockwell was a dark, formidable opponent. Yet he was also capable of tremendous tenderness. His letter to Victor Chapman's mother, written one week after his friend's death, conveyed all the *joie de vivre* and courage that her son had spread to those around him, in particular the effect he had on another American mother who had lost a son in the war—Kenneth Weeks, who had disappeared in the "labyrinth" in the Artois campaign. Kiffin and Victor had kept up a relationship with "Aunt" Alice Weeks: "When

I am in Paris I stay with Mrs. Weeks, whose son was my friend and killed in the Legion. Well, Victor would come around once in a while for dinner with us. Mrs. Weeks always used to say me, 'Bring Victor around; he does me so much good. I like his laugh and the sound of his voice. When he comes in the room it always seems so much brighter.'"[37]

* * *

Thaw returned. Lufberry began to demonstrate the deadly coolness that would make him the match of any German *pilotes de chasse*. And new recruits continued to arrive. One of them was Rockwell's old friend from the Second Company of the *1ᵉʳ étranger*, Paul "Skipper" Pavelka. Few American soldiers who fought in World War I saw more intense fighting than Paul Pavelka. Along with Frank Musgrave, he was one of the few to have taken part in all the major attacks in Artois in May–June 1915 and in Champagne in September 1915. With his hands badly injured from the barbed wire, Palveka asked for a *permission* ("leave" in U.S. military parlance) from the French military authorities to go to Paris in November 1915, "Since before the Champagne offensive he had not had the time or opportunity to change clothes or wash up, and the mud of the trenches and blood of the battlefield clung to his uniform. Almost a pound of shrapnel bullets were picked out of the lining of his greatcoat."[38] Pavelka had earned a shot at the "aviation." He may not have fit Dr. Gros's definition of a gentleman, but as a soldier his bona fides were impeccable. He also had well-connected and persuasive French allies who assisted him in his unlikely quest to become a pilot— French Deputy Georges Leygues, Paris municipal councilor Stephen Jousselin, and diplomat and avid *Escadrille Americaine* supporter, Jarousse de Sillac. When he returned to the 170th Regiment on November 30, 1915, Pavelka found confirmation of his request to transfer to the *Service Aéro-nautique* awaiting him. By August 1916 he had joined N 124 at their base in Behonne.

One of the unwritten rules of World War I air squadrons was that the experienced men got the newest, best "machines," while the new men would have to fly whatever was left. In Pavelka's case it was a dented Nieuport with a checkered past. Thaw had flown it first and been shot up; then Norman Prince had wrecked it. The ground crew patched it up, but everybody was convinced it was "a hoodooed machine."[39] And sure enough on just his second flight Pavelka's plane had its engine burst into flames. At ten thousand feet he was faced with the greatest terror for all pilots: being burned alive—the Nieuport no. 11's rotary engine could catch fire easily if one of the pipes that carried fuel to the cylinders cracked. Pavelka knew that if the flames reached the fuel tank he was finished. In a deft maneuver he turned the plane on its side and descended rapidly, thus keeping the flames away from the fuselage. Then the wings caught fire. Fifty feet above the ground he righted his plane and crash-landed it in a swamp between the lines. Covered with mud he extricated himself from what was left of his plane and ran for the French trenches—as a mighty explosion roared at his back. It had been as close a call as was humanly possible. Then German artillery began shelling the smoking wreckage, barely missing the scorched American.[40] Needless to say, Pavelka's stock rose mete-orically back at Behonne.

Even with Chapman's death, the triumphs of Lufberry, Pavel-ka's miraculous escape, and Thaw's return from Paris, petty grum-blings began to be heard around the aerodrome. One irritant was the behavior of Bert Hall. Hall had proven himself to be a skillful pilot and one not lacking in courage—no one could go up in one of those rickety machines and face enemy fire and be called a coward. But he boasted, exaggerated, cheated at cards, and, perhaps worst of all, was actually able to get confirmation of his kills when others could not. He downed a second plane, a Fokker, on July 23, 1916. His abrasive personality combined with professional envy on the part of his fellow pilots led to a simmering resentment, especially from Norman Prince. Prince had seen Rockwell, Thaw, and now Hall score victories, but his count officially remained at zero, despite the many hours of combat flying he had logged. Both he and Rockwell were frustrated by their failure to be credited with "kills" that they had strong reason to believe they had achieved.[41] But an unconfirmed "kill" was not a kill, period. Edward Jablonski explained how this poisoned the atmosphere at Behonne:

> Meanwhile Norman Prince was brooding. Everyone seemed to have had adventures or accounted for a "Hun" except Norman. As the originator of the squadron, Norman somehow felt that he deserved to win some sort of glory. He flew on all the patrols, came home with bullet holes in his plane, but he seemed immune to German bullets. The Germans were also immune to his. Or else he had bad luck—engine trouble or jammed guns. Something always went wrong. Here it was August, 1916; they had been at Verdun for almost four months. The squadron score stood at ten confirmed victories. Only a plane actually seen to fall and burn or crash was credited to the man who brought it down. In addition, witnesses on the ground had to back up the claim—the man's own

squadron mates would not do. Not one of the ten planes
to the squadron's credit had been knocked down by Norman, and he was not happy about it.[42]

This was one thing Norman Prince's father couldn't buy for
him. Considering how totally committed he was to winning the
air war over Verdun and how many times he had exchanged fire
with the enemy, it isn't surprising that he grew frustrated.

The pilots' eagerness to receive credit for their individual
"kills" is one aspect of World War I air combat that is not particularly admirable in retrospect. The desire of the public—and
the military—to put heroes on pedestals had led to the emphasis
on individual prowess in the air. An "ace's" victories were his
own, not the property of his squadron as a whole. Certainly, there
was squadron pride in the total number of victories achieved by
the group, but it was the individual ace that was singled out for
the greatest adulation. This created an environment where *pilotes
de chasse* could become obsessed with their personal victory
count. And this competition could, in the worst case scenario,
diminish unit cohesion. As the air war progressed into 1917 and
1918 and there were more, and faster, planes with more powerful
guns, fighter pilots often fixated on their individual successes.
This sometimes led to quite elaborate and time-consuming
efforts on their part to obtain confirmation of "kills." When
one pauses to consider what was happening on the ground at
Verdun, the Somme, Flanders, and Soissons during this time,
the effort expended to confirm "kills" becomes unsupportable:
an exercise in extreme egoism, out of all proportion to their
impact on the course of the war. Norman Prince's frustration,
as understandable as it might be, appears selfish, immature,

even childish. One can make a strong argument that it was the observation aircraft that had the larger impact and deserved the lion's share of the laurels. But, alas, they lacked the romantic flair of the *pilotes de chasse*. An artillery barrage delivered with pinpoint precision or crucial evidence of a maneuver the enemy was trying to conceal simply lacked the glamour of a sleek fuselage painted with a snazzy insignia dueling it out in the sky with a similarly colorful foe. And the *Escadrille Americaine* certainly was a colorful bunch.

★ ★ ★

Still, Prince did achieve one of the most gallant, even chivalrous victories of any pilot during the entire war. Well over the German lines, he spotted a two-seater Aviatik observation plane. He dove and fired a short burst, immediately killing the machine gunner-observer. The German pilot was within his sights, but Prince held his fire. Staying on the Aviatik's tail like an angry hornet, he then pulled alongside the German pilot and pointed west. If the German pilot wanted to live he would have to land his plane at a French airfield. This was the "first intact German plane brought down by an American inside the French lines."[43] But when one looks more closely at what transpired that day, it looks decidedly less chivalrous. Prince knew that six miles into German-held territory he was highly unlikely to get his coveted confirmation of a "kill." So with an enemy at his mercy, the only way to get credit for his victory was to bring the plane back with him to France. If he had been over French-held territory, would he have held his fire? He could have made the shot, and the certain result would have been one less experienced German observer pilot to aid the deadly 77s and 105s on the ground in doing their murderous work. The riskier course of action Prince decided on had significant military value—he succeeded in bringing the Aviatik undamaged to be pored over and dissected by personnel from the *Service Aéronautique*—but Prince's apparent chivalry in sparing the pilot's life certainly could have been a self-interested decision. One is forced to consider whether he would have pursued this course of action if not for his desire to achieve his precious "victory." Nonetheless, it was a very impressive achievement in the eyes of the public and his fellow pilots, and contributed to the growing mystique of the squadron.

Another adventure that further contributed to the mystique surrounding the squadron was the pilots' sojourn to Paris in September 1916. Dr. Edmund Gros and Kenneth Weeks's mother Alice had generously opened their homes to the pilots while on leave. "Aunt" Alice Weeks had in fact become something of a godmother to all of the young American men fighting in France. Filling her rooms with "high spirits and eager laughter,"[44] perhaps this was a tribute to her son's memory, or her own way of not dwelling on his death. But the deaths of young men like Victor Chapman must have opened her wounds afresh. In less than a year, a number of the pilots staying at her home that September wouldn't be alive. On the other hand, while they *were* there, they were as full of life as one could possibly be. No morose sorts were tolerated by the men of Squadron N 124.

The luxuries of a hot bath, "a decent cup of coffee and a slice of Boston layer cake" were savored. Then, off to the Chatham Bar or Harry's on the Rue Daunou in the 2nd arrondissement. No one has ever described the scene there better than Herbert Molloy Mason Jr.:

That September in Paris was marked by unseasonably chill winds and an unusual amount of depressing fall rains. Mornings that promised a pleasant, sunny stroll had a nasty way of turning foul, and those who ventured out minus umbrella or cape [in 1916, people still wore capes] risked a sudden drenching. But the weather—so vital a concern while at the Front—was now of little consequence to the Escadrille pilots. Their most cherished hours were spent inside the Chatham Bar, less than a five-minute walk from the Opéra. Indeed, the rain that pelted down outside added extra charm to the Chatham, whose low-ceilinged interior was jammed corner to corner with heavy wooden tables. Here pilots and observers sipped early-morning coffee laced with brandy, vermouth cassis—and with the coming of the Americans, whiskey sours. From their perch on the tall stools at the semicircular zinc bar they watched the crowds of pretty girls hurrying through the rain to meet (or seek) luncheon companions; in the evenings, when the skies were clear, they watched them pass at a more leisurely pace. By 9 p.m. the place was packed, and airmen seeking friends on leave in Paris could almost always find them elbowing their way into the smoky interior....[45]

The *Escadrille Americaine* was the toast of the town. Reporters tried to scoop each other, and in so doing were often taken for a ride by the American pilots. Almost any story, however far-fetched, was generally accepted and often found its way into print back in the U.S. All of this was, of course, heavily lubricated by alcohol. And there was the glamour of it. These pilots in their dark blue uniforms with the red and silver wings on their collars stood in stark contrast to the often shabby and unkempt French soldiers of the line in Paris on leave. The latter often felt like unwanted reminders of something painful and ugly, to be shunned. This disconnect between the Front and the home front was often commented on by French veterans of World War I. Their comrades-in-arms in the air experienced a different Paris when on leave.

One need look no further than Alice Weeks's house guests' decision to pool their funds and purchase a lion cub from a Brazilian dentist for five hundred francs. The squadron needed a mascot, and "Whiskey," as they christened him, would provide that certain ferocious *je ne sais quoi* they were looking for. Bill Thaw brought him back to the base on his lap. When the train conductor inquired as to the antecedents of his "pet," Thaw calmly replied that he was "an African dog."[46] The squadron, with its new addition, decamped to Luxeuil-les-Bains, putting Verdun behind them.

The purpose of their return to Luxeuil was to take part in what was up until then the largest and most daring air raid of the war. The aerodrome at Luxeuil was home to the *Groupe de Bombardment 4* commanded by the daredevil aviator Félix Happe. Forswearing the more nimble and attractive Nieuports, Happe stuck loyally to the almost antique-looking Maurice Farman bombers. (It may seem strange to us that that any aircraft could look "antique" in 1916, as the invention of the first airplane was just over a decade old at that time, but it is a testament to how rapidly the war was pushing advances in aviation technology.) Happe's Farman had additional fuel tanks installed on it, allowing him to penetrate deeper than anyone else behind enemy lines. He now had his eye on his most ambitious target to date: across the Rhine, on the edge of the Black Forest, to the giant Mauser rifle works located in the town of Oberndorf. Squadron N 124 would provide a fighter escort for the great raid. In addition, the Canadian pilots of RNAS no. 3 Wing were posted to Luxeuil for the same purpose. The date was left intentionally vague. In the meantime they trained in formation flying, patrolled, and worked to familiarize themselves with their "machines"—in the Canadians' case, the Sopwith "Strutter"; in the Americans' case, the Nieuport no. 17. Both featured the new synchronized Vickers machine guns that fired through the rotating propeller. The Allies were now poised to take the air war to the Germans.

Kiffin Rockwell, of course, setting aside technological advances and more ambitious strategic objectives, was always ready to take the air war to the Germans. He was a warrior. He wanted to engage the enemy, destroy their aircraft, and kill them. There was little space for nuance or romance in his view of war. And always there was the image of Victor Chapman's body being riddled by German bullets to motivate him. On September 9 over Verdun, Rockwell had recorded his second confirmed "kill." That same day he wrote his brother Paul recounting what had occurred: "This morning I attacked a Boche at three thousand meters high, killed the observateur the first shot. After that, followed the machine down to eighteen hundred meters riddling it with bullets."[47] He was glad to be back in Luxeuil, where he had been so warmly embraced back in the spring. But the six months between his first arrival and his return had noticeably aged him. He looked gaunt, his face creased and lined with worry. He also had grown a mustache, which made him look both older and more Gallic in appearance. At this point Kiffin Rockwell was twenty-four years old, and he looked thirty-four, older even. By one estimate he had taken part in a total of seventy-four aerial combats in July and August alone.[48]

Kiffin Rockwell. Carolinian, *légionnaire*, *pilote de chasse*, knight errant.

Still, he drove himself. When friends questioned his pace, he had a simple reply: "I pay my part for Lafayette and Rochambeau!"[49] From almost anyone else this remark would surely be apocryphal— or, if not, then ridiculous. Attributed to Rockwell, it has the ring of authenticity, and is not the slightest bit funny.

By late September only two of Nieuport no. 17s that had been promised when the pilots were on leave in Paris had arrived. Thénault gave them to his best pilots: Raoul Lufberry and Kiffin Rockwell. On September 23 they took to the early autumn skies over the Vosges in their new "machines." As they made their way in the brilliant morning sunshine towards the Rhine valley, they spotted a group of Fokkers far below, headed west. The two Nieuports dove on the enemy planes. Lufberry fired a burst from his Vickers machine gun, only to have it jam. He broke off the combat, and Rockwell followed suit. The nearby airfield of Squadron N 49 provided Lufberry with a place to see to the necessary repairs before continuing the patrol. Rockwell circled above him, climbing to ten thousand feet. An Aviatik lumbered across the French lines below. Attacking this aircraft from the rear took tremendous nerve. Its rear-mounted machine gun was a formidable weapon, as Rockwell well knew. He pushed down on the stick and went into his dive. German bullets spewed a "stream of lead"[50] at the onrushing Carolinian. On the ground below, a French artillery captain observed a short burst from the Nieuport's gun, then a frantic maneuver by the German pilot to avoid a collision as Rockwell's plane hurtled to earth. A wing ripped away, and the Nieuport began a tight death spiral into the ground. Kiffin Rockwell's body was found in a field full of flowers with a gaping wound in the chest. Lancelot was no more.

News of Kiffin Rockwell's death was carried in newspapers throughout the world. Something about this gallant Southerner and the way he had died, and why he died, touched a nerve. A stunned Georges Thénault, addressing his pilots at the Hôtel Pomme d'Or, could only mutter, "The best and bravest of us is no more."[51] Rockwell's funeral united Frenchmen, Americans,

and Canadians in shared grief and admiration. As Herbert Molloy Mason Jr. has explained, "Rockwell represented more than
an individual who fell in battle; he represented an idea."[52] An
editorial written by Pierre Mille for the Paris daily *Le Temps*
placed his death in a wider historical context: "He fell before
the final victory, he fell for this final victory, and when this victory will be here indeed, it will be the duty of Americans and
French together to say to the ones who gave them birth, as one
would say in the Ancient World: 'blessed are the ones who gave
life to such a son!'"[53] The German press was also aware of the
larger implications of Rockwell's death: "The news of the death
of the famous American aviator, Rockwell, merits the greatest
attention. It is not an isolated case.... America must be made
aware of our profound indignation; she must also be aware that
we consider this participation by her citizens a direct provocation."[54] Kiffin Rockwell wouldn't have had it any other way.
The evening before Rockwell's last patrol, Paul Pavelka recalled
a bottle of cognac being passed around and a pensive Rockwell
uncharacteristically pondering his mortality. Then the old Rockwell reemerged: "And just in case I am killed, I want you all to
take whatever money you happen to find on me and drink to
the destruction of the damned Boche." One can only assume
they did.

★ ★ ★

The weeks following Rockwell's funeral were a period of
waiting—waiting for the new, promised aircraft, waiting for the
"something big" Happe kept alluding to; waiting. The few pilots
who did get into the air saw some action, in particular Norman

Prince, who had the satisfaction of recording his second "victory."
Then, finally, word came down that the operation was on.

The Oberndorf Raid of October 12, 1916, was, frankly, ahead
of its time. Félix Happe was attempting to carry out was what
would later, in World War II, be called "strategic daylight bombing." Some of the raids carried out in that later, even larger struggle could only be described as catastrophic in terms of the number
of aircraft, pilots, and crews lost in the process of completing their
missions. And not all missions were completed. Happe and his
raiders were about to learn something that would then have to be
re-learned by another generation of theorists in military aviation.

One of the major problems with bombing targets deep within
enemy territory was that the fuel tanks of the smaller fighter planes
limited their range (and thus the distance over which they could
provide cover for the larger bombers). By October 12, five Nieuport
no. 17s were ready to escort the Maurice Farmans and Bréguet-
Michelins with their lethal payloads. It was a minimal contribution
to an undertaking with many moving parts. The Canadians of the
RNAS played a major role. Their Sopwith Strutters could either
serve as bombers or provide cover for the larger French planes. In
addition, a group of three dozen planes would attack another target to the south as a diversion. Bert Hall was the *Escadrille Americaine*'s sole representative in this diversionary force. As the
raiders took off in the afternoon, the noise must have been quite
something—the handsome Sopwiths and Nieuports, the lumber-
ing bombers looking like they might not get into the air at all.
The entire contingent, one after the other, forming up above the
aerodrome, then heading east over the Vosges, the Rhine, the Black
Forest, and most ominously, the Fokker base at Colmar. Alfred de
Laage de Meux led N 124's *pilotes de chasse*, including Raoul

Lufberry, Norman Prince, and Didier Masson. The raid suffered complications almost from the start. Aircraft failed to function properly, there was poor coordination, and with the noise and sheer size of the air armada moving east, unsurprised German pilots waited to greet them. One of these pilots was Ernst Udet, at that time a novice fighter pilot, but a man who would become one of the highest scoring and most colorful "aces" of the war; by the war's end in 1918, he was credited with sixty-two confirmed "kills." Udet fired at the engine of one of the Maurice Farmans, disabling and eventually capturing it and its crew intact after landing his plane alongside it. East of the Rhine the fighter escorts had to turn back to refuel, and from that point on the raid became a confused, bloody mess, with some bombers falling from the skies, one group of them getting lost and bombing the wrong town, and some making it through to hit the intended target, only to be destroyed running the gauntlet back across the Rhine. As dusk began to fall the raid "had become a great air battle stretching across most of the flight path."[55]

Bert Hall, flying with the diversionary force, was glad to be clear of the most intense action. He had begun to think that either his, Bill Thaw's, or Norman Prince's number was up. They were the last three surviving members of the original squadron's company (*sans* commanding officers)—and Thaw, for want of a plane, wasn't in the air that day, so Hall was anxious about his odds. But, in the end it was Norman Prince whose number was called. In the running mêlée back from the Rhine, Prince had gotten behind a retiring Fokker and recorded another "kill"—just two shy of the title of "ace" he so coveted. He joined Lufberry for the final leg home, but darkness began to envelop them, and Lufberry signaled that they should land at a smaller advance airfield at Corcieux. He landed, with Prince close behind. In the gloaming, however, Prince failed to see the high-tension cables near treetop level[56] at the unfamiliar field. His plane's wheels caught, and the whole thing—fuselage, wings, engine, propeller, and Prince—went end over end into the ground. His body mangled, he lapsed into a coma and never regained consciousness.

The final summary of the Obendorf Raid does not make for pretty reading: "Of the forty planes sent out, twenty-four actually bombed a target (even if six did bomb the wrong one); nine planes did not make it across the lines and ten planes never returned. The mission to Oberndorf was not a great success."[57] This tally doesn't include losses sustained by fighter escorts, including Norman Prince's death. Though three persons were killed and nine injured at the Mauser rifle works,[58] the plant was up and running at full strength the following day.

★ ★ ★

Félix Happe was blamed for the entire affair and busted back to the infantry from whence he'd come. If it was any solace, his successors in the next war, painting on a larger canvas and with a more varied palate, had little more success than he. It was not until the advent of the American-built P-51 Mustang in World War II that raiders such as Happe's would have something more than a fighting chance to successfully complete their missions and return to base alive.

The raid was the end of the *Escadrille Americaine*'s time in Luxeuil. The squadron was moved to the far less comfortable aerodrome of Cachy in the Somme sector. Other changes were in the air, as well, for N 124. New pilots arrived to replace those lost earlier in the fall. One of them was Bob Soubiron, the former comrade-in-arms of Bill Thaw and Bert Hall in the old Second Company of the *2ᵉ Régiment étranger*. Soubiron had been badly injured in Champagne after joining *les Hirondelles de la Mort* in 1915. In hospital, he awaited word of his request to transfer to the "aviation." On October 28, 1916, the former racecar driver arrived at Cachy.

Inspired by the colorful insignia being adopted by their fellow *groupes des chasse*, both friend and foe, the Americans decided on an Indian head logo as an insignia (one can't help but feel "Whiskey" had been shortchanged as mascot, but he was soon accompanied by a female lion cub, inevitably named "Soda," to assuage any hurt feelings). An enterprising mechanic copied an image from a box of ammunition from the Savage Arms Company bearing a crude visage of a Seminole Indian. The squadron's name also was altered from the *Escadrille Americaine*—in response the political pressure being applied on President Woodrow Wilson's administration by German diplomats looking to rein in Wilson's headstrong countrymen. Thus, *Americaine* became simply *Volantaires*, which pleased no one. Stripping the pilots of their identity clearly wouldn't do. Thus out of the war ministry came a new name: the *Escadrille Lafayette*.[59] This pleased everyone except the Germans. Kiffin Rockwell's claim to honor a historical debt his country owed to France was now embodied in the squadron's name. This was lost on no one that had served with him.

Bert Hall, in stark contrast, had made himself offensive to nearly all of his fellow pilots in N 124. Perhaps the final straw had been his failure to attend Kiffin Rockwell's funeral. Instead he had been in Paris trying to peddle an exclusive on his "friend's" final duel and untimely death to reporters. His anxiety over being one of only two remaining original American members of the squadron also was getting on people's nerves. Finally, matters came to a head. It was unanimous. All of his fellow squadron mates wanted him to go. Thénault could not force Hall to request a transfer. After all, he had been decorated with some of France's highest military honors. He was also a skillful pilot. But the others would not fly with him. One thing that could be said of Bert Hall was that he knew when to cut his losses. He left the squadron with a curse and a threat, transferring to another: N 103. And after only a brief stint with his new outfit, Hall requested a *permission* to return home to the U.S. He never returned. His final act in this drama was as a deserter. For this enigmatic man, it seemed a queer end to what had been, one must admit, a remarkable run.

The "Lafayette Escadrille," as it was known in the United States, drew romantic-minded men to its ranks throughout 1917. Few of the new volunteers had undergone service in the trenches before joining. The pretense of not forgoing one's citizenship to fight for France by joining the *Légion* had been circumvented by the escadrille's wealthy and powerful benefactors—both French and American. The last American volunteer of 1914 to serve in the *Escadrille Americaine* was William Dugan of Rochester, New York. Severely wounded at the Bois de Caillette in the fighting at Verdun, he, like Soubiron, had gotten word of his transfer in hospital and joined the squadron in March 1917 after completing his training. Of the other American volunteers of 1914 to request transfer to the "aviation," none became members of the now world-famous squadron. Fred Zinn of Battle Creek, Michigan, became a widely respected photographic observer for the *Service Aéronautique*, earning the *Croix de Guerre* for his "sang froid" and "contempt of danger."[60] Edgar Bouligny of New Orleans would serve with Squadron N 501; Dennis Dowd, the tragic lovelorn New York, would die in training (a none too rare occurrence) when his plane inexplicably fell from the sky (there was speculation that he may have passed out at the controls, unaccustomed as he was to the high altitude). Herman Chatkoff became an accomplished pilot and served with Squadron C 11 in the Aisne sector, near where he and his comrades had held the line along the Chemin des Dames in the winter of 1914–15. In the summer of 1917, the Lafayette Escadrille had moved yet again, to an aerodrome at nearby Chaudun. Chatkoff flew over whenever he had the time to chat with his fellow Americans. One can't help but wonder if he and Bob Soubiron and Bill Thaw recalled René Phelizot, the big game hunter from Chicago who had taken it in turn with Alan Seeger to carry the American flag that they had all signed that day in Paris when they gaily marched off to the Gare Saint-Lazare, and the war to defend civilization—and died of his injuries in a fight with Arab *légionnaires* in the early days of the war.[61] Soubiron still wore the flag around his waist.

On June 15, 1917, Chatkoff had good-naturedly agreed to take an American visitor aloft in his Caudron. The Caudron was not a nimble, sleek craft like the Nieuports. It was a larger, more ungainly, airplane, but Chatkoff put it through a series of daring maneuvers all the same. The result was an ugly crash. Chatkoff's passenger was cut in half, while Chatkoff sustained severe wounds to head and body. The brain damage he sustained was severe enough to leave him institutionalized for the rest of his life.

These men had served in the French air force (*Service Aéronautique*) with primarily French comrades. They were all officially listed on the roster of the Franco-American Flying Corps—Dr. Edmund Gros's original brainchild of a larger American contingent integrated into the *Service Aéronautique*. He quickly adopted the new name of "Lafayette Flying Corps" once the more famous escadrille was given this moniker. In fact, Dr. Gros himself claimed credit for the name.

One last piece of history regarding Dr. Gros and his Flying Corps took shape at Verdun in 1916, when Eugene Bullard of Columbus, Georgia, first conceived the idea of becoming a pilot. A friend of Victor Chapman before the war, Bullard had been moved by what he had seen in the skies over Vaux and Douaumont while serving with the 170th Regiment. On leave that summer in Paris, he broached the idea to his friends the painters Gilbert White and Moise Kisloing at *La Rotonde*, a street-side café on the Boulevard Montparnasse. Mississippian Jeff Dickson soon joined them, and the talk shifted to Bullard's aspirations. Dickson responded with disbelief. Bullard was black, and there was no way the powers that be would permit a black man to represent the U.S. in such an elite unit. The two made a bet—Dickson certain Bullard would never fly, Bullard more determined than ever that he would.[62]

In the end, Dr. Gros did all in his power to make certain Eugene Bullard lost that bet. He saw himself as a gatekeeper for the American expatriate community in Paris, and he believed that pilots should be gentlemen. Yes, there were cases such as Bert Hall, Paul Pavelka, and Herman Chatkoff who didn't quite meet the standard of "society," but they all had at least one thing going for them that Eugene Bullard did not: they were white. However, Eugene Bullard had allies of his own. Perhaps the most important thing going for him was the French understanding that race was not decisive in determining one's character and capacities—a belief that had been inherited from the Revolution and stood in stark contrast to America's continuing poor record on race, particularly in the South. The

French High Command recognized that Bullard had more than proved his mettle on multiple occasions in both the *Légion* and with the 170th. He deserved a shot at flight school just like any other American fighting for France. The intimations of a preening snob like Dr. Gros proved insufficient to deny Bullard his chance. He seized it, becoming the first black American fighter pilot. One can well imagine the satisfaction that he must have felt collecting on that bet. For sheer perseverance, few stories can match this one.

CHAPTER 10

RENDEZVOUS

Following the bloody offensive in Champagne, the fate of the Foreign Legion in France was very much in doubt. October 1915 would be the last time all of the original volunteers of 1914 were in one place (with the exception, of course, of those already killed, in hospital, or in the "aviation"). The departure of so many of the old guard for the 170th Regiment was an emotional turning point for all of the remaining Americans. Alan Seeger had initially expressed interest in getting out of the *Légion* and its motley collection of mercenaries, Arabs, and assorted riff raff.[1] But over time it grew on the New Yorker. He made friends outside of the relatively small circle of American-born *légionnaires* and began to imbibe some of the Arab culture that the *Légion* had brought with it from North Africa. He also took pride in the history and *esprit de corps* of the unit. Thus, when given a choice, Seeger stayed.

Christopher Charles, Edgar Bouligny, Herman Chatkoff, and Jack Casey—who at the time of their decision were in hospital with wounds or illnesses—also chose to stay, as did a number of other Americans who had joined the *Légion* after 1914. Seeger likely spoke for all of those Americans when he explained his decision in a letter to his mother: "Most of the other Americans have taken advantage of the permission to pass into a regular French regiment. There is much to be said for their decision, but I have remained true to the *Légion*, where I am content and have good comrades. I have a pride particularly in the Moroccan Division, whereof we are the first brigade. Those who march with the Zouaves and the Algerian *tirailleurs* are sure to be where there is most honor."[2]

But it was a former comrade of Seeger's from the pre-war Paris cafés—the Swiss poet Blaise Cendrars—who best captured what it was about *la Légion* that called to those who chose to stay when they could have bid it *adieu*:

> That is what I owe to the Legion, and to the old lascars of Africa, soldiers, NCOs, officers, who came to lead us and mix with us comrades, these desperadoes, these survivors of God knows what colonial epics, but who were all men, all. And that made it all worth the risk of death to meet these damned souls, who smelled of the galleys, were covered with tattoos. None of them ever let us down and each one was willing to sacrifice himself, for nothing, for kudos, because he was drunk, for a challenge, for a laugh, to stick it to someone, by God.[3]

They had littered the fields of Artois and Champagne with their dead, and now they were pulled back to rest, and prepare for the next great attack. Interestingly, the same promise—of being employed only as *troupes d'attaque*—which the Americans that had joined the 170th Regiment had found so attractive, was now made to the *Regiment de Marche de la Légion Étrangère*. When Seeger heard from old friends now in the 170th, still stuck in those cold trenches in Champagne, he had to laugh.[4] The *Légion* was shifted first to Compiègne, then the town of Crevecoeur, in Picardy. It was cold, but they were "warmly quartered in a big town where they could buy all sorts of comforts."[5] New arrivals had also appeared, added to reconstitute at least some of the *Légion*'s strength after the carnage in Champagne. These were old mercenaries that had been serving in Tonkin. Among them was an American soldier-of-fortune from Chicago named Joseph Phillips. Phillips had served in the Philippines with the U.S. Army; then, having acquired a taste for Asia, enlisted in the French Foreign Legion in 1910. He was now a long way from the South China Sea.

Alan Seeger requested and obtained a *permission* to visit Paris for eight days. With the easy duty in Crevecoeur and the anticipation he felt for his trip to Paris, Seeger wrote his mother: "*C'est la bonne vie*"—"Life is good."[6] But as often happens when the body has time to rest following a particularly trying experience that draws on one's reserves, Seeger collapsed with a serious case of bronchitis, something that in 1916—still a number of years from the discovery of antibiotics—could develop quickly into pneumonia if not treated properly, and even take one's life. Pneumonia took a significant portion of the lives of those men listed as "killed" on casualty lists, and the number of deaths it caused were staggering once the Spanish influenza epidemic hit in 1918.

While Seeger was invalided to a hospital to recover, his fellow *légionnaires* moved yet again, this time to the trenches in the

Marest-sur-Matz sector near Compiègne. It was a relatively quiet area on the Western Front in that winter of 1915–16. At one point the various elements of the Division Marocaine organized a soccer league. Christopher Charles and Joseph Phillips were the two American representatives on the *Légion*'s squad. At one point, mid-match, the German artillery opened up on them while they were playing a team of Zouaves. That one was a draw.[7]

* * *

Alan Seeger was physically exhausted, but his mind was at ease knowing that his fellow *légionnaires* were well out of the fighting for the foreseeable future. That also made it the perfect time to recoup his energies and take full advantage of the respite that his condition afforded him. Seeger was not one to shirk combat, but he had come to loathe the training and drill that occupied the men's time when stationed in rear areas.

During his convalescence from bronchitis, he attempted to get ahold of the manuscript book of poems that he had left in Bruges, Belgium, in 1914—something not at all easy to do with the town under German occupation. Seeger contacted the U.S. Embassy, and efforts were made to procure the manuscript, if it still existed. In 1916 the United States was at peace with Germany, and therefore the regular diplomatic channels still functioned. This precarious peace was largely the result of President Woodrow Wilson's determination to not allow the U.S. to be drawn into a war that he believed was being fought to advance selfish European interests. Wilson saw America's role (and his own) as that of a potential peacemaker ready to step in when both sides had exhausted themselves and could not go on. This, of course, was very different from

Alan Seeger's perception of the war—and that of many if not most of his fellow Americans then fighting in France. To them, Wilson's policies were not noble, but shameful. (To be sure, not all of the volunteers of 1914 felt this way. Russell Kelly of the *1er étranger*, who was killed in June 1915 in Artois, wrote his father, "Those who clamor for war most in the states are those who know nothing about it. War is an asinine waste and I take my hat

Woodrow Wilson, president of the United States, 1913–1921.

off to President Wilson for his level headedness.") Largely, they felt that they were risking their lives and spilling their blood to save civilzation—and to redeem their countrymen's honor abroad. Seeger, for one, was frustrated that most Americans seemingly could not concern themselves with what was occurring in France. He addressed this head on in his poem "A Message to America":

> You have the grit and the guts, I know;
> You are ready to answer blow for blow
> You are virile, combative, stubborn, hard,
> But your honor ends with your own backyard;
> Each man intent on his own private goal,
> You have no feeling for the whole;
> What singly none would tolerate
> You let unpunished hit the state,

> Unmindful that each man must share
> The stain he lets his country wear,
> And (what no traveller ignores)
> That her good name is often yours.[8]

The color of "the stain," for Seeger and many of his American comrades, was yellow. When Woodrow Wilson responded to the sinking of the British passenger liner *Lusitania* in May of 1915 with a speech in Philadelphia in which he claimed there was "such a thing as being too proud to fight," it was a moment of disgust and disbelief for many. The liner had been carrying munitions in its hold, and the German Embassy had warned passengers explicitly not to travel in a war zone—but the 1,195 victims of the sinking outweighed these considerations in the public's mind. The fact that many of the 1,195 were women and children, and that 128 of them were U.S. citizens, seemed to almost scream for a forceful response from President Wilson. Kiffin Rockwell wrote his mother that spring from a hospital after being wounded in the Artois Offensive: "We are all watching the U.S. now. If she wants to keep up her name and be respected by other nations, I don't see how she will keep from fighting."[9] But Rockwell misread Woodrow Wilson.

One common misunderstanding about the twenty-eighth president of the United States is that he was from New Jersey. In fact he was a Virginian. In most history books, he suddenly appears, fully-formed, as the progressive governor of New Jersey, reluctantly drafted by the Democratic Party to leave the ivy-covered walls of Princeton. This is all true, up to a point, but Wilson was in no way either a native of New Jersey or reluctant to take power. He had grown up the son of a minister in a South that had been traumatized by the Civil War. He could remember seeing wounded

Confederate soldiers as a boy. It made a powerful impression on his young mind. War was an ugly thing.

Wilson overcame learning disabilities and began a meteoric rise as a scholar of government and law. His work on the British Parliamentary system is still considered a classic of its kind. Of all of his predecessors, Wilson bears closest political resemblance to another Virginian, Thomas Jefferson. Both loved discussing and writing about democratic government, the principles upon which it is based, and the people that it exists to serve. Both were able to articulate idealistic world visions (Jefferson's "Empire of Liberty"; Wilson's "League of Nations") that appealed to many of their contemporaries and still exert a strong appeal on many people today. Yet, both were bigots (in Jefferson's case this was compounded by hypocrisy, as well). They also were both absolutely certain of their own political brilliance. They were very smart men, but they had great difficulty engaging in political debate without personal rancor. In their minds, anyone who disagreed with a policy that they regarded as self-evidentially correct was either stupid, misguided, or disloyal. This characteristic may perhaps have been even more pronounced in Wilson—a self-righteous certainty that was interpreted as either "vision" or narrow-minded arrogance, depending on which side of the political spectrum one viewed him from.

Another historical parallel that links the two Virginians was a common foreign policy dilemma, specifically the question of the American right to conduct maritime trade with Europe in wartime. Jefferson placed a trade embargo on his own ports rather than risk U.S. merchantmen running afoul of the Royal Navy or French privateers. This policy did great damage to the economic well-being of America's port cities (and Jefferson's popularity) at the time, but it kept the U.S. out of a general European war. Woodrow Wilson, faced with nearly the exact same situation, insisted on neutrals' right to trade with Europe, or anywhere else for that matter, as had Jefferson's immediate successor, Madison, who reversed most of Jefferson's policies on the embargo, leading to the so-called "War of 1812" between Britain and the United States. This principle was articulated by President Wilson as the principle of "Freedom of the Seas."

By 1916, the reality was that neither side in the conflict was respecting this principle. The Royal Navy blockaded Germany with its numerically superior surface fleet, and the Kaiser unleashed his *unterseeboots* (U-boat submarines) to torpedo any vessels near the British Isles or French coast. Initially, German U-boat captains had warned vessels before sinking them and allowed time for passengers and crew to get into life boats. After being fired on by concealed deck guns, however the Germans began sinking vessels without warning—as was the case with the *Lusitania*. If Wilson had simply required U.S. nationals not to travel on vessels coming to or from the war zone (as Jefferson had tried to do) and confined U.S. trade abroad to the Western Hemisphere, he might have been able to keep the U.S. out of the war entirely. This, of course, was not what Alan Seeger wanted. He, Rockwell, and many of the other volunteers of 1914 saw this fight as for something more than a single principle like "Freedom of the Seas." They saw it in civilizational terms. To them, France's fight was America's fight. President Wilson never seemed to grasp this.

1916 was a difficult year for President Wilson. Mexico, then in the throes of a ten-year-long civil war, seemed immune to Wilson's attempts to lecture it on its form of government. In January and March of that year forces under the rebel leader

Pancho Villa had murdered U.S. citizens in cold blood. Germany, for its part, was failing to abide by agreements it had reached with Wilson following the sinking of the *Lusitania*. And constantly hounding Wilson in this, the year of his bid for reelection, was his old rival Theodore Roosevelt. Roosevelt had split the Republican Party in 1912 in his bid to return to the White House after an absence of four years. This split—dividing "TR"'s progressive supporters and incumbent William Howard Taft's conservative backers—had opened the door for Wilson to win the election in 1912 with only 42 percent of the popular vote. In retrospect, if the Democrats had nominated nearly anyone other than Wilson— one of the party's better known and more conservative figures— Roosevelt likely would have ridden the progressive tide to victory. But, as a progressive like Roosevelt, Wilson stole much of Roosevelt's radical thunder, relegating him to a humiliating second-place finish. He never forgot, or forgave, Wilson. TR's resentment underlay his positively venomous attacks on Wilson's inability to see what was at stake in Europe, and his unwillingness to prepare America to fight Germany. The *New York Times*, usually sympathetic to the Wilson administration, ran a three-column feature on a speech Roosevelt gave to a large gathering early in 1916 to this effect:

> "If we are really devoted to a high idea," he said, "we must, insofar as our strength permits, aid those who are wronged by others. When we sit idly by when Belgium is being overwhelmed, and, rolling up our eyes, prattle with unctuous self-righteousness about the duty of neutrality, we show that we do not really fear God; on the contrary we show an odious fear of the devil."[10]

Charles Seeger opposed American involvement in the war that his brother Alan had fought beginning in 1914.

TR's rhetoric covered the full spectrum of political discourse from reasoned, statesman-like prose to crude, ugly accusations that seemed beneath the dignity of an ex-president. The pull of Roosevelt's force of character on the American public was, if diminished, still formidable, as Wilson well knew. But at least he didn't have to run against him for president again. Much to the disappointment of Alan Seeger and others, Roosevelt had agreed to stand aside and let another, less charismatic, candidate run on the Republican ticket. He did this not out of conviction, but rather in order to regain the good graces of the party's old guard, still smarting from the split and defeat in 1912 that it blamed on TR. In fact, the Republican candidate, Charles Evans Hughes, barely rated above Wilson in Roosevelt's private ruminations. But TR agreed to go all out for him on the stump in 1916. Thus American voters could easily be excused for thinking that the election was between Roosevelt and Wilson. The election issue was certainly clear: war or no war. In his "Message to America" Alan Seeger made it clear that his sympathies lay with Roosevelt:

> You have a leader that knows—the man
> Most fit to be called American,
> A prophet that once in generations

Is given to point to erring nations
Brighter ideals toward which to press
And lead them out of the wilderness
Will you turn your back on him once again?[11]

For Wilson, he had only scorn:

Will you give the tiller once more to men
Who have made your country a laughing-stock...
A country that turns the other cheek,
Who care not how bravely your flag may float,
Who answer an insult with a note,
Whose way is the easy way in all,
And, seeing that polished arms appall
Their marrow of milk-fed pacifist,
Would tell you menace does exist...
Oh, bury them deeper than the sea
In universal obloquy;
Forget the ground where they lie, or write
For epitaph: "Too proud to fight."[12]

Curiously enough Alan Seeger's older brother Charles disagreed with the necessity and wisdom of America becoming
involved in Europe's suicidal conflict. After graduating from Harvard, Charles Seeger had pursued a career teaching music at the
post-secondary level. In addition to his gifts as a musician, Seeger
had a first-rate mind. His contributions to the study of musicology
advanced the field as a whole. In 1912, he took a position at the
University of California at Berkeley, but nearly threw his career
away for his public stand against the United States' involvement in

World War I—the very thing his younger brother so ardently hoped for. He was fired and returned to the east coast with his pregnant wife and two sons, looking to start over. He was eventually hired at the Julliard School in New York; his third son, Peter, was born in 1919. Pete Seeger grew up to become one of the foremost folk music artists of the twentieth century. Following in his father's footsteps, he took a principled stand against the Vietnam War in the 1960s; following his Uncle Alan, he took a strong stand in support of the war against fascism in World War II and served in the Pacific as an airplane mechanic.

The two brothers' conflicting positions on the war seem a puzzle at first. But when one considers that both were acting on principle—and taking risks to act on their principles—one can see what the brothers shared. Alan Seeger was taking the larger risk, certainly, but his older brother had two children to feed, a pregnant wife, and no job. He placed his promising academic career in jeopardy with his stand against the war. These were men who clearly lived life on a higher idealistic plane. How did Charles view his younger brother's adventures in France? One can't help but be drawn back to that winter long ago on the steep snow-covered hill as Charles and the other boys peeled away on their sleds once they glimpsed the oncoming delivery wagon at the bottom of the run, and Alan went careening on through the horse's legs: "It's hard to explain, Charlie. But I couldn't turn away. Don't you get it? I had to prove to myself that I had the nerve. You know what I mean?"[13] As Charles said, "That was Alan. Tilting against windmills."[14]

Alan Seeger tried to rally his countrymen behind the interventionists. He admitted that he had "been too long from my country's shores":[15]

But as for myself I know right well
I would go through fire and shot and shell
And face new perils and make my bed
In new privations, if ROOSEVELT led;
But I have given my heart and hand
To serve, in serving another land
Ideals kept bright that with you are dim....[16]

The reality was that Seeger and the other American volunteers were largely impotent in the face of the opposition, or simple apathy, towards the war in the United States at the time. In 1916, Theodore Roosevelt did not represent a majority of American public opinion. German-Americans and Irish-Americans largely opposed U.S. intervention for different reasons, as did women (by this time, able to vote in eleven states, including California), socialists, pacifists, and those geographically further removed from the U-boat menace in the Atlantic. All Seeger, Chapman, Bowe, King, and the other remaining volunteers of 1914 could do was lead by example, and plant the seeds that might eventually lead to direct American

Alan Seeger spent his convalescence at this idyllic locale in 1916. He made a full recovery.

involvement. That looked remote indeed as Alan Seeger lay in his hospital bed in the winter of 1916, tilting at windmills.

He recovered from the worst effects of his illness quickly, but a longer recuperation period was mercifully added to his initial stay in hospital. Seeger spent it in truly idyllic surroundings at a chateau in Biarritz owned by a friend of his parents, one Madame de Bonard. Sandwiched luxuriously between the Pyrenees and the Atlantic, Biarritz could not have been further from the front in France, both literally and figuratively. Alan Seeger was treated like a prince. In a letter to his mother he drew a word picture of life in the chateau:

> I don't believe there is a finer site in Biarritz. The house too is the very ideal of comfort and luxury. Fancy me after a year and a half of sleeping with my clothes on in trenches and haylofts, sleeping now in a most volup-tuously soft bed in a pink and white room, with a tiled bathroom adjoining. A little reading lamp is by my pil-low at night; in the morning around ten o'clock I press a button and a maid comes, opens my shutters and brings me café au lait and toast and jam. The view from my window is superb: to the right is a little corner of sea that looks for all the world like the pictures of the Bay of Naples, with a mountain, like Vesuvius, behind. Then all around the rest of the horizon the long line of the Pyrenees, covered with snow now, right to the foot. The air, of course, is fine....[17]

Over a month later he wrote his mother a second letter from Biarritz explaining that since he hadn't been in any danger he had felt no need to write. He would be returning to the *Légion* in May, and had splendid news: "Did I write you that the Embassy have managed to get my MS. from Bruges?"[18] Back in Paris, a fully-recovered Alan Seeger picked up his poems and, after reading through them again for the first time since 1914, "found much that was good" and "much that was juvenile too."[19] A lot had changed since he wrote them. He had changed. On May 1, 1916, Seeger returned to his regiment. In a letter to a friend written at the time, he seemed to be taking leave of the life he had known, explaining that he had "taken his fill of all the pleasures that Paris can give (and it was Paris at its most beautiful). I lived as though I were say-ing goodbye...."[20] A poem he wrote during this period echoed the fatalistic tone in the letter. "Rendezvous with Death" spoke for the soldiers, on both sides, who by now realized that the war would be long and that they likely would not live to see its finish:

> I have a rendezvous with Death
> At some disputed barricade,
> When Spring comes back with rustling shade
> And apple-blossoms fill the air—
> I have a rendezvous with Death
> When Spring brings back blue days and fair.
>
> It may be he shall take my hand
> And lead me into his dark land
> And close my eyes and quench my breath—
> It may be I shall pass him still.
> I have a rendezvous with Death
> On some scarred slope of battered hill,
> When Spring comes round again this year

And the first meadow-flowers appear.

God knows 'twere better to be deep
Pillowed in silk and scented down,
Where love throbs out in blissful sleep,
Pulse nigh to pulse, and breath to breath,
Where hushed awakenings are dear. . .
But I've a rendezvous with Death
At midnight in some flaming town,
When Spring trips north again this year,
And I to my pledged word am true,
I shall not fail that rendezvous.[21]

Did Seeger have a premonition of his own death? It's impossible to say for certain, but if he did he certainly didn't let his foreboding dissuade him from action, either as a poet or as a *légionnaire*. Back with his unit in May, stationed in one of the more quiet sectors of the Front, he likened it to "no more than camping out."[22] They had even left the protection of their bombproof dugouts and pitched tents just back of their trenches. The illusion of safety was abruptly ended when a German airplane bombed their position, leaving eight dead and wounded in its wake. The bombproof dugouts reminded Seeger of "holes like those that I remember pictured in our old natural histories, that show a gopher, an owl, and a snake all living happily together in a burrow. Here it is men, rats, and vermin."[23] He was back home. During this time he penned the poem "Ode in Memory of the American Volunteers Fallen for France," which was intended to first be read at the Memorial Day commemoration to be held among the American expatriate community living in Paris. The ceremony was set for May 30, 1916, at the statue of Washington and Lafayette in the *Place des États-Unis*. As the date approached, Seeger waited anxiously for word that his request for a *permission* to go to Paris and read the poem in person had been granted. No word came. He was deeply disappointed, as he shared with Alice Weeks, the mother of the lost *légionnaire*: "It would have been such an honor and pleasure to have read my verses there in Paris.... To have raised my hopes and then left me in the lurch like that was certainly cruel."[24] According to Seeger biographer Irving Werstein, the oversight was the fault of an official at the foreign ministry who thought that Memorial Day was on the Fourth of July.[25] Whatever the case, Seeger never read the poem in public.

In June 1916 the *Légion* was once again on the move. For reasons that were not yet entirely clear to the men, they had been held out of the terrible fighting that had been raging since February at Verdun. They suspected that General Joffre had done this purposely to have them in peak fighting trim for his next offensive (which would prove to be his last). They were right. As the finest *troupes d'attaque* in the French Army, their presence on the battlefield was deemed necessary for success. After having been held largely in reserve for more than six months, the *Légion* and its diminished but no less committed contingent of Americans was about to get back into the war. On June 22, 1916, they moved out in anticipation of the big push at the Somme. Alan Seeger turned twenty-eight years old that day.

* * *

The Somme River runs through one of the more rural areas in all of France. The British historian Brian Gardner described the region as it existed before the outbreak of war in 1914: "...the River Somme was a minor placid waterway of northern France. It meandered gently through Picardy.... Men fished on its banks. Lovers nestled in the reeds, and punts slipped in and out of its complicated channels. On the uplands to either side villages lay in the folds of undulating slopes.... It was a countryside of singular rural beauty, not unlike parts of Hampshire. The Somme watered it all; the fat orchards, the rich cornfields, the marshy meadows.... Life was a matter of sowing, reaping, and gathering the harvest; of apple-picking, of children's laughter, of fish hiding near the banks, of the sound of church bells drifting over the valley on still Sunday mornings."[26]

That was all gone now. The old Third Company of the *1er étranger* had been stationed in the trenches along the Somme sector in the winter of 1914–1915. It wasn't a pretty sight. The river itself was bisected by the front lines of the French and their British allies to the south and west and the Germans to the north and east. In December 1915 General Joffre had proposed a gigantic offensive to be launched in the Somme sector in the spring of 1916. Initially it was intended to be largely a French show, with the British supporting them on their left flank.[27] But because of the German offensive at Verdun, the French could not commit the number of regiments Joffre had initially hoped to throw at the enemy. Thus by June 1916 the delayed offensive in the Somme sector had increasingly become a British show. The preparations were massive.

After a brutal twenty-kilometer march through blazing heat with a full pack (weighing approximately thirty kilograms, or sixty-six pounds), Alan Seeger and his fellow *légionnaires* arrived at the staging area for the French sector of the great offensive. He quickly recognized that this would "probably be the biggest thing yet."[28] On

July 1, 1916, the Allies went "over the top" early in the morning, following a sustained artillery barrage of the most terrific ferocity. The British Army was full of untried citizen-soldiers fighting in their first battle. Their training had, for the most part, been abysmally lacking in instruction that might have helped them in trench warfare. It seems their sheer numbers, naiveté, and energy were supposed to carry the day once the artillery had finished with its bloody business. The reality was quite different. The Germans, particularly in the front lines, had taken a massive pounding, but once the firing ceased the Germans reemerged to decimate the oncoming British. It's a wonder that any British units were able to seize front-line positions at all. Holding them proved all but impossible.

The Germans had anticipated the attack and planned on launching counterattacks of their own to sweep the survivors from the battlefield. With no food, no water, and no sign of reinforcements, the British attackers were forced to retreat as best they could to their own lines. The losses were appalling. In one sector, two battalions of troops from Sherwood Forest lost 80 percent of their number *killed*.[29] This kind of slaughter for little or no gain was clearly unsustainable, yet the British High Command continued ordering attacks for another five months! The Somme was in many respects a repeat of the ghastly failure at Artois in May–June 1915; once again the generals had failed to recognize that if the attack was going to succeed it would have succeeded on the day it was launched. The subsequent attacks, in which so many men's lives were thrown away, were simply a manifestation of a stubborn unwillingness to admit failure. The heavy initial losses can be attributed to a mistaken understanding of the effect the massed artillery would have on the Germans; but the heavy losses *after* this became clear bordered on the criminal.

The French fared better overall in their sector of the Somme front. That is not to say that their lot was in any way easy, but rather that their losses were not as catastrophic as those of their British allies. On July 1, 1916, the Division Marocaine stormed and held the German front-line trenches opposite them. The *Légion* was called up to reinforce, then relieve, the colonials in front of the small village of Belloy-en-Santerre. On the eve of the battle, Alan Seeger had written a friend that he was "glad to be going in the first wave. If you are in this thing at all it is best to be in to the limit."[30] The Americans had been promised a leave to visit Paris for the Fourth of July, but the exigencies of the war superseded any promises made to them. On the night of July 3 they moved up ready for an attack on the German positions in Belloy-en-Santerre (or what was left of it) the following day. Egyptian *légionnaire* Rif Baer recalled his friend Alan Seeger as "perfectly happy," ready for what lay ahead, and planning a visit to Paris at a later date in lieu of that promised him.[31] The Fourth of July found the Americans awaiting word to go "over the top," across flat farm fields in the sights of German machine-gunners, and take and hold the village. Brooklyn's Christopher Charles, one of the last remaining American volunteers of 1914 still in the *Légion*, had an unparalleled view of the attack, advancing with a machine gun section in support of the first wave:

> July 4 was calm until three o'clock in the afternoon, when our famous seventy-fives began to clear the way for us. The artillery pounded the Germans for more than two hours, and at five o'clock came the order to charge. The boys rose from where they had been lying and started forward. The Germans, seeing us, began a heavy

bombardment with field guns and fusillade with rifles and machine guns, but it did not stop the Legion.... The boys walked at an easy gait until they were within two hundred yards of the enemy. They were then within good range of German rifles and rapid-firers and they began falling fast. When the boys saw their friends falling, they got mad and went forward like a cyclone.[32]

With the German trenches in front of Belloy-en-Santerre now in their hands, the *légionnaires* moved on to the village itself. In twenty minutes of difficult "house to house" fighting in which "every shelter had to be cleared"[33] the *légionnaires* conquered the village and then pursued the retreating Germans nearly three kilometers before the attackers spent themselves. It was a remarkable feat of arms that stood in stark contrast to much of what else had been going on up to that point elsewhere in the Somme offensive. But the cost was high: "The Legion lost in killed, wounded, and missing 25 officers and 844 soldiers," thus sustaining "a 30% casualty rate, in an action considered one of the most glorious in Legion history."[34] Indeed it was, but for the American volunteers of 1914 it represented more than this. It was the end of something.

Alan Seeger had advanced in the first wave, the tallest man in his unit. Rif Baer spotted him across the battlefield. He waved and then "head erect" he ran forward "bayonet fixed" and disappeared.[35] The vanguard of the right flank was cut down by German machine gun fire. Only five of the forty-five men in Seeger's unit survived.[36] He was not among them. Hit by "six explosive bullets,"[37] he crumpled into a shell hole as the second wave advanced past him into the German trenches. Severely wounded in the stomach, Seeger tried to stanch the bleeding, then became delirious.

There was no time for stretcher bearers to extricate him, and he lay there in his final moments in great pain, surrounded by ugliness and death. As historian Tony Geraghty recounts, "Later they heard him cry for water, and his mother. Harvard graduate, Paris poet, Legionnaire no. 19522, Seeger had met his rendezvous with death, and it was neither dulce nor decorum."[38] But in his suffering, in the manner in which he lived his life and died, and in what he believed he had died for, Seeger the man was transformed into Seeger the martyr. On that "disputed barricade" he transcended the war itself. Or rather, he transcended those aspects of it that were sordid, cynical, and devoid of higher meaning.

Today the village of Belloy-en-Santerre sits like an island in a wider sea of flat farmland that stretches on to the horizon, broken here and there by small clumps of trees or structures. It is still as rural as any part of France. A small village school educates all of the community's children in the same shared space. Next to the village church, its steeple twice repaired since Seeger was killed, is a memorial to the poet and his fellow *légionnaires* who died there as well, among them noted poets from other lands. (When it was rebuilt the first time, Alan Seeger's parents donated a bell for the church and planted fruit trees in memory of their son, but both church and trees were destroyed in 1940 when the Germans returned.) After the battle, Seeger's comrades buried him in a common grave outside the village where he fell. It was "later obliterated by a German barrage," and, as Seeger biographer Irving Werstein explains, "An assiduous search over many years revealed no traces of it."[39] Alan Seeger left no relics for pilgrims to venerate. His monument is his poems and the life he led. They speak for themselves.

* * *

When word of Alan Seeger's death reached Paris and New York, initial disbelief—as we have seen, Seeger had been falsely reported killed on a previous occasion—gave way to a profound sense of loss. Seeger, more than anyone else, had been able to articulate to the outside world—and in particular to the United States—what was at stake in France's struggle with Germany. In the weeks that followed, newspapers on both sides of the Atlantic prominently featured stories on Seeger's death, and more importantly on his life. The *New York Sun* placed the story front and center under the headline: *ALAN SEEGER POET WARRIOR DIES FIGHTING FOR FRANCE*. The *Sun*, which had published a number of Seeger's anecdotes of life in the trenches, devoted two columns to him, including an obituary and his poem "Ode in Memory of the American Volunteers Fallen for France." He was described as "one of the first to volunteer" and a "born soldier" whose "enthusiasm for the cause of France, his inherent American sense of humor and his unusual bravery won him the admiration of his comrades and the praise of his superiors."[40] In France, *Le Temps* described him as "one of the most valiant of these Americans willing to fight under the flag of the old ally."[41] Seeger was held up as the embodiment of the dictum of the great French author Alphonse Lamartine's: "Only thought and action together can complement one another."[42] But *Le Figaro* featured perhaps the most moving eulogy to Seeger's memory in print:

> ...a young American poet who deliberately came to fight by our side in France, and was taken while he was

among us, killed at the spring of his life. I ask our sons
not to forget him and their mothers to think about his.

What artists will not be able to express, neither in
marble nor in bronze, because even Michelangelo or
Auguste Rodin would not have been able to do it, the
American poet Alan Seeger clearly wrote....[43]

Seeger penned his last poem in a letter that he wrote to Kenneth
Weeks's mother, Alice, shortly before moving up to the Somme
sector. In it he revealed his unrealized vision of the future he would
not see:

> Beauty of earth, when in thy harmonies
> The cannon's note has ceased to be a part,
> I shall return once more and bring to these
> The worship of an undivided heart.[44]

CHAPTER 11

HAT IN THE RING

For the original American volunteers of 1914, the year 1916 signaled the end of their identity *as a group*. By the beginning of 1917 there were no longer significant numbers of the old guard in any one unit. In addition, the deaths of Victor Chapman in June of 1916, Alan Seeger in July, and finally Kiffin Rockwell in September of that year represented the end of something as well. These men had been the heart and soul of the volunteers of 1914. With them gone, something was lost forever. Yet the light they and their comrades had kindled and nourished for nearly three years on their own would eventually spread across the Atlantic and finally bring the United States into the war to defend civilization.

★ ★ ★

Woodrow Wilson, Alan Seeger's "milk-fed pacifist," won reelection to the White House on November 6, 1916. Election night, November 5, 1916, had begun with great promise for the Republican Party and its candidate, Charles Evans Hughes. The early returns pointed to a Republican victory, but as the vote tally began to come in from the Midwest and finally, the west coast, the possibility of Wilson maintaining his hold on the presidency became less fanciful. In the end, it was California—a state as far removed as was possible from the U-boat menace in the Atlantic, a state in which women voted—that finally tipped the electoral balance in the Democrat's favor.

Wilson had run on the campaign slogan "He Kept Us Out of War." A vote for Wilson was thus a vote for continued U.S. neutrality. No other piece of evidence so convincingly demonstrates Americans' continued reluctance, over two years already into the war, to become directly involved. But a vote for Wilson, ultimately, did not keep the U.S. out of the war. Germany saw to that.

From the perspective of the Kaiser and his generals and diplomats, the U.S. had long ago compromised its neutrality when it meekly submitted to Britain's blockade of German-controlled and German-friendly ports but continued to trade with the Allies. The press coverage of American volunteers openly serving in the trenches and in the skies of France against the German Army only furthered this general impression. Who was Wilson kidding? On February 1, 1917, the German High Command called the president's bluff, launching unrestricted submarine warfare in direct contravention of earlier agreements it had made. Essentially, Germany was at war with the U.S., even if the U.S. was not at war with Germany.

In the weeks that followed, Wilson tried to maintain his policies, but it became increasingly difficult as provocation upon provocation at sea mounted. After severing diplomatic relations with Germany on February 3, 1917, there was little else Wilson could do. His desire to confront Germany over its belligerent policies was tempered by his own prior positions. The *New York Times* reported on February 3, 1917,

> War has not been declared. The President in his address said: "we do not desire any hostile conflict with the German Government. But preparations for war are being made. Many yards have been closed to the public. For the present private shipbuilding concerns and other plants engaged in Government work will take their own precautionary measures...." The President gave a hint of this intention in the address he delivered to Congress today. After he had indicated that he might find it necessary later on that "authority be given to me to use any means that may be necessary for the protection of our seamen and our people to the prosecution of their peaceful and legitimate errands on the high seas," the President said, "I take it for granted that all neutral nations will take the same course."[1]

This tortured rhetoric both encouraged and frustrated interventionists such as Theodore Roosevelt and his close political ally Henry Cabot Lodge. Wilson was moving the U.S. closer to war, but not quickly enough for them, and without the sort of conviction they believed the situation demanded. Then, on February 24, 1917, the British government informed U.S. ambassador Walter Hines Page that they possessed proof that the German foreign ministry had instructed its ambassador in Mexico City to offer military assistance to Mexico in the event of war. In addition, Germany had pledged to restore territory lost by Mexico to the U.S. in the peace that it would dictate once it had emerged victorious over the Allies. This was the notorious "Zimmermann note," named for the German Foreign Minister Arthur Zimmermann, who had conceived the idea. British intelligence had intercepted the note in January 1917 and waited to share it with Wilson until it would have the maximum effect. Essentially, Germany was hedging its bets in the likely event that the U.S. declared war as a result of the resumption of unrestricted submarine warfare. Skeptics both then and now have claimed the note the British had intercepted was a forgery. But the German foreign minister himself admitted on the record, in the *Reichstag* itself, that it was genuine.[2] Wilson was informed of the contents of the intercepted message on February 24, 1917. It was then released to the general public on February 28. War—the war that Bob Scanlon, Jack Bowe, David King, and Bill Thaw had been fighting since 1914—now seemed almost impossible for the United States to resist.

* * *

The fighting in Champagne and at Verdun and the Somme had taken its toll on the volunteers of 1914. Many of the survivors simply were no longer the men they had been in 1914. Many others had been killed. James Bach and Frank Musgrave were in German prisoner-of-war camps. Spanish-American War veteran John Bowe had returned to active duty in 1916 after a long convalescence. Along with fellow Champagne veteran Jack Cordonier, who had also been in hospital, Bowe was sent to the 163rd Regiment in the Vosges. Bowe was now nearly fifty years old.

The 163rd was "composed almost entirely of men from southern France. Most had been enfeebled from bad wounds, or were not quite young enough to be in an attack regiment, but were steady and dependable to hold trenches."[3] Bowe would serve seven months in the front lines before his body finally broke down on him. The fighting in this rugged sector of the Vosges was particularly nasty. As Bowe later recounted, "the trenches were so close together we fought with grenades instead of rifles."[4] The intensity of the

John "Jack" Bowe. Spanish-American War veteran; ex-mayor of Canby, Minnesota; father of four; *légionnaire*; soldier of France.

combat was primarily the result of the fact that the 163rd held the peak known as the *Hartmannsweillerkopf*, from which all of Alsace was visible. Bowe summarized his experience high in the Vosges in his memoir of the war: "We were beyond civilization. Not a flower, a garden, a cow, a chicken, a house with a door or window, or roof, not a civilian or a woman was to be seen.... We had the Boche part of the time, bad weather all the time...."[5]

Reflecting on this wretched setting, John Bowe later penned one of the most vivid descriptions of life in the trenches to come out of the war:

The soldier acquires the habit of noticing little things. He sees a small, starved flower, struggling for sunshine and strength, alongside the trench. He wonders why it chose such an inhospitable home. Next day, there is no flower, no trench—just an immense, gaping hole in the torn ground. He watches the rats, Why are they so impudent and important? He grows so accustomed to them, he does not even squirm, when they run across him in the night. He knows they have enough camp offal and dead men's bodies—they do not eat the living. He watches the cat with interest. She is an old timer and has seen regiments come and go. Her owners are in exile—they have no home—the Germans took it. So, pussy, a lady of good taste, dwells with the French soldiers.[6]

From their position on the peak, the 163rd may have relied almost exclusively on the grenade in attacking the German lines, but the Germans showed a degree of imagination in the various trench-to-trench projectiles they hurled into the French lines. Using trench mortars they threw "aerial torpedoes, crapouillots, and bombs the size of a stovepipe" and others that resembled a "two-gallon demijohn"[7] at the French. As Bowe explained, "They came slow. We could see them—the wide-nosed torpedoes coming direct, the stovepipes hurtling end over end.... We would dodge for one but a half dozen might drop before we could look around."[8] The German heavy artillery also peppered the French positions atop the *Hartmannsweillerkopf*, wreaking great destruction: "Half a dozen men are taking comfort in the shelter of a dugout. The next instant, five are one hundred feet in the air, snuffed out, torn into atoms. But one is left, staring, mouth open."[9]

From their grim post, Bowe and Cordonnier witnessed the final aerial combat of their former comrade, Kiffin Rockwell. His plane would crash at the foot of the mountain.[10]

Remarkably, Bowe and his comrades held onto the peak (there was still something to be said for occupying the high ground in battle, as the Germans had demonstrated at Vimy Ridge in 1915). However, rheumatism finally forced Bowe out of combat altogether. Following another convalescence, he was sent to a territorial unit in the rear, the 92nd, made up of men from forty to fifty-five years of age. For the remainder of his service in the French Army, Bowe performed manual labor: "He helped build roads, dig trenches, unloaded coal and other supplies at the railway stations behind the lines."[11] One night in 1917, after unloading coal in heavy snow with freezing hands, Bowe finally couldn't take it any longer. When the unit's doctor failed to respond to his pleas, Bowe, by his own admission, "went to pieces."[12] After his breakdown he was formally "invalided" out of the army, and eventually made his way home to the United States.

* * *

The country that he had left in 1914 was greatly changed. It had been transformed by war. On April 2, 1917, President Woodrow Wilson had called Congress into extraordinary session to address its members on a matter of the most serious consequence. Over two months since Germany had announced the commencement of submarine warfare, and over one month since being made aware of the Zimmerman note, the president finally decided to ask for a declaration of war. The news was no surprise, but it still had Washington abuzz, such was the gravity of the moment. Wilson had carefully crafted a message that he would read that night, framing his startling about-face on the question of war with Germany in the context of a larger cause than simply national self-interest. The speech was Wilson at his very best. He first summarized the situation at sea and his efforts to make Germany adhere to its agreements. No one could accuse Wilson of not trying to avoid war with Germany. But its leaders had chosen a path that forced the U.S. to either declare war or submit:

> The present German submarine warfare against commerce is a warfare against mankind. It is a war against all nations. American ships have been sunk, American lives taken, in ways which it has stirred us very deeply to learn of, but the ships and people of other neutral and friendly nations have been sunk and overwhelmed in the waters in the same way. There has been no discrimination. The challenge is to all mankind. Each nation must decide for itself how it will meet it. The choice we make for ourselves must be made with a moderation of counsel and a temperateness of judgment befitting our character and our motives as a nation. We must put excited feeling away. Our motive will not be revenge or the victorious assertion of the physical might of the nation, but only the vindication of right, of human right, of which we are only a single champion.[13]

In asking Congress to declare war, Wilson took the grievances of the U.S. and linked them inextricably with the rights of all nations, and all men, in the face of the nakedly autocratic and militaristic power that threatened the world with its limitless ambitions. He pointed out to those assembled that the "wrongs against which we now array ourselves are no common wrongs; they cut to the very roots of human life."[14] The applause that evening was thunderous. The Democrats backed their leader; the Republicans, for the most part, were encouraged by what they had heard. Some sat impassively, more disturbed than inspired by what they were hearing, but they were a distinct minority. The U.S. was going to war because, in perhaps Wilson's most enduring words, "The world must be made safe for democracy. Its peace must be planted upon the tested foundations of political liberty."[15] The fact that in Russia the Czar had recently abdicated and a new provisional government had pledged elections for later in the year, was a convenient turn of events for Wilson. This enabled him to frame the struggle as a stark contrast between democracy on the one hand and autocracy on the other.

Wilson closed on a somewhat somber note. War would mean sacrifice. It was not something one embarked upon lightly—if nothing else, the last two years and eight months in Europe had demonstrated that. The president admitted, "It is a fearful thing to lead this great peaceful people into war," and not just any war but rather the "most terrible and disastrous of all wars" with "civilization itself seeming to be in the balance."[16] It's curious to think what Bill Thaw or John Bowe would have made of these powerful closing words in Wilson's message, if they read them. They had grasped with absolute clarity that civilization was in the balance back in August of 1914. It was heartening to see that Wilson had finally brought the U.S. into the war, but they could certainly be forgiven for asking what had taken him so long.

Within days both houses of Congress voted to declare war on Germany. Uncle Sam's hat was now definitively in the ring. But what would this mean exactly? When looking back at 1917, Americans of today need first to try and forget the large defense establishment of the twenty-first century. The United States did possess a world-class navy. Its army, however, was small and poorly equipped. Only once in its history had the United States mobilized a significant percentage of its population to fight a war. Though there were many Civil War veterans still living in 1917, Americans for the most part had no experience fighting a war on the scale that it had been raging in Europe since 1914. In many respects, commander-in-chief Wilson's military organization was similar to that of the Spanish-American War in 1898—that is to say, unprepared. There were 127,588 officers and enlisted men in the U.S. Army when war was declared. These forces were supplemented by a poorly trained and often physically unfit National Guard of 80,446 men.[17] The United States' aerial forces numbered a mere handful of planes that were embarrassingly backward by 1917 standards. Any kind of meaningful American contribution on the Western Front would certainly be some time away.

Germany was counting on that. They knew that the U.S. was in no position to fight a war in France in 1917—and perhaps not even in 1918. For his part, Wilson initially seemed to have believed that the U.S. could limit its role to supplying the Allies and fighting the Germans at sea. The Europeans soon disabused him of this notion. Both France and Britain were reaching a critical stage in the war. Mutiny had swept much of the French Army in 1917 following the disastrous Nivelle Offensive. The mutiny had been suppressed, but in April 1917 the restoration of order in the trenches seemed more indefinite than permanent. Britain too, was absolutely stretched. Its riches had been greatly depleted to fight the war. Essentially, what Wilson's new allies (Wilson preferred to call the

United States an "associated power" rather than an ally) were telling him was that they might lose the war. The uncertain situation in Russia also took a turn for the worse when the provisional government's great offensive against Germany sputtered and died in July 1917. Thus what had initially seemed to call for a relatively limited American role, now seemed to demand a gigantic U.S. commitment. The U.S. would have to raise and train an army of millions of men and safely transport it across the Atlantic before Germany could win the war. This was a daunting task, to put it mildly.

A call for one million volunteers went out, but when the number of new recruits initially fell far short of what was required, conscription was enacted by Congress. Legitimate worries over whether the draft would lead to societal unrest plagued the government. In the end, though, most of the 2.8 million American men who received their notice reported for duty at the specified time and place, much to the great relief of Wilson and the U.S. High Command. There were not insignificant numbers of socialists actively resisting the draft, most notably their leader, sixty-three-year-old Eugene Debs—but their resistance did not seriously disrupt it. Debs was eventually tried and convicted under the sedition provisions of the Espionage Act and

General John J. Pershing, commander of the American Expeditionary Force in France.

received a sentence of ten years in prison.[18] There were also the so-called "shirkers" who took jobs in the defense industry to avoid military service—notable among them the baseball player Babe Ruth and the prizefighter Jack Dempsey. But by the end of 1917, the U.S. had approximately 1.5 million men under arms. But most weren't in France. And that was where the war was going to be won or lost.

As overall commander of this new army, eventually known as the American Expeditionary Force (AEF), Wilson chose a tall, mustachioed Missourian with a ramrod-straight posture named John Pershing. He was not necessarily the obvious choice. General Leonard Wood was seen by many as the more likely candidate for this difficult post, but his close ties to the Republican leadership, including Theodore Roosevelt, disqualified him in the president's estimation. Pershing looked like a soldier, he had no overt politics of his own, and he had acquitted himself with some degree of distinction when leading the frustrating Punitive Expedition into Mexico in 1916 to try and apprehend Pancho Villa. In May 1917 Pershing secretly departed New York for Europe, arriving first in England on June 8. Addressing the assembled press, Pershing, "said he and his men were glad to participate 'in this great war for civilization.'"[19] Five days later, Pershing and his staff arrived to great fanfare in the French port of Boulogne. The French people expected a savior, and Pershing certainly looked the part. In Paris, Pershing and the modest-sized first contingent of the AEF were greeted with near euphoria that reached its climax when Pershing held the French tricolor, brought it to his lips, and kissed it. In a country and city that nearly invented romance, this romantic gesture touched something elemental in the French soul.

In 1917, David King was still fighting in the French Army. The 170th Regiment, *les Hirondelles de la Mort*, had been sent into the Somme inferno in August 1916 and had taken part in the assault on Clery with great loss of life. The shelling from the German lines was ferocious. King recounted a young soldier "standing with his back to the parapet, breathing spasmodically, a glassy look in his eye and the whole back of his head blown off."[20] A wound in the groin eventually forced King to seek medical attention. He endured a harrowing ride back to the rear and a decidedly unromantic hospital experience before being discharged. As King explained, "Military hospitals are wonderful things—in novels. Spotless sunlit wards, sympathetic doctors, charming Red Cross nurses.... Emergency hospitals don't come up to scratch.... Doctors are overworked—efficient but hectic; and the charming nurse is replaced by some fat old orderly, who, as a great favor, smuggles in wine— at a price."[21]

Judged unfit for further duty in the infantry, King was placed in artillery school in anticipation of his transfer to a new outfit. The school was in Vincennes, near Paris, and King and a few collaborators figured out quickly how to get out of the barracks by marching out as if on duty. When challenged at the gate, they replied "'Fatigue to get hay!'" then they "swung smartly out of the barracks, dispersing two hundred yards down the street, for the four corners of Paris."[22] King recalled a night with William Dugan, the shoe manufacturer's son from Rochester, New York, and some Canadian Highlanders that started at a bar called "The Hole in the Wall" and devolved into a mock naval battle with carriages on the Champs-Elysées. King was named "admiral" and his "flagship" was amply stocked with "rum, whiskey, and H. E. Brandy."[23]

The local gendarmes put up a fight, but ultimately were no match for this "flotilla."

Things were more grim for David King at Vincennes. A number of military executions took place at the barracks during this time—usually men found guilty of desertion or cowardice. It was an ugly business, and King's role was to stand guard as the condemned was brought before the firing squad. To someone that had seen so much death on the battlefield, as King had, there was a pointlessness to these proceedings. Later the notorious German spy Mata Hari was executed at Vincennes.

Back at the Front, King was placed in a Sound Ranging section. The unit's task was to assist the gunners in improving their accuracy and to help them determine where German artillery fire was coming from. As King admitted, the unit was a group of "mixed pickles" thirty-five strong, with a handful of mathematics specialists and young kids—otherwise "we were all cripples."[24] This sort of duty was a long way indeed from being one of the *troupes d'attaque*. Like the much older John Bowe, David King was now seen as only being useful for certain types of support duty. He was a very different man from the one who had marched across Paris to the Gare Saint-Lazare in August 1914. Lingering issues with his right eye as a result of a shell blast meant that a career in the "aviation" was not open to him. The French Army clearly felt it had gotten the best it was going to get out of King. It looked like he would end the war cooped up in an observation post, measuring wind speed and temperature for the French artillery.

But with the entry of the United States into the war, King's opportunities expanded. The U.S. Army accepted applications from Americans abroad to serve in their own country's military. Initially, King was given the runaround, but ultimately—likely due to the fact that he was a member of a wealthy and prominent family—King was summoned to Paris to appear before a three-member panel of officer-examiners. By his own admission, they really didn't know what to make of him, but he was recommended for a first lieutenant's commission nonetheless.

But King's was an unusual story. Those Americans still serving in *la Légion Étrangère*—the "advanced guard of the American forces" as they referred to themselves—had written as a group offering their services to President Wilson, only to be coldly dismissed: "The subject of utilization of the services of Americans serving abroad has received the careful consideration of the War Department in a number of instances, and the conclusion has been reached that it is not deemed for the best interest of the United States for the War Department to request the discharge of the Americans serving in the Allied armies...."[25]

For artist Jack Casey, mechanic Christopher Charles, and their fellow remaining volunteers of 1914, this was a bitter pill to have to swallow. Here were men who had seen and acted on the wisdom of fighting to stop German aggression long before their president. Here were men who had learned, in the most difficult circumstances possible, lessons in trench warfare that could only be acquired through actual combat. And yet it seemed that Uncle Sam had no use for them. But over time, many of the Americans serving in the *Légion* or with the French Army would be incorporated into the ranks of the AEF, including West Pointer Charles Sweeney. Sweeney, who had drilled the motley collection of poets, painters, and adventurers in front of the Palais Royal in August 1914 entered the AEF with a major's commission and rose to the rank of lieutenant colonel by the war's end. For his part, King finally received his actual transfer in December 1917 and spent his first night as a U.S.

Army officer in a French officers' mess before boarding a train the next day. He bid farewell to the French Army with a final salute: "*Vive l'Amérique! Vive la France! Adieu—bonne chance! À bas les Boches! Adieu, adieu!*"

★ ★ ★

The Boches, for their part, were busy negotiating a peace treaty with Bolshevik Russia. Sensing the moment was propitious, the German High Command had offered transport and money to Bolshevik leader Vladimir Lenin in 1917 in the hope that he might seize power and pull Russia out of the war. The Germans' investment in Lenin succeeded beyond their wildest dreams. After taking power in a carefully planned *coup d'état*, Lenin quickly moved to pull Russia out of the war in order to consolidate the Bolsheviks' power back home. After months of haggling, in March 1918 the advancing Germans forced Russia to cede vast amounts of its European territory to Germany and satellite states that it would establish on Russia's borders. The Treaty of Brest-Litovsk was a "victor's peace" in the truest sense of the term. If one were ever to wonder what peace with a victorious Germany would have looked like in the west, one need look no further than this treaty—a fact certainly not lost on the leaders of the Allied countries.

This treaty was crucial in the German High Command's strategy to finally win the war because it allowed them to transfer millions of battle-hardened veterans from the Eastern Front to the Western Front, erasing any manpower advantage that the Allies enjoyed. The capture of Paris and with it the ability to dictate terms to the Allies seemed a very real possibility. On March 21, 1918, the Germans' great Spring Offensive began. General Pershing, who did not yet have his forces up to full strength, made it clear to the French and British that his men were not ready—and even when they were, they would fight only as an American Army, and not be fed piecemeal into the lines. In the weeks and months that followed, as the Germans continued to hammer the Allied line, Pershing's resolve on this issue would be sorely tested, but he would not be moved, at least not to any large degree.

The mix of volunteers and draftees, black and white, found France to be a welcoming place in which their horizons were greatly broadened. For many, even the time spent in a city such as New York where they embarked for their trans-Atlantic crossing was completely out of their realm of experience. France and Paris were exponentially more so. If one could have gotten all of them to reflect on what they were doing there, the answers likely would have been a mix of patriotism, the desire to get away from home, and a difficult-to-articulate idealism fired by President Wilson's appeal. The volunteers, in particular, were more susceptible to Wilson's rhetoric. At Princeton, where his word and example carried such great weight with the student body, officer candidates drilled in expectation of receiving their appointments. F. Scott Fitzgerald recounted those heady, anxious days in his semi-autobiographical novel, *This Side of Paradise*: "…war rolled swiftly up the beach and washed the sands where Princeton played. Every night the gymnasium echoed as platoon after platoon swept over the floor and shuffled out the basket-ball markings…. In Princeton everyone bantered in public and told themselves privately that their deaths at least would be heroic. The literary students read Rupert Brooke passionately; the lounge lizards worried over whether the government would permit English-cut uniform for officers; a few of the hopelessly lazy wrote the War Department, seeking an easy commission and a soft berth."[26]

One of those who answered Wilson's call to help make the world safe for democracy: John Elco of Donora, Pennsylvania, AEF.

But most Americans who fought in World War I weren't Ivy Leaguers. These young Americans from all walks of life were embarking on an adventure in which they would set the world to rights, or so they were told. The ships that took them across the ocean braved Atlantic gales and the ever-present danger of German torpedoes. In one of the more remarkable though often underappreciated feats of World War I, two million American soldiers were safely transported to France with minimal loss of life. Homesick and seasick, the "doughboys," as they soon were called, quickly absorbed the beauty and antiquity of the French countryside once ashore. Many also acquired a taste for French wine—this, at a time when the U.S. itself was in the process of adopting Prohibition. There were many pretty French girls without beaus to court them; many widows; many orphans. In general, the U.S. troops had a good time, but underneath the surface gaiety was a sadness that one didn't have to look very hard to see and feel. In a sense, France was one big, beautiful, haunted house. Too many had been lost. Too many had suffered. Too many were grieving. But by the spring of 1918 the long-awaited Americans were finally there in force. Alan Seeger's call to his countrymen was about to be answered.

Germany's vaunted Spring Offensive of 1918 was in fact a series of thrusts over a period of months in which different sectors of the Allied line were targeted and penetrated. In late May 1918, the situation for the French Army was critical. Driven off the Chemin des Dames which it had recaptured in 1917, it now retreated toward the Marne River, where Joffre had made his stand in 1914. Once across this river in large enough numbers, the German Army could fall on Paris within a matter of days. It was at this point that the AEF got into the war in a serious and decisive manner for the first time. American troops had served alongside the French on the Chemin des Dames to gain experience in trench warfare firsthand, and at Cantigny on May 28, 1918, the AEF had launched its first modest-sized offensive against the Germans.

The town of Château-Thierry on the Marne represented the deepest penetration by the German Army. It was here that the U.S. Third Division joined the French in a heroic stand beginning on May 31, 1918. Then three days later the American counterattack, carried out by both "doughboys" and a contingent of U.S. Marines in nearby Belleau Wood, began to push the Germans back. The cost in human life was appalling for what was in certain respects a small action. But the immediate danger to Paris had been averted. The American contribution at Château-Thierry and Belleau Wood had large-scale significance: What if the Americans hadn't been there to help stop and then force back the Germans? Small actions, certainly, but in the larger historical context of the war, small actions with big consequences. Regardless, though, the overall German threat remained.

The German High Command had decided on a massive blow to be directed at the British in Flanders in July 1918, with a feint towards the Marne to temporarily occupy the French Army and ensure it could not come to its British ally's aid. But much to their surprise the feint was far more successful than anticipated. The German High Command sensed opportunity. The decisive moment had arrived: the Germans would either capture Paris and win the war, or they would be stopped and forced to eventually seek the best terms they could get from the Allies. At this crucial juncture, the French, with General Charles Mangin and the Division Marocaine playing a leading role, decided to hit back, hard. The U.S. First and Second Divisions joined them. On July 18, 1918, the "doughboys" attacked the Germans at Soissons with remarkable ferocity, taking heavy losses. The Germans, caught flat-footed, rallied, but never fully recovered from this counterattack. In the annals of U.S. military history the Battle of Soissons rarely receives the sort of attention reserved for Catigny, Château-Thierry, Belleau Wood, and the first and only major U.S. offensive of the war in the Meuse-Argonne. But it should. More than any other engagement the AEF was involved in, it was at Soissons that it made its greatest battlefield contribution to the Allied victory in the war. After Soissons, the German High Command abandoned its planned offensive in Flanders and never made another serious attempt to break the Allied line. The best it could hope for was to hold onto as much French territory as possible and negotiate the best terms it could get. The Battle of Soissons was eventually lumped together with a number of other engagements being fought at approximately the same time that are now known collectively as the Second Battle of the Marne, which represented the high water mark for the Germans. Their gamble to win the war had failed, and millions of U.S. soldiers were now in France, with millions more slated to follow them. Germany was going to lose the war. Paris would be spared, and civilization saved.

In the air, the U.S. war effort was, in the beginning, embarrassingly behind the times. Though the expectations of an airborne armada of American planes never materialized, the U.S. did eventually design and mass-produce the Curtis JN or "Jenny" for training its pilots. But in France it was forced to purchase French aircraft if it wanted to get into the fight. The pilots of SPA 124 (named for their new SPAD VIIs), the famed Lafayette Escadrille, had tried to offer their services as a group to the AEF, only to face discouraging and demoralizing delays. No group of Americans in France was better known, or had more specific skills to offer, yet they fought on as a French unit until finally, in January 1918, the pilots began to receive word of their appointments to the United States Army Air Service. Squadron ace Raoul Lufberry was given command of the new 94th pursuit squadron. With its famous "hat in the ring" logo painted on the fuselages of all its planes, the 94th became the most successful American squadron in the war, with former racecar driver Eddie Rickenbacker eventually eclipsing Lufberry as the greatest of all American aces (Lufberry was killed when he leapt from his flaming plane a mile above a small French village named Maron). Bill Thaw was given command of the new 103rd pursuit squadron, composed of the remaining pilots of the Lafayette Escadrille. The famous Indian head logo was painted on the fuselages of its planes. Of the volunteers of 1914, only former playboy Thaw, racecar driver Bob Soubiron, and the diminutive William Dugan, the shoe manufacturer's son from Rochester, New York, remained in the air. In July, 1918, Thaw was promoted to command an entire pursuit group composed of four separate squadrons. The 103rd final commander was Bob Soubiron, who had been there on August 25, 1914,

Bob Soubiron standing next to his SPAD XIII armed with twin mounted Vickers machine guns.

when the Americans marched across Paris to the Gare Saint-Lazare. Flying first the SPAD VII, then the sleek SPAD XIII, by war's end the squadron could boast of over forty confirmed kills, with an equal number unconfirmed. Among its many aces was its first commander, Bill Thaw of Pittsburgh, Pennsylvania.

By war's end in November 1918, airpower had begun to be used in a manner that anticipated what was to come in the 1930s and 1940s, with coordinated ground-air operations and mass aerial bombardments. Even from the vantage point of 1918, the Caudrons that the original American pilots had flown seemed to be from another, vanished age. Which, of course, they were.

★ ★ ★

There would be no return to the front in American uniform for David King. His wounds, including the lingering condition with his right eye, meant either desk duty or a role with intelligence. Fortunately for King, it was the latter. Posted to G2B, also known as the counterespionage section, he soon found himself in Bern, Switzerland, ostensibly to look into matters related to American prisoners of war, but in reality to check on his German counterparts there: "Bern was a maelstrom of intrigue and comedy. Most of the diplomatic corps lived at the Bellevue Palace. Allies on one side of the dining room—enemies on the other. Mutual glaring and hate fests before meals. In the lounge every other chair was occupied by a widespread newspaper, from which stuck out mysterious legs. If conversation turned to interesting topics, a pair of ears would protrude beyond the paper, betraying the presence of the enemy."[27]

The absurdity of Bern was replaced by some genuine counterintelligence work in its lovelier sister city of Geneva, which King described as being "filled with deserters, professional spies, renegades and dope fiends." The shadow war there was played for keeps.

★ ★ ★

When the real war ended in November 1918, King helped organize the repatriation of his countrymen held in German prisoner of war camps. Two of the thousands of American prisoners that made their way back to France were James Bach and "Lucky" Frank Musgrave.

The war's end meant very different things to different people. Germany, with its Kaiser abdicated and a new republic in place, felt it deserved the type of peace given to France after Napoleon had been defeated in 1814–1815—that is to say, a peace in which the nation's political system and its autocratic and militaristic leaders were held responsible, not an entire people. Woodrow Wilson seemed to have supported this idea in his call for a peace without victors. But for France, it was a victory not only of the nation but of the race—and at a tremendous price: France had mobilized a total of 8.41 million men to fight the war. Of these, fully 60 percent were either killed or wounded. In comparison, Britain lost 37 percent of those mobilized killed or wounded; and Germany 41 percent.[28] The United States, in contrast, whose "decisive addition to Allied strength," as French historian Marc Ferro explained, was "the determining factor in the Central Powers' defeat,"[29] emerged from the war in a position of strength. America had entered the war with an enormous industrial advantage, a key contribution to the Allied cause. In 1915 the Central Powers had held a 355–346 edge (in millions of tons) in coal; a 24–13 edge in steel, and a 25–16 edge in iron. In 1918 the Allies, including the United States, outpaced the Central Powers 841–340, 58–16, and 50–15, respectively.[30] Yet because of the enormous suffering of its people, and because the majority of the fighting had taken place on its soil, France possessed a moral authority that compensated for its weakness in real terms. Its leader, octogenarian Georges Clemenceau, wanted reparations and a permanently weakened Germany, so this sort of thing could never happen again. Britain, for its part, had spent so much of its young men's blood and so much of its treasure in meeting the German challenge that at the very least it expected to be permitted to compensate itself at the expense of Germany and its allies. Nineteen-eighteen would see the beginning of the British myth that it had won the war. At sea, with the crippling blockade imposed by the Royal Navy, this certainly had some merit. But in France and Flanders, one is hard pressed to find a decisive British victory. Only the rear guard actions at Mons and Le Cateau and the stand on the Marne in 1914 would seem to justify the British claim. The so-called "Blackest Day" of the German Army, which resulted from British General Douglas Haig's counter-offensive near Amiens in August 1918, occurred *after* the German offensive was already broken by the French and Americans at Soissons. And one could make a case that Haig should have been court-martialed for his insistence on continuing near suicidal attacks at the Somme and in Flanders earlier in the war, long after it was clear the larger objectives there could not be realized. The British Prime Minister, Welshman David Lloyd George, recognized all this, but never sacked Haig. He was a pragmatist. The British people had suffered too—an entire generation ripped up from the roots while still in full flower. Victory was not enough. In the heat of the moment, Britons and their leader felt Germany must pay as well.

President Wilson arrived in this roiling European political environment in December 1918. Earlier in the year he had issued his so-called "Fourteen Points," in which he claimed the moral high ground from Germany's leaders. The document was a mix of broad statements of policy and detailed agenda items regarding a post-war European settlement. It was the former that got the world's attention. His strong remarks regarding "open covenants openly arrived at," "freedom of the seas," and "self-determination"[31] for all peoples inspired people the world over, as did his call for a new international peacekeeping body, a "League of Nations" to ensure a world war would never happen again.

In the end, Woodrow Wilson failed to achieve most of his cherished ideas. Germany's new leaders were never invited to participate in the negotiations, and France and Britain wore the inexperienced Wilson down until he was left with little but his now-flawed League. In retrospect, it's easy to recognize the errors

Wilson made. The overwhelming public adulation he experienced personally in Europe's capitals convinced him he had the continent's people on his side. But the continent's people had conflicting aims. He failed to include any prominent Republicans in his delegation even though he knew he would need their votes in the Senate to ratify the treaty he was negotiating. Theodore Roosevelt died suddenly while Wilson was in Paris, but Henry Cabot Lodge would have made an outstanding foil to the hard-boiled Clemenceau and slippery Lloyd George. This would have meant Wilson would have had to share the spotlight with a rival that he loathed, but by letting his rival take ownership of the treaty he would have almost certainly assured its passage. In the end, for all of Wilson's inspiring and idealistic rhetoric, he could be quite petty. And physically he was not a well man. If he had stayed in Washington he could have conserved his strength and blamed any shortcomings in the negotiations on Lodge, but it was not in his character to do so. As Thomas Fleming, in his revisionist history of Wilson and the war, explained, "He saw himself leading the entire world to a new spiritual level, a global incarnation of American idealism. But he was a very tired man. His words did not come close to matching his vision, nor did the text of the league, which had not a single soaring phrase...."[32]

Perhaps the most insightful analysis of Wilson came from the two men with whom he spent the most time, negotiating for months in Paris. Clemenceau: "I never saw a man talk more like Jesus Christ and act more like Lloyd George." And Lloyd George's assessment: "He believed in mankind but distrusted all men...."[33]

The Treaty of Versailles officially ended World War I, but it left Germany humiliated and angry. The United States never joined the League of Nations, and Britain soon withdrew from Europe as well, leaving France to enforce the treaty on its own. Wilson suffered a stroke and served out the remainder of his term an invalid. Fashionable opinion in Britain turned against the treaty when a member of the delegation to Paris quit in disgust over its crippling reparations and then wrote a pamphlet outlining his criticisms: economist John Maynard Keynes's *The Economic Consequences of the Peace* was widely read and set the debate over the treaty, reparations, and German war guilt for decades to come, even convincing the ever malleable Lloyd George that Germany had been no more to blame for causing the war than any other country. It was not until Fritz Fischer's work in the 1960s–70s that this consensus was finally challenged and overturned, at least to a certain extent. And, of course, the historical assessment of World War I was highly colored after 1945 by what Adolf Hitler had done. Some blamed the treaty, while others saw continuity between the Kaiser's Germany and Hitler's Third Reich. The debate lingers.

For the United States, World War I soon soured public opinion toward not only Wilson and the treaty but Europe more generally. Within months, the great boom of the Twenties was on, Wilson was out, and idealism was passé.

Over one hundred thousand "doughboys" never made it home from France. About half died in combat, the other half from disease, as the Spanish Influenza epidemic took its toll in the barracks and in the trenches. In Paris, a new generation of expatriates would find inspiration in its streets, museums, and cafés. But for those that had been there before 1914, it wasn't the same. The artist Jack Casey, who had finally been accepted into the AEF only to be refused active duty and asked to lead its art department, left Paris. Finding "Montparnasse spoiled" he "sought inspiration for his work in Cuba and Spain."[34] Casey and his comrades had won, but ultimately they couldn't save what they had fought for. It was already past them, back there somewhere before August 1914.

EPILOGUE

The surviving volunteers of 1914, for the most part, returned from whence they had come after the war. The indomitable Bob Scanlon, considered a good luck charm by his wartime companions, returned to the ring to resume his career.

What German bullets and shells could not do, a woman nearly did—he was shot by his jealous ex-lover in 1920 but survived.

William Thaw would play a role in laying the groundwork for the U.S. Air Force before returning to his native Pittsburgh. Eugene Bullard had gained considerable fame as a French *pilote de chasse*, but would find no interest in his skills when he offered them to the embarrassed Americans. It would seem Edmund Gros and Woodrow Wilson were not alone in their bigotry. "Skipper" Paul Pavelka transferred to fly in Greece in 1917 on the Salonika Front. In one of the most unbelievable turns of events surrounding the volunteers of

Bob Scanlon.

1914, this son of a farmer was killed when trying to ride a friend's unruly mount. A man who had escaped death in the grand assaults in Artois and Champagne, a man who had brought a broken plane with a flaming wing into a crash landing in No Man's Land, had died when a horse fell on him. After publishing his own memoir in 1918, Jack Bowe drifted back into the obscurity from which he had emerged in 1914, his duty done. And Paul Rockwell would document it all. Were they foolish dreamers? Sober-minded realists? Reckless adventurers? Ultimately these distinctions matter less than the whole of their story. And it's important to keep in mind that history has vindicated their personal assessments about the situation when they initially volunteered. They did not abandon their own judgment. There is a lesson in that for all people.

In the autumn of 1918, as the war was moving inexorably toward defeat for Germany, Madeleine Chevrel wrote a front page article for *Le Gaulois*. She had just finished reading a copy of Alan Seeger's collected poems. Intoxicated with the anticipation of victory, she reflected on what they meant to her:

He composed them as a long love letter to the sweet French land. And he sang this land until he died. I opened this book and I felt I heard the music of the stars.... the soldier-poet is not the dead young man in a village in the Somme, his soul is still in the wind, running to victory....[1]

* * *

After the war, both the French people and the American expatriate community made lasting gestures to the memory of the Americans that had fallen under French colors. The most grandiose was a memorial to the pilots of the Lafayette Escadrille built in a small wood near the village of Marnes-la-Coquette in 1928, just west of Paris. A grand triumphal arch is framed by stately columns on either side. There are references to Washington and Lafayette and the Revolution. In a crypt below the arch are the coffins of the pilots that perished. Most contain actual remains. Some are empty. A stained glass window filters the light that falls on the floor below the coffins. Even on a warm spring day, the entrance to the crypt is cold.

The *Place des États-Unis* is located in the 16th arrondissement of Paris. There is a park there. At one entrance is a statue with a winged figure bringing two comrades-in-arms together at its base. Behind the statue the smell of urine, left by some drunk or a homeless person, is unmistakable. There are names etched in stone, some fading with time.

On July 4, 1923, the French people unveiled a monument to memorialize and honor the American volunteers who had sacrificed for France, and "for civilization" itself, in the war. The names of the Americans who were killed fighting for France are inscribed on the reverse side of the monument. A statue by sculptor Jean Boucher with the likeness of Alan Seeger stands atop the monument. In an interview after its first viewing, Boucher explained why: "From the moment the commission came to me, I have been inspired by thought of the young poet, Alan Seeger, who it was my good fortune to know and love. It was inevitable that I should, in seeking to express the essential qualities of the spirit of these young American volunteers in the first dark and terrible days of the Great War—the qualities that so entirely command the veneration of the French people—reproduce as symbol of the central altar fire of France's memorial the head and the features of the author of 'I Have a Rendezvous With Death.' And, dear friend, I have a strong impression, that as time goes on both France and America will take from this modest reminder of the days that tried men's souls as they were never tried before, some suggestion of the grand truth that in nobility of these devoted sons shone the true soul of America."[2] Boucher statue's arm is raised in greeting…or is it a farewell?

Memorial to the American Volunteers, *Place des États-Unis*, Paris.

ACKNOWLEDGMENTS

It has been such an enjoyable experience researching and writing this book. There are many people I would like to thank, but my wife Katie comes first. She is my unwavering ally. I would also like to thank my brother Josh for proofreading each chapter and suggesting changes that improved the narrative. Thanks also to my mother, Carolyn Hanna, for her encouragement and support.

In addition I would like to thank my agent, Farley Chase, for believing in this project, and for putting in so much time making sure we got the proposal right. Most agents wouldn't put that much effort into one writer's proposal. I am fortunate that he does things the old fashioned way. I'd also like to thank my publisher, Alex Novak, for recognizing what a good story this is, and my editor, Elizabeth Kantor, for forcing me to think about every aspect of it. I hope my writing does it justice.

In France, Claire Khelfaoui was the researcher-interpreter-fixer-translator extraordinaire. I cannot say enough about how thorough she has been throughout. And her studio in Montmartre made it possible for my wife to join me in Paris, which was wonderful. Jean Luc Despocq, groundskeeper at the Chateau du Blanc Sablon, shared his knowledge of the original chateau with us, and made us feel very welcome. Yves Fohlen at the Musée du Chemin des Dames / Caverne du Dragon also was very generous with his time and expertise. I admire his passion for, and knowledge of, his subject. I also would like to express how pleasant our research trip as a whole was. Whether in Picardy, Champagne, Lorraine, Artois, or Paris and its environs, the French people that we encountered were unfailingly helpful and gracious. I would also like to thank the guide at Fort Vaux, whose name I'm embarrassed to say I don't recall, that gave us the map of the Verdun battlefield. This was typical of what we experienced. The French government and people also deserve praise for the care with which they have preserved and honored the memory of World War I. Driving around the countryside to the north and east of Paris, this is so evident. Visiting Verdun was something that I will never forget. My esteemed colleague at Stuyvesant, Dr. Lisa Greenwald, made the whole trip to France possible in the form that it ultimately took by sharing her contacts with me. *Merci!*

Nick Valldejuli, ex-*légionnaire* and fellow author, took time to read through chapter 3. Discussing his time in the Foreign Legion, particularly his story of the march in the Pyrenees, gave me a sense of that intangible quality its members possess. Christopher Bulko, Ken Cassens, and Dave King at the Old Rhinebeck Aerodrome in Red Hook, New York answered all of my questions about the aircraft flown during World War I. Their passion and meticulousness were an inspiration. There aren't many people that can tell you what it is like to fly a Nieuport no. 11 or a Caudron, or a SPAD VII. They can.

Lastly, I would like to recognize the following for their efforts on my behalf during the research process, some of whom (as I mentioned in the acknowledgements for my previous book) I have not had the pleasure to meet face-to-face (a wonder and a symptom of the age of the Internet in which we all now live): Maureen Maryanski and Chelsea Frosini at the New-York Historical Society, Bev Benz at the Canby Public Library (Minnesota), historian Harry Crocker, the Morris County (New Jersey) Interlibrary Loan program, Mary Laura Kludy at the Virginia Military Institute Archives, Colonel Vincent Scarniet *Armée belge* (ret.) for taking the time to explain the larger meaning of the events of 1914 for the Belgian people, and Rich McErlean for his sound advice and generosity of spirit.

NOTES

CHAPTER 1: *BELLE ÉPOQUE*

1. Irving Werstein, *Sound No Trumpet: The Life and Death of Alan Seeger* (New York: Thomas Y. Crowell Company, 1967), 6.
2. Ibid.
3. Ibid., 3.
4. Ibid.
5. Alan Seeger, *Poems* (New York: Charles Scribner's Sons, 1916), xv–xvi.
6. Werstein, *Sound No Trumpet*, 8.
7. Seeger, *Poems*, 10.
8. Barbara Tuchman, *The Proud Tower: A Portrait of the World Before the War 1890–1914* (New York: The Macmillan Company, 1966), 307.
9. Ibid., 249.
10. Ibid., 300.

11. John Bowe, *With the Thirteenth Minnesota in the Philippines* (Minneapolis, MN: Press of A. B. Farnham PTG & Stationery Co., 1905), 33–37.

12. Walter LaFeber, "Vice Presidential Nominee: Theodore Roosevelt," Interview transcripts for American Experience, "America 1900," available at www.pbs.org/wgbh/amex/1900/filmmore/reference/interview/lafeber_vpnomineetr.html.

13. Kiffin Yates Rockwell and Paul Ayres Rockwell, *War Letters of Kiffin Yates Rockwell: Foreign Legionnaire and Aviator France, 1914–1916, with Memoir and Notes by Paul Ayres Rockwell* (Garden City, NY: Doubleday, Page & Company, The County Life Press, 1925), xii.

14. Ibid., xiii.

15. Ibid., xv.

16. Ibid.

17. "Lynchings: By Year and Race," the Archives at Tuskeegee Institute, February 1979.

18. Werstein, *Sound No Trumpet*, 42.

19. Victor Emanuel Chapman and John Jay Chapman, *Victor Chapman's Letters from France: With Memoir* (New York: The Macmillan Company, 1917), 8.

20. Ibid., 21.

21. Alan Seeger, Letter to Guy Emerson, May 28, 1913.

22. Werstein, *Sound No Trumpet*, 40.

23. Ibid.

24. Ibid., 41–42.

25. "Bob Scanlon," BoxRec.com Boxing Encyclopaedia, available at boxrec.com/media/index.php?title=Human:45817.

26. Tuchman, *The Proud Tower*, 32–33.

27. Mary A. McAuliffe, *Twilight of the Belle Epoque: The Paris of Picasso, Stravinsky, Proust, Renault, Marie Curie, Gertrude Stein, and Their Friends through the Great War* (New York: Rowan & Littlefield, 2014), 235.

28. Ibid.

29. Ibid., 61–62.

30. Tuchman, *The Proud Tower*, 463.

31. "How Love Made a War Hero of Pittsburgh's Wealthy Scapegrace," *Richmond Times-Dispatch*, June 13, 1915.

32. "William Thaw Ends Air Journey Here; Passes Under East River Bridges on Last Lap of Flying Boat Trip from Newport," *New York Times*, October 6, 1913.

33. Herbert Molloy Mason Jr., *The Lafayette Escadrille* (New York: Random House, 1964), 9–10.

34. Tuchman, *The Proud Tower*, 250.

35. Ibid., 229.

36. Helmuth von Moltke quoted by Admiral Georg Alexander von Müller, December 8, 1912, in Fritz Fischer, *War of Illusions: German Policies from 1911 to 1914* (New York: W. W. Norton & Company 1975), 162.

37. Kaiser Wilhelm II, 1899, quoted in Tuchman, *The Proud Tower*, 266.

CHAPTER 2: ERUPTION

1. David Fromkin, *Europe's Last Summer: Who Started the Great War in 1914?* (New York: Alfred A. Knopf, 2004), 124–25.

2. Ruth Henig, *The Origins of the First World War*, 3rd ed. (London and New York: Routledge, 2002), 47.

3. Ibid., 40.

4. Fromkin, *Europe's Last Summer*, 271–75.

5. Herbert Molloy Mason Jr., *The Lafayette Escadrille* (New York: Random House, 1964), 6.

6. Ibid., 5–6.

7. "The Tour: Year 1914," available at www.letour.fr/HISTO/us/TDF/1914/index.html.

8. Irving Werstein, *Sound No Trumpet: The Life and Death of Alan Seeger* (New York: Thomas Y. Crowell Company, 1967), 46–47.

9. Kiffin Yates Rockwell and Paul Ayres Rockwell, *War Letters of Kiffin Yates Rockwell: Foreign Legionnaire and Aviator France, 1914–1916, with Memoir and Notes by Paul Ayres Rockwell* (Garden City, NY: Doubleday, Page & Company, The County Life Press, 1925), xviii–xix.

10. John Bowe, *Soldiers of the Legion* (Chicago: Press of Peterson Linotyping Co., 1918), 229.

11. Paul Ayres Rockwell, *American Fighters in the Foreign Legion* (Boston: Houghton Mifflin Company, 1930), 3.

12. Victor Emanuel and John Jay Chapman, *Victor Chapman's Letters from France: With Memoir* (New York: The Macmillan Company, 1917), 22.

13. Werstein, *Sound No Trumpet*, 51.

14. Ibid.

15. Rockwell, *American Fighters in the Foreign Legion*, 201–2.

16. Mason, *The Lafayette Escadrille*, 12–13.

17. Alan Seeger in the *New Republic*, May 22, 1915, and in Alan Seeger, *Poems* (New York: Charles Scribner's Sons, 1916), xxv.

18. Eileen Reynolds, "MCMXIV: It Wasn't Called Great for Nothing: The First World War Changed Far More Than Lines on a Map," *New York University Alumni Magazine* (Winter 2014).

19. Kenneth E. Silver, quoted in Reynolds, "MCMXIV: It Wasn't Called Great for Nothing."

20. Bowe, *Soldiers of the Legion*, 92–93.

21. Werstein, *Sound No Trumpet*, 58–59.

CHAPTER 3: *LA LÉGION*

1. Herbert Molloy Mason Jr., *The Lafayette Escadrille* (New York: Random House, 1964), 8.

2. David King, *Ten Thousand Shall Fall* (New York: Duffield & Company, 1927), 6.

3. William Thaw, Letter, August 30, 1914, in Edwin W. Morse, *The Vanguard of American Volunteers in the Fighting Lines and in Humanitarian Service, August 1914–April 1917* (New York: Charles Scribner's Sons, 1918), 15.

4. Barbara Tuchman, *The Guns of August* (New York: The Macmillan Company, 1962), 316.

5. Ibid., 226.

6.   Douglas Porch, *The French Foreign Legion: A Complete History of the Legendary Fighting Force* (New York: HarperCollins, 1991), 141–42.

7.   John Bowe, *Soldiers of the Legion* (Chicago: Press of Peterson Linotyping Co., 1918), 23–24.

8.   Porch, *The French Foreign Legion*, 340.

9.   Ibid., 334–43.

10.   Mason, *The Lafayette Escadrille*, 13–14.

11.   King, *Ten Thousand Shall Fall*, 9.

12.   Irving Werstein, *Sound No Trumpet: The Life and Death of Alan Seeger* (New York: Thomas Y. Crowell Company, 1967), 67–68.

13.   Bowe, *Soldiers of the Legion*, 25.

14.   Mason, *The Lafayette Escadrille*, 15.

15.   Ibid.

16.   King, *Ten Thousand Shall Fall*, 15–16.

17.   Ibid., 12.

18.   Kosta Todorov, *Balkan Firebrand*, in Douglas Porch, *The French Foreign Legion*, 342–43.

19.   Alan Seeger, *Letters and Diary of Alan Seeger* (New York: Charles Scribner's Sons, 1917), 153.

20.   Blais Cendrars, *La Main coupée*, in Porch, *The French Foreign Legion*, 342–43.

21.   Tuchman, *The Guns of August*, 395–99.

22.   Ibid., 400.

23.   Mason, *The Lafayette Escadrille*, 16.

24.   Ibid.

25.   Geoffrey Bocca, *La Légion! The French Foreign Legion and the Men Who Made It Glorious* (New York: Thomas Y. Cromwell & Company, 1964), 112–13.

26.   "Le Boudin" lyrics and translation may be found at https://en.wikipedia.org/wiki/Le_Boudin.

27.   Seeger, *Letters and Diary*, 2.

28.   King, *Ten Thousand Shall Fall*, 14.

29.   Ibid., 15.

30.   Ibid.

31.   Ibid., 20–21.

32. Mason, *The Lafayette Escadrille*, 18.
33. King, *Ten Thousand Shall Fall*, 18.

CHAPTER 4: CHEMIN DES DAMES

1. David King, *Ten Thousand Shall Fall* (New York: Duffield & Company, 1927), 24.
2. Ibid., 29.
3. John Bowe, *Soldiers of the Legion* (Chicago: Press of Peterson Linotyping Co., 1918), 39.
4. Herbert Molloy Mason Jr., *The Lafayette Escadrille* (New York: Random House, 1964), 21.
5. Alan Seeger, *Poems* (New York: Charles Scribner's Sons, 1916), xxx.
6. King, *Ten Thousand Shall Fall*, 26–27.
7. Mason, *The Lafayette Escadrille*, 25.
8. King, *Ten Thousand Shall Fall*, 33.
9. Ibid., 40.
10. Ibid., 34.
11. Bowe, *Soldiers of the Legion*, 44.
12. Mason, *The Lafayette Escadrille*, 29.
13. Bowe, *Soldiers of the Legion*, 18–19.
14. Ibid., 133.
15. King, *Ten Thousand Shall Fall*, 29.
16. Ibid., 42.
17. Bowe, *Soldiers of the Legion*, 131.
18. King, *Ten Thousand Shall Fall*, 42.
19. Mason, *The Lafayette Escadrille*, 32.
20. "New York Recruit Wounded in Battle," *New York Sun*, January 14, 1915.
21. Ibid.
22. King, *Ten Thousand Shall Fall*, 44.
23. Ibid., 46–47.
24. Ibid., 46.
25. Douglas Porch, *The French Foreign Legion: A Complete History of the Legendary Fighting Force* (New York: HarperCollins, 1991), 346.
26. Edward Jablonski, *Warriors with Wings: The Story of the Lafayette Escadrille* (New York: Bobb-Merrill Company, 1966), 44.

27. "Menu de Luxe for Foreign Legioners," *New York Sun*, April 25, 1915.

28. Seeger, *Poems*, xxxi.

29. "Menu de Luxe."

30. Seeger, *Poems*, 131, 133.

31. Geoffrey Bocca, *La Légion! The French Foreign Legion and the Men Who Made It Glorious* (New York: Thomas Y. Cromwell & Company, 1964), 50.

32. Ibid.

33. King, *Ten Thousand Shall Fall*, 56.

34. Mason, *The Lafayette Escadrille*, 34.

35. King, *Ten Thousand Shall Fall*, 46.

36. Bowe, *Soldiers of the Legion*, 95.

37. King, *Ten Thousand Shall Fall*, 62.

38. Ibid.

39. Irving Werstein, *Sound No Trumpet: The Life and Death of Alan Seeger* (New York: Thomas Y. Crowell Company, 1967), 109.

40. Bocca, *La Légion!*, 51–52.

41. Werstein, *Sound No Trumpet*, 108.

42. Ibid., 112.

43. Mason, *The Lafayette Escadrille*, 34.

44. Kiffin Yates Rockwell, Letter to Paul Ayres Rockwell, February 16, 1915, in Kiffin Yates Rockwell and Paul Ayres Rockwell, *War Letters of Kiffin Yates Rockwell: Foreign Legionnaire and Aviator France, 1914–1916, with Memoir and Notes by Paul Ayres Rockwell* (Garden City, NY: Doubleday, Page & Company, The County Life Press, 1925), 26.

45. Paul Ayres Rockwell, *American Fighters in the Foreign Legion* (Boston: Houghton Mifflin Company, 1930), 50–51.

CHAPTER 5: *SANS PEUR SANS PITIÉ*

1. Kiffin Yates Rockwell, Letter to the Vicomte de Peloux, April 22, 1915, in Kiffin Yates Rockwell and Paul Ayres Rockwell, *War Letters of Kiffin Yates Rockwell: Foreign Legionnaire and Aviator France, 1914–1916, with Memoir and Notes by Paul Ayres Rockwell* (Garden City, NY: Doubleday, Page & Company, The County Life Press,

1925), 36; Paul Ayres Rockwell, *American Fighters in the Foreign Legion* (Boston: Houghton Mifflin Company, 1930), 89.

2.   Kenneth Weeks, Letter to Alice Weeks, 1914, in ibid.

3.   Ibid., 66–67.

4.   Ibid., 66.

5.   Russell Anthony Kelly and James Edward Kelly, *Kelly of the Foreign Legion: Letters of Légionnaire Russell A. Kelly* (New York: Mitchell Kennerley, 1917), 25.

6.   Ibid, 63.

7.   Ibid, 78.

8.   Ernst Jünger, *Storm of Steel* (New York: Penguin Books, 2004), 39.

9.   Rockwell, *American Fighters in the Foreign Legion*, 70.

10. Ibid., 71.

11. Ibid., 72.

12. Rockwell and Rockwell, *War Letters of Kiffin Yates Rockwell*, 73.

13. Kiffin Yates Rockwell, Letter to Paul Ayres Rockwell, May 13, 1915, in ibid.

14. Rockwell, *American Fighters in the Foreign Legion*, 72.

15. Kiffin Yates Rockwell, Letter to Paul Ayres Rockwell, May 13, 1915, in Rockwell and Rockwell, *War Letters of Kiffin Yates Rockwell*, 43.

16. Ibid.

17. Herbert Molloy Mason Jr., *The Lafayette Escadrille* (New York: Random House, 1964), 39.

18. Kiffin Yates Rockwell, Letter to Paul Ayres Rockwell, May 13, 1915, in Rockwell and Rockwell, *War Letters of Kiffin Yates Rockwell*, 44.

19. Mason, *The Lafayette Escadrille*, 40.

20. Edward Jablonski, *Warriors with Wings: The Story of the Lafayette Escadrille* (New York: Bobb-Merrill Company, 1966), 48.

21. Kiffin Yates Rockwell, Letter to Paul Ayres Rockwell, May 13, 1915, in Rockwell and Rockwell, *War Letters of Kiffin Yates Rockwell*, 44.

22. Rockwell, *American Fighters in the Foreign Legion*, 77.

23. Ibid.

24. Ibid, 78.

25. Georges Blond, *Verdun* (New York: The Macmillan Company, 1964), 155–56.

26. Rockwell, *American Fighters in the Foreign Legion*, 81–82.

27. Ibid., 82–83.

28. Ibid., 84.

29. Ibid.

30. Alan Seeger, *Poems* (New York: Charles Scribner's Sons, 1916), 171.

CHAPTER 6: *ESCADRILLE AMERICAINE*

1. Kiffin Yates Rockwell, Letter to Paul Ayres Rockwell, May 13, 1915, in Kiffin Yates Rockwell and Paul Ayres Rockwell, *War Letters of Kiffin Yates Rockwell: Foreign Legionnaire and Aviator France, 1914–1916, with Memoir and Notes by Paul Ayres Rockwell* (Garden City, NY: Doubleday, Page & Company, The County Life Press, 1925), 44.

2. Kiffin Yates Rockwell, Letter to Paul Ayres Rockwell, June 15, 1915, in ibid., 52.

3. Kiffin Yates Rockwell, Letter to the Vicomte de Peloux, May 18, 1915, in ibid.

4. Edward Jablonski, *Warriors with Wings: The Story of the Lafayette Escadrille* (New York: Bobb-Merrill Company, 1966), 61.

5. Kiffin Yates Rockwell, Letter to Paul Ayres Rockwell, June 22, 1915, in Rockwell and Rockwell, *War Letters of Kiffin Yates Rockwell*, 54.

6. Jablonski, Warriors with Wings, 49, 51.

7. Edwin W. Morse, *The Vanguard of American Volunteers in the Fighting Lines and in Humanitarian Service, August 1914–April 1917* (New York: Charles Scribner's Sons, 1918), 19–20.

8. Jablonski, *Warriors with Wings*, 50.

9. Ibid.

10. Herbert Molloy Mason Jr., *The Lafayette Escadrille* (New York: Random House, 1964), 26.

11. Ibid., 41.

12. Ibid., 43.

13. Ibid., 43–45.

14. Jablonski, *Warriors with Wings*, 34–35.

15. Jarousse de Sillac, Letter to Colonel Paul Victor Bottieaux, May 20, 1915, in Mason, *The Lafayette Escadrille*, 48.

16. Ibid., 53.

17. Ibid.

18. Kiffin Yates Rockwell, Letter to Paul Ayres Rockwell, September 6, 1915, in Rockwell and Rockwell, *War Letters of Kiffin Yates Rockwell*, 69.

19. Kiffin Yates Rockwell, Letter to his mother, September 8, 1915, in ibid., 70.

20. Kiffin Yates Rockwell, Letter to Paul Ayres Rockwell, September 27, 1915, in ibid., 76–77.

21. Rockwell, *American Fighters in the Foreign Legion*, 92.

22. Ibid., 93.

23. "Memorial for Sons of Harvard Who Fell in War," *Princeton Union*, December 28, 1916.

24. Henry Weston Farnsworth, in Edwin W. Morse, *The Vanguard of American Volunteers: in the Fighting Lines and in Humanitarian Service August 1914–April 1917* (New York: Charles Scribner's Sons, 1918), 29.

25. Rockwell, *American Fighters in the Foreign Legion*, 100.

26. Jablonski, *Warriors with Wings*, 55.

27. Ibid., 62.

28. Ibid., 60.

29. Kiffin Yates Rockwell, Letter to Paul Ayres Rockwell, October 12, 1915, in Rockwell and Rockwell, *War Letters of Kiffin Yates Rockwell*, 83.

30. Jablonski, *Warriors with Wings*, 66.

31. Ibid., 67.

CHAPTER 7: CHAMPAGNE

1. Alan Seeger, *Poems* (New York: Charles Scribner's Sons, 1916), 134.

2. Russell Anthony Kelly and James Edward Kelly, *Kelly of the Foreign Legion: Letters of Légionnaire Russell A. Kelly* (New York: Mitchell Kennerley, 1917), 39.

3. Alan Seeger, *Letters and Diary of Alan Seeger* (New York: Charles Scribner's Sons, 1917), 110.

4. Paul Ayres Rockwell, *American Fighters in the Foreign Legion* (Boston: Houghton Mifflin Company, 1930), 121.

5. Seeger, *Letters and Diary*, 117–18.

6. John Bowe, *Soldiers of the Legion* (Chicago: Press of Peterson Linotyping Co., 1918), 121.

7. Seeger, *Letters and Diary*, 128–29.

8. Bowe, *Soldiers of the Legion*, 125–26.

9. Ibid., 126.

10. Seeger, *Letters and Diary*, 129.

11. Bowe, *Soldiers of the Legion*, 127–28.

12. Victor Emanuel Chapman and John Jay Chapman, *Victor Chapman's Letters from France: With Memoir* (New York: The Macmillan Company, 1917), 128.

13. Seeger, *Letters and Diary*, 135.

14. David King, *Ten Thousand Shall Fall* (New York: Duffield & Company, 1927), 67.

15. Seeger, *Letters and Diary*, 137.

16. King, *Ten Thousand Shall Fall*, 71–72.

17. "Henry Weston Farnsworth," in Edwin W. Morse, *The Vanguard of American Volunteers in the Fighting Lines and in Humanitarian Service, August 1914–April 1917* (New York: Charles Scribner's Sons, 1918), 34–36.

18. Seeger, *Letters and Diary*, 139.

19. King, *Ten Thousand Shall Fall*, 69.

20. Ibid.

21. Seeger, *Letters and Diary*, 140.

22. Ibid., 141.

23. Marc Ferro, *The Great War: 1914–1918* (London: Routledge & Kegan Paul, 1973), 63–64.

24. King, *Ten Thousand Shall Fall*, 76.

25. Seeger, *Letters and Diary*, 162; Bowe, *Soldiers of the Legion*, 127–28.

26. Seeger, *Letters and Diary*, 163.

27. Alan Seeger, Letter to his mother, October 25, 1915, in Seeger, *Letters and Diary*, 165.

28. Bowe, *Soldiers of the Legion*, 149.

29. Ibid., 151.

30. Seeger, *Letters and Diary*, 166–67.

31. King, *Ten Thousand Shall Fall*, 81.

32. Ibid., 83.

33. Paul Rockwell, *American Fighters in the Foreign Legion*, 113.

34. Bowe, *Soldiers of the Legion*, 153.

35. Seeger, *Poems*, 141–43.

36. Seeger, *Letters and Diary*, 167.

37. Bowe, *Soldiers of the Legion*, 154.

38. Rockwell, *American Fighters in the Foreign Legion*, 113.

39. King, *Ten Thousand Shall Fall*, 87–88.

40. Bowe, *Soldiers of the Legion*, 155.

41. Rockwell, *American Fighters in the Foreign Legion*, 113–14.

42. Ibid., 111–12.

43. Bowe, *Soldiers of the Legion*, 55.

44. "Frank Musgrave," in Rockwell, *American Fighters in the Foreign Legion*, 115.

45. King, *Ten Thousand Shall Fall*, 89.

46. Ibid.

47. Rockwell, *American Fighters in the Foreign Legion*, 117.

48. Ibid., 118.

49. Ibid., 119–20.

50. Ibid., 119.

51. Ibid., 120.

52. Ferro, *The Great War*, 64.

53. Geoffrey Bocca, *La Légion! The French Foreign Legion and the Men Who Made It Glorious* (New York: Thomas Y. Cromwell & Company, 1964), 53.

54. King, *Ten Thousand Shall Fall*, 90.

55. Chapman and Chapman, *Victor Chapman's Letters from France*, 158.

56. "Champagne 1914–15," *New York Sun*, October 6, 1915.

57. Alan Seeger, Postcard to his family, October 30, 1915, in Seeger, *Letters and Diary*, 174.

58. Alan Seeger, Letter to his mother, October 25, 1915, in ibid., 165.

59. Rockwell, *American Fighters in the Foreign Legion*, 128–29.

60. Ibid., 159.

CHAPTER 8: VERDUN

1. John Bowe, *Soldiers of the Legion* (Chicago: Press of Peterson Linotyping Co., 1918), 163.
2. Ibid., 164.
3. Georges Blond, *Verdun* (New York: The Macmillan Company, 1964), 176.
4. David King, *Ten Thousand Shall Fall* (New York: Duffield & Company, 1927), 96.
5. Paul Ayres Rockwell, *American Fighters in the Foreign Legion* (Boston: Houghton Mifflin Company, 1930), 160–62.
6. Bowe, *Soldiers of the Legion*, 165.
7. Ibid.
8. King, *Ten Thousand Shall Fall*, 98.
9. Rockwell, *American Fighters in the Foreign Legion*, 162.
10. Ibid., 164.
11. Ibid., 165.
12. King, *Ten Thousand Shall Fall*, 103.
13. Ibid., 104–5.
14. Ibid., 105.
15. Rockwell, *American Fighters in the Foreign Legion*, 166.
16. King, *Ten Thousand Shall Fall*, 106.
17. Ibid., 114.
18. Ibid.
19. Rockwell, *American Fighters in the Foreign Legion*, 166.
20. King, *Ten Thousand Shall Fall*, 116.
21. Ibid., 117.
22. Ibid., 118.
23. "Joseph Joffre" in Rockwell, *American Fighters in the Foreign Legion*, 166.
24. David King, Letter, March 2, 1916, in King, *Ten Thousand Shall Fall*, 118–19.
25. King, *Ten Thousand Shall Fall*, 119.
26. Blond, *Verdun*, 173.
27. Ibid., 169.
28. King, *Ten Thousand Shall Fall*, 103.
29. Ibid., 123.

30. Ibid., 125.

31. "Ferdinand Capdevielle" in Rockwell, *American Fighters in the Foreign Legion*, 167–68.

32. King, *Ten Thousand Shall Fall*, 131–33.

33. Rockwell, *American Fighters in the Foreign Legion*, 168–69.

34. Blond, *Verdun*, 211.

35. King, *Ten Thousand Shall Fall*, 135.

36. Marc Ferro, *The Great War: 1914–1918* (London: Routledge & Kegan Paul, 1973), 77.

37. Blond, *Verdun*, 210–11.

38. Rockwell, *American Fighters in the Foreign Legion*, 170.

CHAPTER 9: KNIGHTS OF THE AIR

1. Edward Jablonski, *Warriors with Wings: The Story of the Lafayette Escadrille* (New York: Bobb-Merrill Company, 1966), 20.

2. Herbert Molloy Mason Jr., *The Lafayette Escadrille* (New York: Random House, 1964), 56.

3. Ibid.

4. Ibid., 59.

5. Ibid., 59–60.

6. Georges Blond, *Verdun* (New York: The Macmillan Company, 1964), 149.

7. Mason, *The Lafayette Escadrille*, 61.

8. Ibid.

9. Victor Chapman, Letter to Elizabeth Chapman, May 14, 1916, in Victor Emanuel Chapman and John Jay Chapman, *Victor Chapman's Letters from France: With Memoir* (New York: The Macmillan Company, 1917), 179.

10. Jablonski, *Warriors with Wings*, 73.

11. Kiffin Yates Rockwell, Letter to Paul Ayres Rockwell, May 18, 1916, in Kiffin Yates Rockwell and Paul Ayres Rockwell, *War Letters of Kiffin Yates Rockwell: Foreign Legionnaire and Aviator France, 1914–1916, with Memoir and Notes by Paul Ayres Rockwell* (Garden City, NY: Doubleday, Page & Company, The County Life Press, 1925), 109.

12. Mason, *The Lafayette Escadrille*, 63.

13. Victor Chapman, Letter to his cousin, May 23, 1916, in Chapman and Chapman, *Victor Chapman's Letters from France*, 182.

14. Mason, *The Lafayette Escadrille*, 67–68.

15. Kiffin Yates Rockwell, Letter to his mother, May 23, 1916, in Rockwell and Rockwell, *War Letters of Kiffin Yates Rockwell*, 111.

16. Mason, *The Lafayette Escadrille*, 74–75.

17. Blond, *Verdun*, 204.

18. Jablonski, *Warriors with Wings*, 81.

19. Ibid., 82.

20. Ibid., 83.

21. Victor Chapman, Letter to his father, June 1, 1916, in Chapman and Chapman, *Victor Chapman's Letters from France*, 182–83.

22. Ibid., 184.

23. Ibid., 185.

24. Kiffin Yates Rockwell, Letter to Paul Ayres Rockwell, June 2, 1916, in Rockwell and Rockwell, *War Letters of Kiffin Yates Rockwell*, 113.

25. Victor Chapman letter to his father, June 2, 1916, in Chapman and Chapman, *Victor Chapman's Letters from France*, 186.

26. Ibid.

27. Jablonski, *Warriors with Wings*, 84.

28. Ibid., 86.

29. Ibid., 87.

30. Mason, *The Lafayette Escadrille*, 74.

31. Jablonski, *Warriors with Wings*, 84.

32. Ibid., 89–91.

33. Mason, *The Lafayette Escadrille*, 81.

34. Kiffin Yates Rockwell, Letter to Paul Rockwell, June 23, 1916, in Rockwell and Rockwell, *War Letters of Kiffin Yates Rockwell*, 117–18.

35. Ibid., 118.

36. "Neutral and Heroes: the American Volunteers," *Le Petit Parisien*, November 1, 1916.

37. Kiffin Yates Rockwell, Letter to Elizabeth Chapman, June 30, 1916, in Rockwell and Rockwell, *War Letters of Kiffin Yates Rockwell*, 120.

38. Paul Ayres Rockwell, *American Fighters in the Foreign Legion* (Boston: Houghton Mifflin Company, 1930), 162.

39. Mason, *The Lafayette Escadrille*, 96.

40. Jablonski, *Warriors with Wings*, 104–5.

41. Kiffin Yates Rockwell, Letter to Paul Ayres Rockwell, August 4, 1916, in Rockwell and Rockwell, *War Letters of Kiffin Yates Rockwell*, 128–29.

42. Jablonski, *Warriors with Wings*, 105–6.

43. Ibid., 107.

44. Ibid., 110.

45. Mason, *The Lafayette Escadrille*, 102.

46. Ibid., 111.

47. Kiffin Yates Rockwell, Letter to Paul Ayres Rockwell, September 9, 1916, in Rockwell and Rockwell, *War Letters of Kiffin Yates Rockwell*, 132.

48. Jablonski, *Warriors with Wings*, 116.

49. Ibid., 115.

50. Ibid., 120.

51. Mason, *The Lafayette Escadrille*, 119.

52. Ibid., 120.

53. "The Americans Who Died for France," *Le Temps*, November 4, 1916.

54. Editorial from Duetsche Tageeszeitung, quoted in Mason, *The Lafayette Escadrille*, 120.

55. Jablonski, *Warriors with Wings*, 131.

56. Ibid., 152.

57. Ibid., 150.

58. Mason, *The Lafayette Escadrille*, 145.

59. Ibid., 160–61

60. Rockwell, *American Fighters in the Foreign Legion*, 294.

61. John Bowe, *Soldiers of the Legion* (Chicago: Press of Peterson Linotyping Co., 1918), 95.

62. Craig Lloyd, *Eugene Bullard: Black Expatriate in Jazz Age Paris* (Athens, GA: University of Georgia Press, 2006), 50–51.

CHAPTER 10: RENDEZVOUS

1. Alan Seeger, Letter to his mother, March 12, 1915, in Alan Seeger, *Letters and Diary of Alan Seeger* (New York: Charles Scribner's Sons, 1917), 74.

2. Alan Seeger, Letter to his mother, October 25, 1915, in Seeger, *Letters and Diary*, 172–73.

3. Blais Cendrars, *La Main coupée*, in Douglas Porch, *The French Foreign Legion: A Complete History of the Legendary Fighting Force* (New York: HarperCollins, 1991), 368.

4. Alan Seeger, Letter to his mother, November 30, 1915, in Seeger, *Letters and Diary*, 175.

5. Paul Ayres Rockwell, *American Fighters in the Foreign Legion* (Boston: Houghton Mifflin Company, 1930), 136.

6. Alan Seeger, Letter to his mother, November 30, 1915, in Seeger, *Letters and Diary*, 176.

7. Rockwell, *American Fighters in the Foreign Legion*, 136.

8. Alan Seeger, *Poems* (New York: Charles Scribner's Sons, 1916), 162.

9. Kiffin Yates Rockwell, Letter to his mother, June 8, 1915, in Kiffin Yates Rockwell and Paul Ayres Rockwell, *War Letters of Kiffin Yates Rockwell: Foreign Legionnaire and Aviator France, 1914–1916, with Memoir and Notes by Paul Ayres Rockwell* (Garden City, NY: Doubleday, Page & Company, The County Life Press, 1925), 49.

10. "Roosevelt Urges Full Readiness," *New York Times*, January 21, 1916.

11. Seeger, *Poems*, 164.

12. Ibid.

13. Irving Werstein, *Sound No Trumpet: The Life and Death of Alan Seeger* (New York: Thomas Y. Crowell Company, 1967), 6.

14. Ibid.

15. Seeger, *Poems*, 165.

16. Ibid.

17. Alan Seeger, Letter to his mother, March 7, 1916, in Seeger, *Letters and Diary*, 188.

18. Alan Seeger, Letter to his mother, April 13, 1916, in ibid., 190.

19. Ibid.

20. Alan Seeger, Letter, May 12, 1916, in Seeger, *Letters and Diary*, 192.

21. Seeger, Poems, 144.
22. Alan Seeger, Letter, May 19, 1916, in ibid., 196.
23. Ibid., 197.
24. Alan Seeger, Letter to Alice Weeks, June 1, 1916, in ibid., 202.
25. Werstein, *Sound No Trumpet*, 126.
26. Brian Gardner, *The Big Push: A Portrait of the Battle of the Somme* (New York: William Morrow and Company, 1963), 4.
27. Ibid., 11.
28. Alan Seeger, Letter, June 28, 1916, in Seeger, *Letters and Diary*, 211.
29. Gardner, *The Big Push*, 81.
30. Alan Seeger, Letter, June 28, 1916, in Seeger, *Letters and Diary*, 211.
31. Rif Baer, in Seeger, *Letters and Diary*, 213.
32. "Christopher Charles," in Rockwell, *American Fighters in the Foreign Legion*, 173.
33. Ibid., 174.
34. Porch, *The French Foreign Legion*, 368.
35. Rif Baer, in Seeger, *Letters and Diary*, 214–15.
36. Rockwell, *American Fighters in the Foreign Legion*, 180.
37. Ibid.
38. Tony Geraghty, *March or Die: A New History of the French Foreign Legion* (New York: Facts on File Publications, 1986), 143.
39. Werstein, *Sound No Trumpet*, 129.
40. "Alan Seeger Poet Warrior Dies Fighting for France," *New York Sun*, July 23, 1916.
41. "An American Judgment on French Soldiers," *Le Temps*, August 23, 1916.
42. Ibid.
43. "Soldier of France," *Le Figaro*, September 1, 1916.
44. Alan Seeger, Letter to Alice Weeks, June 24, 1916, in Seeger, *Letters and Diary*, 210.

CHAPTER 11: HAT IN THE RING

1. "Relations with Germany are Broken Off," *New York Times*, February 3, 1917.
2. Barbara Tuchman, *The Zimmermann Telegram* (New York: The Macmillan Company, 1966), 194–95.

3. Paul Ayres Rockwell, *American Fighters in the Foreign Legion* (Boston: Houghton Mifflin Company, 1930), 208.

4. John Bowe, *Soldiers of the Legion* (Chicago: Press of Peterson Linotyping Co., 1918), 137.

5. Ibid., 136–37.

6. Ibid., 197.

7. Ibid., 143.

8. Ibid., 144.

9. Ibid., 195.

10. Rockwell, *American Fighters in the Foreign Legion*, 210.

11. Ibid.

12. Bowe, *Soldiers of the Legion*, 168.

13. Woodrow Wilson, "President Wilson's Declaration of War Message to Congress," April 2, 1917 (Washington, DC: The National Archives).

14. Ibid.

15. Ibid.

16. Ibid.

17. Thomas Fleming, *The Illusion of Victory: America in World War I* (New York: Basic Books, 2003), 87.

18. Ibid., 247.

19. Ibid., 112.

20. David King, *Ten Thousand Shall Fall* (New York: Duffield & Company, 1927), 144.

21. Ibid., 148.

22. Ibid., 154.

23. Ibid., 155.

24. Ibid., 158.

25. War Department A.G.O. letter to Captain Carl Boyd, Third Cavalry Military Attaché, American Embassy, Paris, in Rockwell, *American Fighters in the Foreign Legion*, 258.

26. F. Scott Fitzgerald, *This Side of Paradise* (New York: Barnes & Noble Classics, 2005), 135.

27. King, *Ten Thousand Shall Fall*, 177–78.

28. Marc Ferro, *The Great War: 1914–1918* (London: Routledge & Kegan Paul, 1973), 226.

29. Ibid., 111.

30. Ibid., 121.

31. Woodrow Wilson, "The Fourteen Points, 8 January, 1918," the Avalon
     Project at Yale University.

32. Fleming, *The Illusion of Victory*, 340.

33. Ibid., 363.

34. Rockwell, *American Fighters in the Foreign Legion*, 349.

EPILOGUE

1.   "Dream of Hero," *Le Gaulois*, October 8, 1918.

2.   "Honor for the 'Comrades of the stars,'" *Dearborn Independent*, June
     25, 1921.

SELECTED
BIBLIOGRAPHY

BOOKS

Blond, Georges. *Verdun*. New York: The Macmillan Company, 1964.

Bocca, Geoffrey. *La Légion! The French Foreign Legion and the Men Who Made It Glorious*. New York: Thomas Y. Cromwell & Company, 1964.

Bowe, John. *Soldiers of the Legion*. Chicago: Press of Peterson Linotyping Co., 1918.

———. *With the Thirteenth Minnesota in the Philippines*. Minneapolis, MN: Press of A.B. Farnham PTG & Stationery Co., 1905.

Chapman, Victor Emanuel, and John Jay Chapman. *Victor Chapman's Letters from France: With Memoir*. New York: The Macmillan Company, 1917.

Ferro, Marc. *The Great War: 1914–1918*. London: Routledge & Kegan Paul, 1973.

Fischer, Fritz. *Germany's Aims in the First World War*. New York: W. W. Norton & Company, 1967.

———. *War of Illusions: German Policies from 1911 to 1914*. New York: W. W. Norton & Company, 1975.

Fitzgerald, F. Scott. *This Side of Paradise*. New York: Barnes & Noble Classics, 2005.

Fleming, Thomas. *The Illusion of Victory: America in World War I*. New York: Basic Books, 2003.

Fromkin, David. *Europe's Last Summer: Who Started the Great War in 1914?* New York: Alfred A Knopf, 2004.

Gardner, Brian. *The Big Push: A Portrait of the Battle of the Somme*. New York: William Morrow and Company, 1963.

Geraghty, Tony. *March or Die: A New History of the French Foreign Legion*. New York: Facts on File Publications, 1986.

Henig, Ruth. *The Origins of the First World War*. 3rd edition. London and New York: Routledge, 2002.

Jablonski, Edward. *Warriors with Wings: The Story of the Lafayette Escadrille*. New York: Bobb-Merrill Company, 1966.

Jonnes, Jill. *Eiffel's Tower: And the World's Fair Where Buffalo Bill Beguiled Paris, the Artists Quarreled, and Thomas Edison became a Count*. New York: Viking, 2009.

Jünger, Ernst. *Storm of Steel*. New York: Penguin Books, 2004.

Kelly, Russell Anthony, and James Edward Kelly. *Kelly of the Foreign Legion: Letters of Légionnaire Russell A. Kelly*. New York: Mitchell Kennerley, 1917.

King, David. *Ten Thousand Shall Fall*. New York: Duffield & Company, 1927.

Lloyd, Craig. *Eugene Bullard: Black Expatriate in Jazz Age Paris*. Athens, Georgia: University of Georgia Press, 2006.

Mason, Herbert Molloy, Jr. *The Lafayette Escadrille*. New York: Random House, 1964.

McAuliffe, Mary A. *Twilight of the Belle Epoque: The Paris of Picasso, Stravinsky, Proust, Renault, Marie Curie, Gertrude Stein, and Their Friends through the Great War*. New York: Rowan & Littlefield, 2014.

McCullough, David. *The Greater Journey: Americans in Paris*. New York: Simon & Schuster, 2011.

Meigs, Mark. *The Americans from the Chemin des Dames to the Marne*. Aisne Département, February 2015.

Porch, Douglas. *The French Foreign Legion: A Complete History of the Legendary Fighting Force*. New York: HarperCollins, 1991.

Reynolds, Eileen. "MCMXIV It Wasn't Called Great for Nothing: The First World War Changed Far More Than Lines on a Map." *New York University Alumni Magazine* (Winter 2014).

Rickenbacker, Eddie V. *Fighting the Flying Circus*. Garden City, NY: Doubleday & Company, 1965.

Rockwell, Kiffin Yates, and Paul Ayres Rockwell. *War Letters of Kiffin Yates Rockwell: Foreign Legionnaire and Aviator France, 1914–1916, with Memoir and Notes by Paul Ayres Rockwell*. Garden City, NY: Doubleday, Page & Company, The County Life Press, 1925.

Rockwell, Paul Ayres. *American Fighters in the Foreign Legion*. Boston: Houghton Mifflin Company, 1930.

Seeger, Alan. *Letters and Diary of Alan Seeger*. New York: Charles Scribner's Sons, 1917.

———. *Poems*. New York: Charles Scribner's Sons, 1916.

Silver, Kenneth E. *Esprit De Corps: The Art of the Parisian Avant-Garde and the First World War, 1914–1925*. Princeton, NJ: Princeton University Press, 1992.

Tuchman, Barbara. *The Guns of August*. New York: The Macmillan Company, 1962.

———. *The Proud Tower: A Portrait of the World Before the War 1890–1914*. New York: The Macmillan Company, 1966.

———. *The Zimmermann Telegram*. New York: The Macmillan Company, 1966.

Udet, Ernst. *Ace of the Iron Cross*. Garden City, NY: Doubleday & Co., 1970.

Werstein, Irving. *Sound No Trumpet: The Life and Death of Alan Seeger*. New York: Thomas Y. Crowell Company, 1967.

Whitehouse, Arch. *Decisive Air Battles of the First World War*. New York: Duell, Sloan and Pearce, 1963.

Wortman, Marc. *The Millionaires' Unit: The Aristocratic Flyboys Who Fight the Great War and Invented American Airpower*. New York: Public Affairs, 2006.

FILMS

America: 1900. Produced and directed by David Grubin. WGBH Boston, 1998.

Apocalypse WWI. Produced by Louis Vaudeville and Josette D. Normandeau. Directed by Isabelle Clarke and Daniel Costelle. A CC&C/Ideacom International/ECPAD co-production in collaboration with France Télévisions & TV5 Québec Canada, 2014.

Hell's Angels. Produced and directed by Howard Hughes. United Artists, 1930.

Paths of Glory. Produced by James B. Harris. Directed by Stanley Kubrick. United Artists, 1957.

Wings. Produced by Lucien Hubbard. Directed by William A. Wellman. Paramount Pictures, 1927.

DOCUMENTS

Kipling, Rudyard. "Recessional." The Kipling Society, 1897.

"Lynchings: By Year and Race." The Archives at Tuskegee Institute: February, 1979.

Seeger, Alan. Letter to Guy Emerson 28 May 1913. Spartanburg, SC: Sandor Teszler Library Collection, Wofford College.

Wilson, Woodrow. "The Fourteen Points, 8 January 1918." The Avalon Project at Yale University.

Wilson, Woodrow. "President Wilson's Declaration of War Message to Congress, 2 April 1917." Washington, DC: The National Archives.

PERIODICALS

"À la Comédie-Française—La matinée en l'honneur des volontaires américains." *Le Petit Parisien*, January 22, 1917.

"Alan Seeger, Poet Warrior Dies Fighting for France." *New York Sun*, July 23, 1916.

"Alan Seeger Unscathed." *New York Sun*, October 16, 1915.

"American Author Killed in France." *New York Times*, January 17, 1916.

"Arms and the Man Who Writes." *New York Tribune*, July 28, 1918.

"Champagne 1914–'15." *New York Tribune*, October 6, 1915.

"Colonel Thaw, War Ace, Dies After Week's Illness." *Pittsburgh Post-Gazette*, April 23, 1934

"Honor for the Comrades of the Stars." *Dearborn Independent*, June 25, 1921.

"How Love Made a War Hero of Pittsburgh's Wealthy Scapegrace." *Richmond Times-Dispatch*, June 13, 1915.

"Les Américains morts pour la France." *Le Temps*, November 4, 1916.

"Les neutres héroïques—Volontaires américains." *Le Petit Parisien*, November 1, 1916.

"Le Soldat de France." *Le Figaro*, September 1, 1916.

"Lettres américaines—Harvard et la guerre." *Le Temps*, October 13, 1918.

"Memorial for Sons of Harvard Who Fell in the War." *Princeton Union*, December 28, 1916.

"Menu De Luxe for Foreign Legioners." *New York Sun*, April 25, 1915.

"New York Recruit Wounded in Battle." *New York Sun*, January 14, 1915.

"Nos amis américains—Les fêtes de La Fayette à New York." *Le Figaro*, September 8, 1916.

"Pete Seeger, Champion of Folk Music and Social Change, Dies at 94." *New York Times*, January 28, 2014.

"Relations With Germany Are Broken Off." *New York Times*, February 3, 1917.

"Rêve de héros." *Le Gaulois*, October 8, 1918.

"Roosevelt Urges Full Readiness." *New York Times*, January 21, 1916.

"Undying Record of American Legionaries." *New York Sun*, March 24, 1918.

"Un jugement américain sur le soldat français." *Le Temps*, August 23, 1916.

"William Thaw Ends Air Journey Here; Passes Under East River Bridges on Last Lap of Flying Boat Trip from Newport." *New York Times*, October 6, 1913.

INTERVIEWS

Christopher Bulko, airshow director, pilot. Interviewed by David Hanna,
    August 1, 2015. Old Rhinebeck Aerodrome. Red Hook, New York.
Dave King, pilot. Interviewed by David Hanna, August 1, 2015. Old
    Rhinebeck Aerodrome, Red Hook, New York.
Jean-Luc Despocq. Interviewed by David Hanna, April 7, 2015. Chateau
    du Blanc Sablon, Craonelle, France.
Ken Cassens, director of aircraft maintenance, pilot. Interviewed by
    David Hanna, August 1, 2015. Old Rhinebeck Aerodrome, Red Hook,
    New York.
Nicholas Valldejuli, *1ᵉʳ Régiment étranger de cavalerie, 1ᵉʳ Régiment
    étranger, Légion Étrangère ret*. Interviewed by David Hanna, April 4,
    2015.
Yves Fohlen. Interviewed by David Hanna, April 7, 2015. Musée du Che-
    min des Dames / Caverne du Dragon, Chemin des Dames, France.

INTERNET SITES

American Volunteers in the French Foreign Legion: 1914–1917, http://
    www.monongahelabooks.com/amvol.html.
"Bob Scanlon." BoxRec.com Boxing Encyclopaedia. boxrec.com/media/
    index.php?title=Human:45817.
"The Internet Classics Archive: *The Art of War* By Sun Tzu Translated by
    Lionel Giles." classics.mit.edu/Tzu/artwar.html.
LaFeber, Walter. "Vice Presidential Nominee: Theodore Roosevelt."
    Interview transcripts. *American Experience: America 1900*. www.
    pbs.org/wgbh/amex/1900/filmmore/reference/interview/lafeber_
    vpnomineetr.html.
Le Ministère de la Défense, *Mémoire des Hommes*. www.memoiredeshommes.
    sga.defense.gouv.fr/fr/article.php?laref=1.
"L'Offensive en Artois, En Mai et Juin 1915." chtimiste.com/
    batailles1418/1915artois1.htm.
"The Tour: Year 1914." www.letour.fr/HISTO/us/TDF/1914/index.html.

LIST OF ILLUSTRATIONS AND SOURCES

Some images are used in this book under Creative Commons licenses. The Creative Commons Attribution 2.0 Generic license can be found at https://creativecommons.org/licenses/by-sa/2.0/; the Creative Commons Attribution-ShareAlike 3.0 Unported license can be found at http://creativecommons.org/licenses/by-sa/3.0/legalcode; the Creative Commons Attribution 3.0 Unported license can be found at https://creativecommons.org/licenses/by/3.0.legalcode; and the Creative Commons Attribution ShareAlike 4.0 International can be found at http://creativecommons.org/licenses/by-sa/4.0/legalcode.

CHAPTER 1: *BELLE ÉPOQUE*

Claude Monet, *La Gare Saint-Lazare*, oil on canvas, 1877. *The National Gallery, London.*

View of the Eiffel Tower and the grounds of the *Exposition Universelle* on the Champs de Mars with the Seine and the Pont d'Iena in the foreground, 1889. *Public domain image available courtesy of Wikimedia Commons.*

The Moulin Rouge, Montmartre, Paris, 1900. *Public domain image available courtesy of Wikimedia Commons.*

Alan Seeger in Paris, 1912. *Public domain image.*

Those magnificent men in their flying machines—William Thaw (at right) after successfully flying under the four bridges spanning the East River, New York, 1913. *Public domain image available courtesy of Wikimedia Commons.*

CHAPTER 2: ERUPTION

Princip is apprehended after firing his fatal shots in Sarajevo, June 28, 1914. *Public domain image available courtesy of Wikimedia Commons.*

Kaiser Wilhelm II (left) and Army Chief of Staff Helmuth von Moltke. Both felt war was necessary and "the sooner the better." *Getty Images.*

The American volunteers cross the Place de l'Opera on their way to the Gare Saint-Lazare on August 25, 1914. *Public domain image.*

CHAPTER 3: *LA LÉGION*

Nineteenth-century illustration of a *légionnaire* in the field. *Public domain image available courtesy of Wikimedia Commons.*

Pérignon barracks, Toulouse, France, circa 1910. *Author's collection.*

Joseph Joffre, the French commander who ordered the counterattack at the First Battle of the Marne in 1914. *Public domain image available courtesy of Wikimedia Commons.*

CHAPTER 4: CHEMIN DES DAMES

Reims Cathedral, Champagne, bombed, 1914. *Public domain image uploaded by user "Gerald Garitan" and reproduced here under the Creative Commons Attribution-Share Alike 3.0 Unported license.*

Craonelle, Picardy, 1914. *Public domain image uploaded by user "vassse nicolas, antoine" and reproduced here under the Creative Commons Attribution-Share Alike 2.0 Unported license.*

In the ruins of the *Belle Époque*, 1914. *Public domain image uploaded by user "vassse nicolas, antoine" and reproduced here under the Creative Commons Attribution-Share Alike 2.0 Unported license.*

Kiffin Rockwell in the foreground (with Dennis Dowd to his immediate right) holding the line along the Chemin des Dames, 1914. *Virginia Military Institute archives.*

Alan Seeger. Warrior-bard, New Yorker, citizen of Paris, worshipper of beauty. *Public domain image.*

Baby-faced David King holding the line along the Chemin des Dames, with Fred Zinn in the foreground. *Public domain image.*

CHAPTER 5: *SANS PEUR SANS PITIÉ*

Scene of the Second Battle of Artois, May–June 1915. *Public domain image available courtesy of L'offensive en Artois, http://chtimiste.com/batailles1418.1915artois1.htm.*

Kenneth Weeks. Architect, author, Bostonian, *légionnaire. Public domain image.*

The memorial at Vimy Ridge. *Image uploaded by user "Labatt-blueboy" and reproduced here under the Creative Commons Attribution-Share Alike 2.0 Canada license.*

CHAPTER 6: *ESCADRILLE AMERICAINE*

Roland Garros. French racing pilot, aviation pioneer, war hero. *Public domain image available courtesy of Wikimedia Commons.*

Dr. Edmund Gros. *Public domain image available courtesy of Wikimedia Commons.*

CHAPTER 7: CHAMPAGNE

Suippes, Champagne, France. *Author's collection.*

Scene of Battle, Champagne, September–October 1915. *Public domain image available courtesy of Wikimedia Commons.*

Monument de la Ferme de Navarin, *Aux Morts des Armées de Champagne. Author's collection.*

CHAPTER 8: VERDUN

Erich von Falkenhayn, architect of the German offensive against Verdun. *Public domain image available courtesy of Wikimedia Commons.*

Scene of battle, Verdun, February–December 1916. *Image drawn by "Gdr," uploaded by user "Fanghong" and reproduced here under the Creative Commons Attribution-Share Alike 3.0 Unported license.*

The cratered and pitted ruins of Fort Vaux, Verdun, France. *Author's collection.*

CHAPTER 9: KNIGHTS OF THE AIR

The "Bébé," the Nieuport no. 11. *Public domain image available courtesy of Wikimedia Commons.*

From left to right, James McConnell, Victor Chapman, and Kiffin Rockwell at the Hôtel Pomme d'Or, 1916. *Virginia Military Institute archives.*

The *pilotes de chasse* of N 124, spring 1916. From left to right, Kiffin Rockwell, Georges Thénault, Norman Prince, Alfred de Laage de Meux, Elliott Cowdin, Bert Hall, James McConnell, and Victor Chapman. *Public domain image available courtesy of Wikimedia Commons.*

Victor Chapman. Artist, *légionnaire, pilote de chasse. Public domain image available courtesy of Wikimedia Commons.*

Kiffin Rockwell. Carolinian, *légionnaire, pilote de chasse,* knight errant. *Virginia Military Institute archives.*

CHAPTER 10: RENDEZVOUS

Woodrow Wilson, president of the United States, 1913–1921. *Public domain image available courtesy of Wikimedia Commons.*

Charles Seeger opposed American involvement in the war that his brother Alan had fought beginning in 1914. *Public domain image available courtesy of Wikimedia Commons.*

Alan Seeger spent his convalescence at this idyllic locale in 1916. He made a full recovery. *Public domain image available courtesy of Wikimedia Commons.*

CHAPTER 11: HAT IN THE RING

John "Jack" Bowe. Spanish-American War veteran; ex-mayor of Canby, Minnesota; father of four; *légionnaire*; soldier of France. *Public domain image.*

General John J. Pershing, commander of the American Expeditionary Force in France. *Public domain image available courtesy of Wikimedia Commons.*

One of those who answered Wilson's call to help make the world safe for democracy: John Elco of Donora, Pennsylvania, AEF. *Author's collection.*

Bob Soubiron standing next to his SPAD XIII armed with twin mounted Vickers machine guns. *Public domain image available courtesy of Wikimedia Commons.*

EPILOGUE

Bob Scanlon. *Author's collection.*

Memorial to the American Volunteers, *Place des États-Unis*, Paris. *Author's collection.*

INDEX

323